TREASURES OF
Oklahoma

Oklahoma State Capitol, located in Oklahoma City

by William Faubion

a part of the Morgan & Chase Treasure Series
www.treasuresof.com

MORGAN & CHASE PUBLISHING INC.

© Copyright 2007 by Morgan & Chase Publishing, Inc.
All rights reserved.
No portion of this book may be reproduced or utilized in any form,
or by any electronic, mechanical or other means without the prior written permission of the publisher.

Published by:
Morgan & Chase Publishing, Inc.
531 Parsons Drive, Medford, Oregon 97501
(888) 557-9328
www.treasuresof.com

Printed by:
Taylor Specialty Books - Dallas TX

First edition 2007
ISBN: 978-1-933989-10-5

THE TREASURE SERIES

*I gratefully acknowledge the contributions
of the many people involved in the writing and production of this book.
Their tireless dedication to this endeavour has been inspirational.*
—Damon Neal, *Publisher*

Managing Editor:
John Gaffey

Senior Story Editor:
Gregory Scott

Senior Writer:
Megan Glomb

Proof Editors:
Avery Brown, Clarice Rodriguez, Robyn Sutherland

Graphic Design:
C.S. Rowan, Tamara Cornett , Michael Frye, Jesse Gifford, Jacob Kristof, Mary Murdock, Chris Rose-Merkle

Image Coordinators:
Wendy Gay and Donna Lindley

Website:
Molly Bermea, Ben Ford

Morgan & Chase Home Team
Cindy Tilley Faubion, Emily Wilkie, Pam Hamilton, Heather Allen , Virginia Arias, Ray Ackerman,
Danielle Barkley, Anne Boydston, Sue Buda, Casey Faubion, Shauna O'Callahan, Cari Qualls, Terrie West

Contributing Writers:
Dusty Alexander, Cory Bernhardt, Carol Bevis, Mark Allen Deruiter, Claudia Van Dyke, Lanette Fadley,
Dori Graham, Paul Hadella, Mary Knepp, Lynda Kusick, Lonnie Larson, Mary Beth Lee, Nancy McClain, Maggie McClellen,
Sandy McLain, Kevin Monk, Damon Peterson, Mary Sandlin, Timothy Smith, Susan Vaughn, Todd Wels

Special Recognition to:
Gene Mitts

We dedicate this book to the generous citizens of Oklahoma who shared their stories with us, and also to the state's next 100 years. We hope they are as grand as the last 100.

Our thanks to Lonnie Larson, a life-long resident of Oklahoma who is the personification of OK!

Finally, our gratitude goes to Pam Hamilton, because without her help this book could not have been completed.

Table of Contents

V Table of Contents

- VI Oklahoma Map
- VIII Oklahoma Fact
- 1 Forward

2 Central

Frontier Country

- 4 Accommodations & Resorts
- 18 Galleries & Fine Art
- 30 Museums, History & Culture
- 48 Restaurants, Bakeries & Cafés
- 54 Shopping & Services
- 63 Wines & Specialty Foods

68 Western

Red Carpet Country & Great Plains Country

- 70 Accommodations & Resorts
- 73 Attractions & Recreation
- 74 Galleries & Fine Art
- 75 Museums, History & Culture
- 81 Shopping & Services
- 85 Wines & Specialty Foods

88 Northeastern

Green Country

- 90 Sapulpa, Oklahoma
- 97 Accommodations & Resorts
- 112 Attractions & Recreation
- 130 Galleries & Fine Art
- 132 Museums, History & Culture
- 146 Restaurants, Bakeries & Cafés
- 168 Shopping & Services
- 183 Wines & Specialty Foods

188 Southern

Lake & Kiamichi Country

- 190 Accommodations & Resorts
- 196 Attractions & Recreation
- 197 Galleries & Fine Art
- 199 Museums, History & Culture
- 200 Restaurants, Bakeries & Cafés
- 202 Shopping & Services
- 203 Wines & Specialty Foods

204 Indices

- 204 Index by Treasure
- 209 Index by City

How to use this book

Treasures of Oklahoma is divided by region and category. Categories range from accommodations to wines, with headings such as attractions, galleries, museums, restaurants and shopping in between.

In the index, all of these Treasures are listed alphabetically by name as well as by the city where you can visit them.

We have provided contact information for every Treasure in the book.
These are places and businesses that we encourage you to visit on your travels through Oklahoma.

Central
Frontier Country

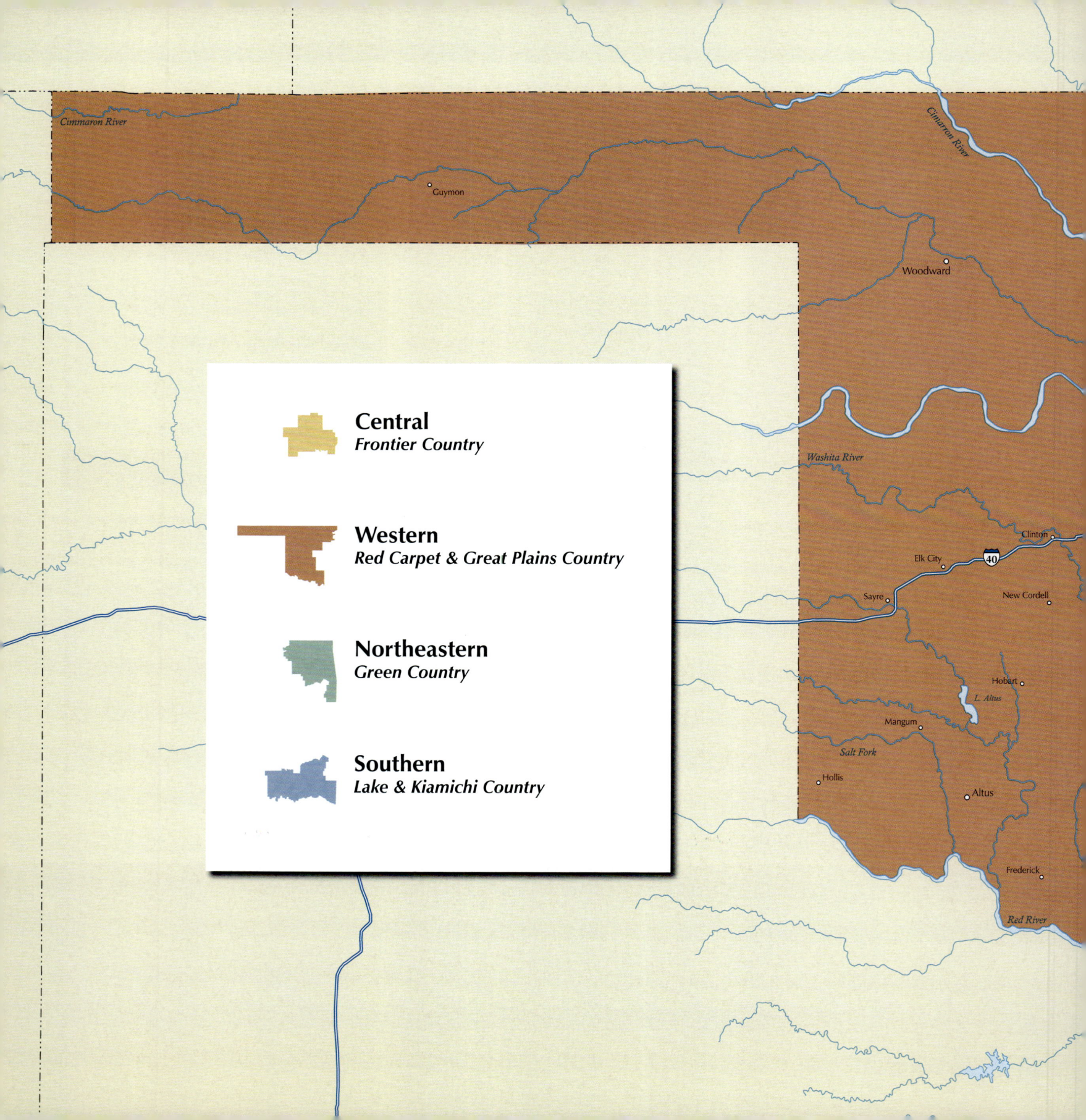

Western
Red Carpet & Great Plains Country

Northeastern
Green Country

Southern
Lake & Kiamichi Country

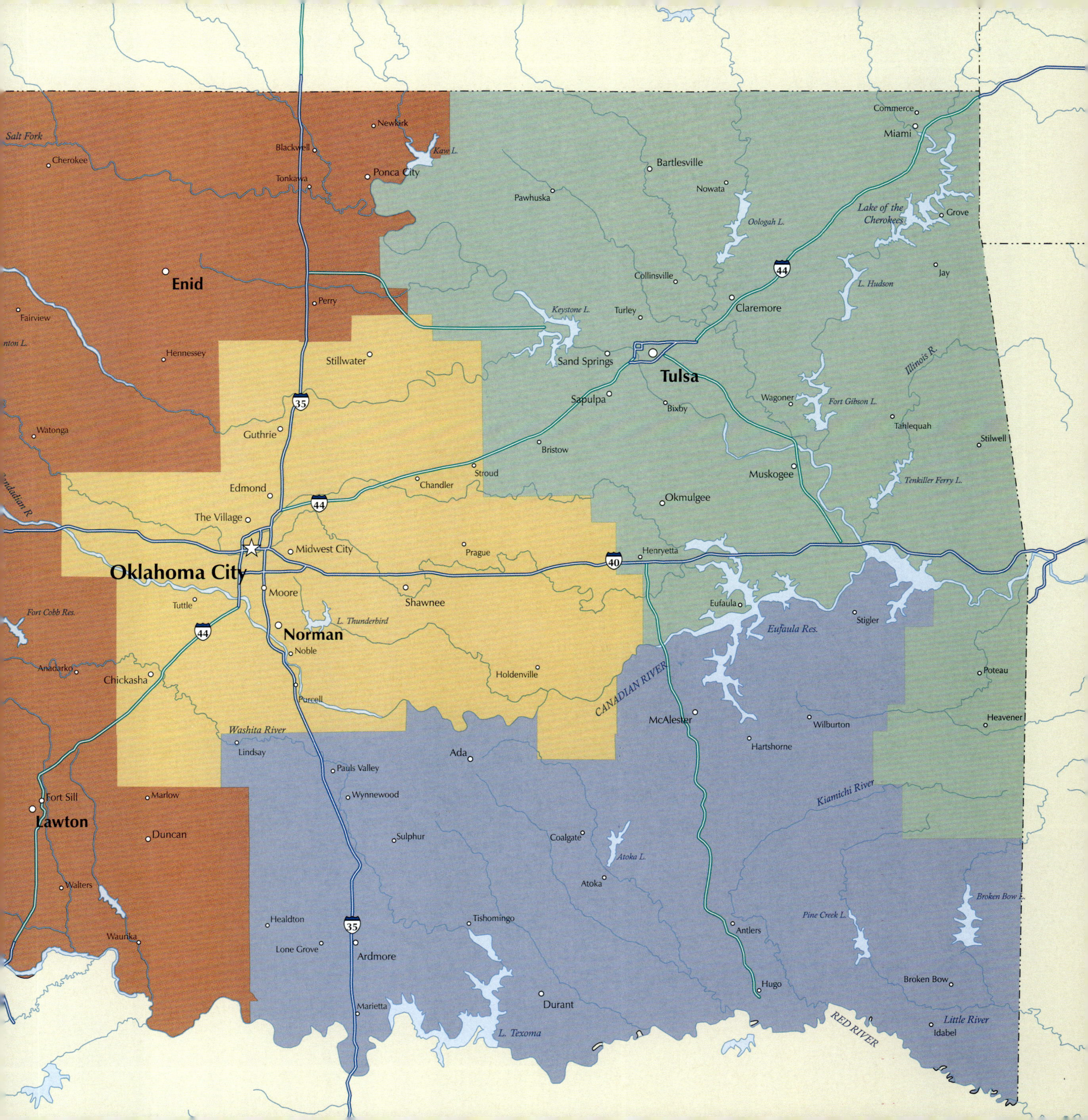

Salt Fork
Cherokee
Newkirk
Blackwell
Kaw L.
Tonkawa
Ponca City
Enid
Perry
Fairview
Hennessey
Watonga
Commerce
Miami
Bartlesville
Nowata
Pawhuska
Oologah L.
Lake of the Cherokees
Grove
Jay
L. Hudson
Collinsville
Claremore
Keystone L.
Turley
Sand Springs
Tulsa
Sapulpa
Bixby
Illinois R.
Wagoner
Fort Gibson L.
Tahlequah
Stilwell
Stillwater
35
Guthrie
Bristow
Stroud
Chandler
Edmond
44
Muskogee
Tenkiller Ferry L.
Okmulgee
The Village
Midwest City
Prague
Henryetta
40
Oklahoma City
Moore
Shawnee
Tuttle
Eufaula
Stigler
Fort Cobb Res.
L. Thunderbird
Eufaula Res.
44
Norman
Noble
Anadarko
Chickasha
Holdenville
Poteau
Canadian River
Purcell
McAlester
Wilburton
Heavener
Washita River
Lindsay
Hartshorne
Ada
Pauls Valley
Fort Sill
Marlow
Wynnewood
Kiamichi River
Lawton
Duncan
Sulphur
Coalgate
Atoka L.
Walters
Atoka
Broken Bow L.
Healdton
Tishomingo
35
Pine Creek L.
Waurika
Antlers
Lone Grove
Ardmore
Hugo
Broken Bow
Durant
Marietta
Little River
Red River
Idabel
L. Texoma

Scissor-tailed Flycatcher

OKLAHOMA FACTS:

Admitted to the Union: 1907, the 46th state
Population (2006): 3,579,212
Largest City: Oklahoma City, 531,324
Largest Metro Area: Oklahoma City, 1,172,339
Highest Mountain: Black Mesa, 4,973 feet

Animal: American Buffalo (Bison)
Bird: Scissor-tailed Flycatcher
Fish: White Bass
Floral Emblem: Mistletoe (*Phoradendron serotinum*)
Fossil: Saurophaganax maximus
Gemstone: Barite Rose
Motto: *Labor Omnia Vincit* (Labor Conquers All Things)
Nickname: Sooner State
Tree: Redbud (*Cercis canadensis*)

Foreword

Welcome to *Treasures of Oklahoma*, Centennial Edition. This book is a resource that can guide you to some of the best places in Oklahoma, a state of great diversity. Oklahoma's 11 distinct ecoregions range from the high plains of the Panhandle to the cypress swamps and forests of the southeast corner of the state. The Midwest, West, South and Southwest all meet in Oklahoma, yielding a sparkling cultural mosaic, just as colliding cold and warm air masses produce the most spectacular thunderstorms in the world.

Few states have a more distinctive history. This was once Indian Territory, the land of exile for the Five Civilized Tribes and other nations. Today, as many as a quarter of the state's population may be able to claim some Indian ancestry. In 1889, lands that include modern Oklahoma City were opened to white settlers in the first of a series of great Land Rushes. Some settlers crossed the line ahead of time—the Sooners. In the 20th century, newcomers flooded into Oklahoma after oil was discovered, but the drought and dust storms of the Dirty Thirties hit the state hard. Today, Oklahoma is booming again and the bustling metropolises of Oklahoma City and Tulsa are as cosmopolitan as any place on earth.

2007 is a special year to visit Oklahoma while it celebrates 100 years as part of the Union. Countless attractions await visitors to the state. See astonishing displays at the Stafford Air & Space Center in Weatherford or the Will Rogers Memorial Museum in Claremore. Visit Sapulpa, the Heart of Route 66, or the National Route 66 Museum in Elk City. For football action, cheer for the University of Oklahoma Sooners, national champions more times since World War II than any other team.

Oklahoma is home to the nicest people you'll ever meet. In preparing this book, we talked to thousands of small-business people about their products, their services and their vision. We visited art galleries in Norman and shopped for furniture in Oklahoma City. We visited wineries along the Turner Turnpike and enjoyed great Italian dining in suburban Tulsa. You are holding the result of our efforts in your hands. *Treasures of Oklahoma* is a 213-page compilation of the best places in Oklahoma to eat, shop, play, explore, learn and relax. We did the legwork. All you have to do now is enjoy

—John Gaffey

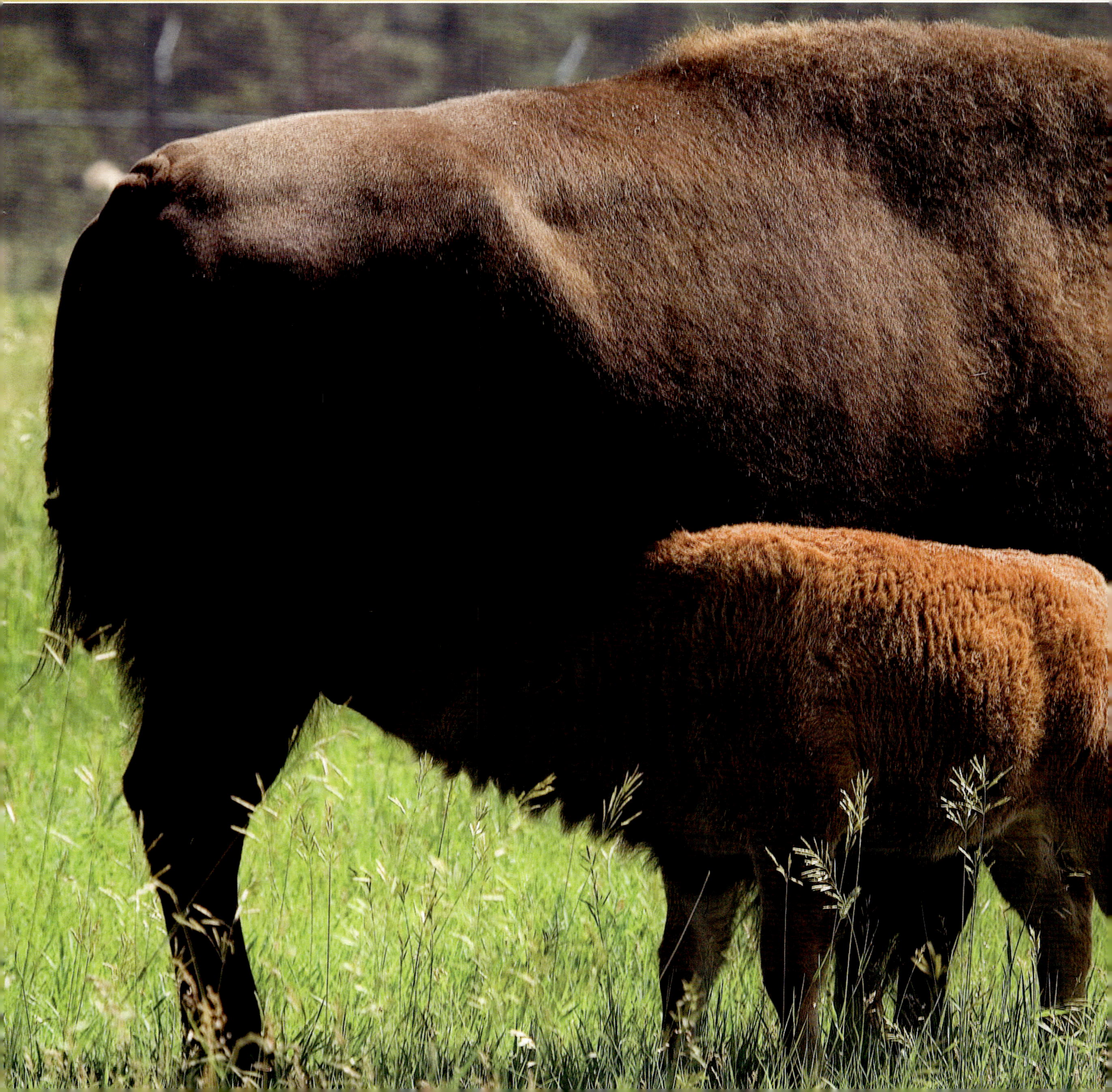

Central Oklahoma
Frontier Country

American Buffalo—Oklahoma State Animal

Accommodations & Resorts

Red Stone Inn Bed & Breakfast

What better way to explore Oklahoma City than from a restored 1930s mansion! The Red Stone Inn Bed & Breakfast, once the home of Territorial doctor Wyatt Slaughter, has been restored to its former splendor, thanks to the efforts of Ann and Mark Amme, who purchased the distinctive stone structure in 1996 and spent three years on renovations. Today, four guest rooms treat visitors to secluded acreage and views of downtown Oklahoma City. For all its peace and quiet, the Red Stone Inn is just minutes from favorite tourist destinations like the Zoo, Bricktown, the National Cowboy Museum, Remington Park and the Omniplex. All rooms feature jetted tubs and television, VCR and DVD players. Each room has its individual charms. Consider a suite in rich browns and golds with a king size pillow top bed, a private balcony and a panoramic view or a room with a Western theme and warm country antiques. The rooms and suites are spacious, elegantly appointed with family heirlooms and remarkably uncluttered. The breakfast room is stocked with homemade cookies, popcorn, tea, coffee and bottled drinks. Ann and Mark enjoy hosting weddings and retreats and won the 2004 Book of Lists Best for Wedding Services award. The ponds and wooded grounds make beautiful photo backdrops. Mark is an accomplished chef with a reputation for wedding cakes, hors d'oeuvres and even full-course meals. Enjoy today's entertainments and yesterday's quiet elegance at the Red Stone Inn.

3101 Northeast 50th Street, Oklahoma City OK
(405) 427-0383
www.redstoneinnokc.com

Renaissance Oklahoma City Convention Center Hotel

Renaissance Oklahoma City Convention Center Hotel brings elegance and comfort to your stay in the city. In the heart of downtown and just minutes from the Bricktown Canal and Entertainment District, this AAA four-diamond Marriott hotel will surpass your expectations for an upscale hotel experience. From the moment you enter the building and take in the stunning 15-story atrium, you will be treated like royalty. You can enjoy world-class dining at the Falling Water Grill or relax with a spa treatment from Tuo Bellaza. Whether you choose to work out in the health club or simply lie by one of the pools, the Renaissance makes your happiness a top priority. The rooms and suites, filled with tasteful furniture and décor, offer guests such thoughtful luxuries as high-speed Internet access, a complimentary daily newspaper and refrigerators. You can start each morning off right at Caffeina's Coffee Shop, where you can pick up freshly baked treats and Starbucks coffee products. For business travelers, the hotel offers many meeting rooms and a distinguished boardroom. If you have time to get outdoors, nearby activities include biking trails, tennis and golfing. At the Water's Edge Lounge, you will find a comfortable chair and a drink for unwinding after a busy day. Stay at the Renaissance Oklahoma City Convention Center Hotel, where your expectations for excellence will be satisfied.

10 N Broadway, Oklahoma City OK
(405) 228-8000
www.marriott.com

The Arcadian Inn Bed & Breakfast

When you need a day or two away from your ordinary routine, consider the charms of the Arcadian Inn Bed & Breakfast, located in the heart of Edmond. The building itself has a lot of history behind it, beginning back in 1902 when Dr. Ruhl began construction of a one-story home on property that had been deeded to his wife Edith. Later, the first story was raised and a second floor built underneath it. The house served as a family dwelling for many years, but was in a state of disrepair before preservation efforts began in 1989. A visit to the Arcadian Inn is a step back in time and a window on a world of yesterday lost to most of us. Spending a couple of days at the Arcadian Inn is an opportunity to enjoy a quiet retreat and old-fashioned hospitality. Couples appreciate soaking in a whirlpool for two and cuddling by the fire. You can even have a candlelight breakfast delivered to your room, featuring the inn's signature vanilla butter sauce, served on pancakes or waffles. Sophisticated casual dining is close by as well, and most Monday through Thursday guests can enjoy a free meal at Lottinville's Wood Grille as part of their getaway experience. While perhaps most appealing as a couple's getaway, visitors of all backgrounds and ages will enjoy stepping over a threshold into the past with a visit to the Arcadian Inn, where memories of your visit are certain to linger long after checkout.

328 E First Street, Edmond OK
(405) 348-6347
www.arcadianinn.com

America's Best Value Inn

With its 106 guestrooms, America's Best Value Inn is Shawnee's largest full-service hotel. The inn offers hospitality, affordable rates and a caring, efficient staff. It's also packed with entertainment options, including a glass-enclosed indoor pool surrounded by lavish greenery. Guests who want to socialize will enjoy the inn's disco club, open seven nights a week. The spacious rooms come equipped with high-speed Internet access, cable television with HBO and microwaves. Each room also has its own iron and ironing board, coffeemaker and hairdryer. The hotel's on-site restaurant offers complete brunch and dinner buffets, with room service available 24 hours a day. Conference rooms accommodate wedding receptions, family reunions and business meetings. The inn is just minutes away from local casinos, golf courses and a convenient shopping mall. Make reservations quickly and easily on the website or by telephone. Enjoy all that Shawnee has to offer while enjoying the comforts of America's Best Value Inn.

4900 N Harrison Avenue, Shawnee OK (405) 275-4404 (888) 315-BEST (2378) *www.americasbestvalueinn.com*

Accommodations & Resorts • 7

Holiday Inn at Norman

The Holiday Inn at Norman is perfect for those seeking an affordable stay in an upscale hotel. The only full-service hotel in the vicinity, it's located only minutes from the University of Oklahoma and a short drive to downtown Oklahoma City and the Will Rogers International Airport. In 2004, all 149 rooms in the hotel were redecorated and upgraded with such features as data ports, coffeemakers and Nintendo equipment. Thirteen suites are available, and seven rooms are designed to accommodate accessibility equipment for the handicapped. A free *USA Today* is delivered each weekday to all rooms. Whether you are traveling for business or pleasure, you'll find many comforts and extras here. You can order room service or visit the full-service restaurant and lounge. A computer in the lobby is available for guest use, and guests traveling with their own laptops will appreciate the hotel's free high-speed wireless Internet access. An exercise facility and an indoor pool and spa will keep you trim and relaxed during your stay. The Holiday Inn at Norman offers 7,000 square feet of meeting space to accommodate groups of any size. General Manager Penn Davidson says he runs the Norman Holiday Inn like a home away from home to entice his guests to keep coming back. The hotel makes an excellent base of operations for anyone attending one of the exciting athletic events hosted by the University of Oklahoma Sooners. When your travels take you to Norman, spend the night at the Holiday Inn.

1000 N Interstate Drive, Norman OK
(405) 364-2882
www.holiday-inn.com/normanok

Elk City/Clinton KOA

When you're traveling across country it's a special blessing to end your day at a place with standards you can trust. This is especially true of the Elk City/Clinton KOA. Just off Interstate 40, this campground is halfway between the two towns for which it is named. This is Route 66 country, and both towns have museums dedicated to the Mother Road. The campground is a short walk from Clinton Lake, which offers great sand bass and crappie fishing, and is a short drive to Foss Lake, also known for bass fishing. Cabins are available and come equipped with heat and air conditioning. You can park your RV on one of the many long, level, paved and shady RV sites or pitch a tent on a grassy site. The Elk City/Clinton KOA provides 30 or 50 amp service for RV sites, wireless Internet and cable television. You'll find the sparkling clean pool open May through September, a children's playground and a fenced pet area where the family hound can romp freely. Enjoy breakfast or dinner in the dining room or at your site. Be sure to save room for the exceptional homemade pie. If you're a stranger in the land, stop in and make a friend at the Elk City/Clinton KOA.

I-40, Exit 50 (Clinton Lake Road), Canute OK
(580) 592-4409

Casa Bella Bed & Breakfast

What do you do if you live next door to an unattractive tract home that has been abused over the years by a steady procession of renters? If you are Larry and Tricia Forbes, you buy the ugly little thing and renovate it until it emerges as the beautiful Casa Bella Bed & Breakfast. The transition was difficult and expensive, but the lovely Casita, meaning *little house*, that emerged from the renovation justified the effort, which included stripping the house to the bare studs and replacing all of the plumbing before rebuilding. The interior offers rich detail with Mexican art pieces, elegant antiques and intricate trim work. The outdoors with its lovely Mediterranean gardens offers a quiet retreat, punctuated by waterfalls, streams and stone paths. Guests enjoy an oversized hot tub, a large stone fire pit and an enticing hammock. The casita includes two bedrooms with queen size beds, luxurious linens and a double shower with Mexican tile. You can relax in an open living area with a serving bar and a kitchenette with a coffee maker and a microwave. Modern amenities abound, including satellite television, a VCR/DVD player and a stereo system. Each morning, a Continental breakfast is delivered to the Casita for dining at your leisure. The Casita's grounds offer space for a small wedding or party. For larger groups, you can arrange to rent the main hacienda's grounds. For a private, Mexican-style retreat in Norman, visit Casa Bella Bed & Breakfast.

638 E Brooks, Norman OK
(405) 329-2289
www.casabellabedandbreakfast.com

Rosewood Inn Bed and Breakfast

The Rosewood Inn Bed and Breakfast is among the most romantic places to stay in the Oklahoma City area. The inn's three guest accommodations are beautifully furnished. All have fireplaces, elegant beds and private baths. Whirlpool tubs for two come with scented bath salts and spa bathrobes. Each room has a microwave, refrigerator and video library. The romantic and spacious Friendship Suite displays elegant walls of burgundy and forest green. Daybreak's décor includes sport memorabilia that will rekindle youthful memories. The Simplicity Room soothes your spirit. The Rosewood Inn's signature homemade peanut butter chocolate chip cookies await you in your room. In the morning, wake up to the aroma of coffee and a homemade breakfast served at the time of your choice. You can enjoy breakfast in your room, in the Gathering Room or outside in the Rosewood Gardens. You can stroll through the gardens, relax in the shade of a 60-year-old pecan tree and listen to the babbling brook. The Rosewood was the project of innkeepers Val and Dana Owens, who completely rebuilt the house beginning in 1993. Val recently passed on, and his son Garrett is now the manager. The inn continues to show the same attention to detail and pampering of its guests that it did under Val. Even the cookie recipe remains the same. Be sure to ask your hosts about dinner options, in-room massages and other amenities. The inn frequently hosts weddings and similar gatherings. Visit the Rosewood Inn Bed and Breakfast, where you can turn hectic moments into pleasant memories.

7000 NW 39th Street, Bethany OK
(405) 787-3057 or (888) 786-3057
www.rosewoodinnbb.com

Oklahoma City Zoological Park and Botanical Garden

It's often been said that kids love zoos, wherever they are and whatever creatures they happen to star. At the Oklahoma Zoological Park and Botanical Garden, you will find that this adage applies to adults as well, and spending a day here allows a visitor to see why the staff claims to be part of one of the best zoological facilities in America. The zoo features a varied assortment of beasts and critters, including some of the world's most exotic animals, on 110 lushly planted acres. In 2004, Child magazine honored the zoo as the third-best family-friendly zoo in the country, against some very stiff competition. With great amenities and interesting displays around every corner, kids of any age will have a spectacular experience. Beyond animals, you'll find many amusements, including a tram, a rock climbing wall, a children's train and swan-shaped paddleboats. When it comes time to feed the beast within, the on-site Canopy Food Court offers climate-controlled comfort and a variety of food options. It pays to plan ahead for a visit here, especially if you have kids along. You can access a map and exploration guide on the zoo's website that will help you get the lay of the land. So put together your visiting strategy and take some time out of the daily grind to spend a few hours with the engaging wildlife at the Oklahoma City Zoological Park and Botanical Garden. Everyone in the family is sure to have a wonderful time!

2101 NE 50th Street, Oklahoma City OK 405-424-3344
www.okczoo.com

City of Guthrie

Plenty of history and civic enthusiasm make Guthrie, the first state capital of Oklahoma, an ideal place to celebrate the Centennial and to explore Oklahoma's rich heritage year-round. Guthrie was born of the Land Run of 1889, when President Benjamin Harrison opened two million acres of Indian Territory for homesteading on a first-arrival basis. This dusty prairie stop along the AT&SF railroad became home to more than 10,000 settlers in a single day. Within months, Guthrie was an elegant, fully functioning Victorian city. Careful restoration has preserved this architectural legacy in one of the largest designated historic district in the United States. Downtown Guthrie itself is a National Historic Landmark, where history comes alive each day in six unique museums and hourly Historic Trolley Tours. Landmarks such as the Oklahoma Territorial Museum, the Frontier Drugstore Museum and the world's largest Scottish Rite Masonic Temple add to the historical wealth of the town. Guthrie celebrates heritage festivals throughout the year. Its 89er Celebration commemorating the Land Run boasts Oklahoma's largest 89er Day parade. During the Territorial Christmas Celebration, citizens don period dress for the Victorian Walk through the streets of downtown, where store windows feature live exhibits depicting 19th century Guthrie. Visitors can enjoy world-class bluegrass music at the annual Oklahoma International Bluegrass Festival and year-round at the Double Stop Fiddle Shop & Music Hall. Explore Oklahoma's cultural heritage in historic Guthrie.

212 W Oklahoma Street, Guthrie OK
(405) 282-1947 (Chamber of Commerce)
www.guthrieok.com

Attractions & Recreation

Oklahoma State University Botanical Garden

Envision a creation of loveliness beckoning you to wander its paths and explore its courtyards and niches. You'll find this and more at the Oklahoma State University (OSU) Botanical Garden, which offers visitors peaceful repose, solitude, contemplation and many educational opportunities. The garden, located on 100 acres west of the OSU campus, contains display gardens with an abundance of annuals and perennials. You'll see a water, rock and wildscape gardens. There's a Japanese tea garden, patio garden and six to seven yearly theme gardens. The permanent plant collections and seasonal gardens at the research facility serve as living laboratories for students and visitors. The educational site contains more than 1,000 species of herbaceous and woody plants, an arboretum, turf and nursery research centers, and the set of the *Oklahoma Gardening* television show. The studio gardens cover three acres and include vegetable, herb, formal, annual and perennial gardens, plus a fruit orchard and a compost demonstration site. There is even a chicken moat garden and a fantasy theme garden for children. The OSU Botanical Garden is also the headquarters for the Oklahoma Botanical Garden & Arboretum, the statewide arboretum system. Visit the OSU Botanical Garden and enjoy the diverse beauty that Oklahoma has to offer.

3425 W Virginia, Stillwater OK
(405) 744-6460

Myriad Botanical Gardens

A breathtaking urban paradise lies nestled in the heart of downtown Oklahoma City. The Myriad Botanical Gardens provides 17 acres of landscaped lawns and lush gardens surrounding a two-acre sunken lake teeming with fish and water loving plants. In the center is the Gardens' gem—the Crystal Bridge Tropical Conservatory—a living plant museum housing more than 1,000 species of tropical and sub-tropical plants. This cylindrical glass structure is organized into two distinct habitat regions: the Tropical Rainforest Zone and the Arid Tropical Zone. Each habitat features outstanding collections of plants found in their respective biomes, with the dominant types being palms, orchids, gingers, bromeliads, begonias, euphobias and cycads. Outside the conservatory, on the northeast corner of the grounds, you'll find the Meinders Garden. Each spring, this garden explodes in a riot of color and boasts an array of some of the most outstanding perennials and flowering shrubs recommended for use in Oklahoma. Throughout the year, the Gardens' Water Stage, a lake-side amphitheater, hosts many events, including twilight concerts and Oklahoma Shakespeare in the Park. Many of the garden areas are available for wedding and event bookings. What started as a collective dream for early city leaders is now an exotic reality for citizens and tourists alike. A visit to Oklahoma City is not complete until you experience the Myriad Botanical Gardens.

301 W Reno (corner of Reno and Robinson),
Oklahoma City OK
(405) 297-3995
www.myriadgardens.com

Attractions & Recreation • 13

Photo by KB35

Water Taxi of Oklahoma City

Want to see Oklahoma City in an entirely new way? Hail a taxi, a Water Taxi, that is. Since 2002, Water Taxi of Oklahoma City has provided residents and visitors with a tantalizing glimpse of the capital city as they ride along the manmade Bricktown Canal. The Bricktown Canal was one of the major components that transformed a former warehouse district into a thriving entertainment district. Just as a flower receives nourishment from the rain, the canal helped grow new business in formerly abandoned buildings. From April through October, the distinctive yellow Water Taxi boats run from 10 am to 10 pm with extended hours during July and August. During the regular season, you can board a Water Taxi every 10 to 15 minutes at the firm's landing on the Bricktown Riverwalk. During the off-season, Water Taxi's schedule is weather-dependent. Passengers can also board a water taxi at other dock locations by hailing the taxi from the shore. You'll find restaurants, entertainment venues and other businesses along the canal. You will get a glimpse of some lovely parkland, and a guide will provide historical information and entertaining commentary as you travel. The entire round trip takes approximately 40 minutes. In addition to its normal services, Water Taxi offers cocktail and catered dinner cruises as well as private charters. Let Water Taxi of Oklahoma City take you on an unforgettable voyage through the splendid scenery, shopping and entertainment opportunities of Oklahoma City.

115 E California Avenue, Suite 300, Oklahoma City OK
(405) 234-TAXI (8294)
www.watertaxi.com

Oklahoma Centennial Freedom Festival

The city of Bethany's annual 4th of July Freedom Festival is bigger than ever in Oklahoma's Centennial year. The fest combines old-fashioned family fun with one of the state's most impressive fireworks displays. The day begins with a traditional morning flag-raising ceremony and recognition of soldiers past and present. Then the festivities kick off with the Bethany Centennial Freedom Run beginning at 7:30 am. At 10, the Oklahoman Centennial Parade marches from Southern Nazarene University to Eldon Lyon Park, where carnival rides, food and novelty vendors await the revelers. Leading the schedule of games throughout the day is the 3-on-3 Nothin' but Net Basketball Tournament, followed by the Fox 25 Oklahoma Idol and So You Think You Can Dance contests. Entertainment includes Winter Circle, Fresh Sunday, Maci Wainwright and Harvey and the Wallbangers. One of the special Centennial events is a Land Run Re-enactment. All are invited to come dressed in period costumes and race on foot or haul their wagon to the plot of land they want to homestead. As evening sets in, guests enjoy a barbecue dinner by the lake as the sky darkens for the fireworks finale.

6700 NW 36th Street, Bethany OK
(405) 789-5005

Remington Park Racetrack & Casino

For many, a visit to the racetrack is a simple chance to enjoy a nice day outdoors soaking in the ambiance of the sports entertainment world. For others, the thrill is in the attempt to try to figure out which proud steed will win each of the many equine competitions taking place on any given day. Both types of race fans are quite welcome at Remington Park Racetrack & Casino, a large but comfortable facility sitting on 375 prime acres in the heart of Oklahoma City's well named Adventure district. Founded by the late Edward DeBartolo, Sr., Remington Park consists of a stable area with 18 barns and more than 1,300 stalls, as well as a main one-mile oval track with room to accommodate over 20,000 fans. A recent $35 million renovation transformed the old Grandstand floor into the Remington Park Casino, thus expanding the operation to what it is today. Despite the variety of activities that are usually going on all around, it is possible to settle in and enjoy a memorable horse race in a beautiful setting before heading off to hit the slots and other games of chance.

One Remington Place, Oklahoma City OK
(405) 424-1000
www.remingtonpark.com

FireLake Grand Casino

The latest accomplishment of the Citizen Potawatomi Nation, FireLake Grand Casino is taking Oklahoma gaming to the next level. The first true Las Vegas-style casino in Oklahoma, FireLake Grand Casino boasts beautiful architecture inside and out. More than 125,000 square feet of premier gaming space supports 1,800 of the newest games—all Class 3, Vegas style. In addition to the wide variety of slots, the casino has 100 table games including blackjack, poker and Ultimate Texas Hold'Em. Try craps or Spinette, similar to roulette. Dining options at the casino are as great as the games. The Grand Buffet is a delight to the senses. Wall-to-wall plasma screens in the Grandstand Sports Grille ensure you'll catch all the action while you enjoy your favorite food and drink. Embers Steakhouse offers the finest cuts of meat, seafood and an extensive wine collection. Perched atop the second floor balcony, the Fire & Ice Bar is the hot spot for cooling off. Finally, the Roasted Bean Café will wake you up with the finest gourmet coffee and desserts. The casino hosts top-notch special promotions, plus the biggest names in entertainment. Wayne Newton, Randy Travis and Three Dog Night are among the recent headliners. A seven-story hotel and a coliseum are under development for the site. For a night you'll remember, come to the FireLake Grand Casino.

777 Grand Casino Boulevard, Shawnee OK
(405) 96-GRAND (964-7263)
www.firelakegrand.com

Citizen Potawatomi Nation Cultural Heritage Center

The Citizen Potawatomi Nation Cultural Heritage Center houses the nation's museum, library, veteran's memorial and much else. The museum's facilities, a source of pride, are absolutely state-of-the-art. As a result, the museum will be able to accept exhibitions from everywhere. The Citizen Potawatomi are a dynamic people with a bright future, and the museum emphasizes the connection between the nation's ancestors and the people of today. The theme is not Who We Were, but Who We Are. The permanent collection features Potawatomi artifacts drawn from the museum's collections, along with interpretive displays. Revolving exhibits in the Long Room consist of thematically grouped displays, for example, everyday textiles and how they changed over the years. The museum is digitally capturing its entire collection, and the results in time will be available over the Internet. The Long Room, a meeting hall that can seat up to 1,000, is also the site of the veteran's memorial, the Wall of Honor. This moving display of photos, framed letters, awards and decorations pays homage to the warriors who stepped forward when called. The center also houses offices, a genealogical research facility, a language classroom and a recording site for the Tribal Heritage project. Come see the Citizen Potawatomi Nation Cultural Heritage Center, one of the most impressive museum complexes in Oklahoma.

1899 S Gordon Cooper Drive, Shawnee OK
(405) 275-3121 or (800) 880-9880
www.potawatomi.org/Culture/default.aspx

Attractions & Recreation

The Chesapeake Boathouse

The Chesapeake Boathouse welcomes you to the Oklahoma River in downtown Oklahoma City with a combination of dramatic architecture and fun family activities. The Chesapeake Boathouse has quickly become the center of activity on the newly rejuvenated river and offers rowing, kayaking, dragon boating and bicycling for ages eight to 80. Visitors to the river can take a tour of the boathouse, rent bicycles to explore 13-plus miles of trails or kayaks for a little on-the-water fun. If you have a larger group, consider a dragon boat excursion. You'll need 16 to 20 paddlers to keep this colorful 60-foot boat moving down the river. The boathouse can also be reserved for special events and offers day passes for its state-of-the-art fitness facility. Even if you're not a candidate for the more active side of the boathouse, make a point to visit just to experience the art and architecture of rowing. Hailed by many as a landmark presence, the Chesapeake Boathouse design represents a sleek rowing shell with 16 columns of light highlighting the reflecting pool at the bow of the building. Inside, you'll find a magnificent display of rowing shells and a rowing community eager to share their passion for the sport with you. Early mornings and late afternoons, you'll be likely to see rowers of all ages on the water. The Chesapeake Boathouse is Oklahoma City's community boathouse and has something for everyone, so visit it soon.

725 S Lincoln Boulevard, Oklahoma City OK
(405) 552-4040
www.chesapeakeboathouse.org

Attractions & Recreation • 17

Oklahoma Opry

Are you ready for Oklahoma's best-kept secret? Then you won't want to miss Oklahoma's largest and longest-running country music show, the Oklahoma Opry. Founded in 1977, the Opry showcases outstanding talent from Oklahoma and the surrounding states at its Friday and Saturday night music shows. Country, gospel, oldies and comedy shows promise a good time for the whole family in a non-smoking, alcohol-free environment. Up to nine performers may appear each night, backed by the house band. The Opry has introduced more than 20,000 entertainers to the Oklahoma public, including such greats as Edgar Cruz, Carrie Underwood, Bryan White and Reba MacEntire. The theater offers padded seats and concession stand with mouth-watering snacks for intermissions. After the show, guests can check out merchandise at the Entertainers' Table. The Opry provides front-curbside parking and accommodations for tour buses. For affordable, family entertainment, visit the Oklahoma Opry and enjoy Oklahoma's finest talent.

**404 SW 25th Street,
Oklahoma City OK
(405) 632-8322
www.okopry.com**

Galleries & Fine Art

Norman Gallery Association

A wide variety of quality visual art is available throughout the year in these Norman galleries

Downtown Art and Frame

An informal mix of gallery and workshop space, Downtown Art and Frame showcases original works by new and established Oklahoma artists. Owner Barney Gibbs has been framing treasures for museums, galleries and the public for 29 years. He consults closely with conservators and museum professionals to ensure that Downtown Art and Frame takes every step necessary for the long-term preservation of valuable art and documents.

115 S Santa Fe Avenue, Norman OK
(405) 329-0309

Performing Arts Studio

In addition to ongoing gallery exhibitions, the Performing Arts Studio (PAS) offers two free concerts each month from May through September for the Summer Breeze Concert Series. Poetry readings offered each month are also free and open to the public. The public can purchase tickets for the Winter Wind Concert Series held on Sundays from October through April. In addition, Oklahoma's passenger rail connection, the Heartland Flyer, stops each morning at the Depot on its 419-mile journey from Oklahoma City to Ft. Worth. Departing passengers enjoy coffee at the gallery while viewing the exhibitions at the PAS.

200 S Jones Avenue, Norman OK
(405) 307-9320

Shevaun Williams & Associates

Shevaun Williams is an award-winning fine-art and commercial photographer who has provided her clients with the highest quality photography for more than 20 years. Shevaun Williams & Associates is housed in a 4,500 square-foot historic building in downtown Norman. The renovated space includes a staging area, plus four separate studio spaces and galleries to display Williams' art. Exhibitions displaying a variety of fine art are held in conjunction with the art walks, which are free and open to the public.

221 E Main Street, Norman OK
(405) 329-6455

The Norman Gallery Association is a non-profit organization that promotes original fine art in Norman. The member galleries and museums sponsor programs most of which are located in Norman's historic downtown arts district. The galleries offer free refreshments during

Galleries & Fine Art • 19

The Crucible Gallery and Sculpture Garden

The Crucible Gallery and Sculpture Garden exhibits work created in Norman's Crucible Foundry. This facility attracts talented artists from across the country to practice the ancient art of casting monumental bronze sculpture. The Crucible had the honor of pouring the Guardian, the Native American statue that sits on the top of the new Oklahoma State Capitol dome. As a reflection of the talent it has gathered, the Crucible Gallery and Sculpture Garden has quickly become a destination point for hundreds of arts patrons who visit each month. The exhibits at the Gallery, which rotate seasonally, present a broad range of style, motion and expression.

110 E Tonhawa Street, Norman OK
(405) 579-2700

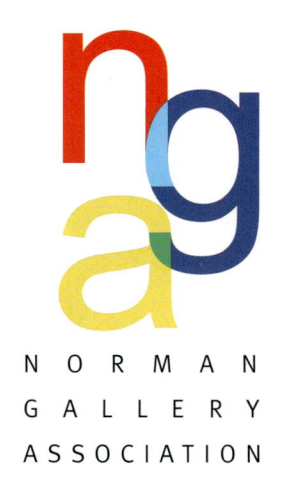

NORMAN GALLERY ASSOCIATION

Come to the Heart of Norman for the Arts!

Mainsite Contemporary Art Gallery

Owner Gary Clinton established Mainsite Contemporary Art in the late 1990s to highlight the work of living artists. Located in the heart of the downtown arts district, the gallery features regionally emerging artists, as well as recognized national and international artists. The gallery exhibits eight shows each year.

122 E Main Street, Norman OK
(405) 292-8095

Dreamer Concepts Studio and Foundation

Dreamer Concepts Studio and Foundation opened its doors in December 2006. The mission of this non-profit foundation is to encourage and promote new artists in the community. Through the studio, Dreamer Concepts offers emerging artists a critical and receptive environment in which to display their work. The foundation works with artists to help them develop the professional and business skills necessary to succeed. As a community of artists, the foundation provides a meaningful framework for networking and access to a wide variety of specialized speakers and cultural events. Visitors to Dreamer Concepts Studio and Foundation will find a colorful array of affordable, one-of-a-kind gift items.

324 E Main Street, Norman OK
(405) 701-0048

and exhibitions that introduce Norman artists to the public. During its seasonal art walks, the Gallery Association invites everyone to browse its member galleries, the walks and display art in a wide variety of media and styles. Let the Norman Gallery Association show you what Norman artists have to offer.

20 • Galleries & Fine Art

Norman Gallery Association

A wide variety of quality visual art is available throughout the year in these Norman galleries

Ring of Fire Studio

The Ring of Fire Studio has some of the finest pieces of blown glass and sculptures in Oklahoma. Owners Craig and Allison Clingan have been making glass works of art together for more than 10 years. Although they enjoy creating a wide variety of glass art, their main focus is on illuminated sculpture and lighting.

318 E Main Street, Norman OK
(405) 701-5300

Jacobson House Native Art Center

The Jacobson House Native Art Center is on the National Register of Historic Places and the Oklahoma Historical Society's Landmarks List. Jacobson House stands as a living symbol of the recognition of Native American art, a medium that speaks to the spirit of every person. Bringing art exhibits, cultural activities, lectures and workshops to the public, Jacobson House continues the tradition begun by Oscar and Jeanne d'Ucel Jacobson and their Native American student artists.

609 Chautauqua Avenue, Norman OK
(405) 366-1667

Firehouse Art Center

Since 1971, the Firehouse Art Center (FAC) has served Norman and surrounding communities with visual art classes and gallery exhibitions of high quality. The FAC brings guest artists of national renown to Norman to teach weekend workshops while the gallery exhibits their work. It attracts art students from a three-state region. The many community events the FAC produces are well known, and include the Chocolate Festival and Gala, ArchitecTour, Midsummer Nights' Fair, the Ceramic Art Auction and the Holiday Gift Gallery.

444 S Flood Avenue, Norman OK
(405) 329-4523

The Norman Gallery Association is a non-profit organization that promotes original fine art in Norman. The member galleries and museums sponsor programs most of which are located in Norman's historic downtown arts district. The galleries offer free refreshments during

Galleries & Fine Art • 21

Norman Arts Council

One of the Norman Arts Council's (NAC) community projects is the NAC gallery. In 2005, the NAC opened its office space to local community residents as an art gallery in an outreach effort to provide a space to exhibit their work. The NAC works with the Firehouse Art Center to secure local artists and their work for display. Because Norman is truly a community of artists, the NAC seeks to promote and encourage budding artists through the gallery project.

220 E Main, Suite 101, Norman OK
(405) 360-1162
www.normanarts.org

NORMAN GALLERY ASSOCIATION

Come to the Heart of Norman for the Arts!

Moore-Lindsay House Historical Museum

The Moore-Lindsay House Historical Museum offers visitors an excellent glimpse of late-Victorian lifestyles as well as the early history of Norman. After years of neglect, the period home was purchased by the City of Norman in 1973. The city renovated it and opened it to the public in 1975. The turn-of-the-century Queen Anne-style Victorian dwelling features shingled siding, expansive porches, stained glass windows and a turret. Now home to the Cleveland County Historical Society, the house serves as a showroom for the society's collection of territorial-era artifacts and furnishings. As a result, the Moore-Lindsay House Historical Museum is a living demonstration of urban domestic life during Oklahoma's Territorial Era, 1889 to 1907.

508 N Peters Avenue, Norman OK
(405) 321.0156

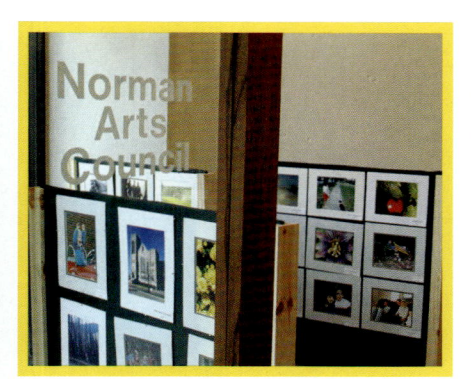

Blue Apples Gallery

Norman Artist Ron Radcliff, whose work has won praise over 30 years, owns Blue Apples Gallery. The gallery features artists from Oklahoma, Colorado, Texas, Kansas, Iowa and British Columbia, Canada. Over 50 artists have shown their work in the gallery since it opened in April 2005. The consignment artists of the Apple Core exhibit in mediums ranging from jewelry, photography and sculpture to fine pottery and paintings. Work is rotated every two to three months.

800 W Rock Creek Road, Suite 117, Norman OK
(405) 321-0342

Hall of Tattoos

Hall of Tattoos is the gallery and studio of Kenny Hall and staff, award-winning artists with 42 years of tattoo experience between them. Specializing in both black and gray and color work, the Halls draw custom designs for 40 percent of their clients. Examples of their small, full sleeve and back pieces line the walls of the studio. In addition to tattoo designs, Hall of Tattoos displays a wide range local artwork in mediums ranging from sculpture to prints, paintings and jewelry.

328 E Main Street, Norman OK
(405) 364-7335

and exhibitions that introduce Norman artists to the public. During its seasonal art walks, the Gallery Association invites everyone to browse its member galleries, the walks and display art in a wide variety of media and styles. Let the Norman Gallery Association show you what Norman artists have to offer.

22 • Galleries & Fine Art

Photos by Jai Gronemeier

Galleries & Fine Art • 23

MSB Art Gallery

Ed Crane's MSB Art Gallery specializes in creative custom and conservation framing, large oil paintings and beautiful, ready-made frames. Do you like dreamy Tuscan landscapes with fields of rich red poppies? Perhaps you enjoy Native American art, something whimsical or inspirational art. Whatever you seek, you'll find it here. The gallery features oils and giclee prints by Oklahoma artists such as Janet Loveless and Brad Price. It stocks more than 1,500 prints from artists that include Guilloume, G. Harvey, Jose Candia and many others. You can also use a computerized database to search through more than 200,000 prints you can special-order. MSB Art Gallery's custom framing includes dry mounting, glass selection and matting. Choose among hundreds of moldings and mat boards. Consider a custom shadow box to exhibit three-dimensional mementoes such as your baby's shoes, rattle and first hair clipping. You'll also find contemporary-looking wraparound giclee canvases that need no framing at all. MSB Art Gallery also shows bronze sculptures by Oklahoma artist Sandra Van Zandt, whose commissioned artworks are on display in public buildings and museums throughout the U.S. For a great gift, check out the handmade glass paperweights from Glass Eye Studio. Owner Ed Crane has developed a lease-to-own program through which businesses and organizations can adorn their walls with upscale art without immediately paying the entire cost of the works. Come see what Ed has on display. Whatever your preferences, MSB Art Gallery, located in Chatenay Square Shopping Plaza, has something for you.

10600 S Pennsylvania Avenue, Oklahoma City OK
(405) 692-0087
www.msbartgallery.com

Firehouse Art Center

Firehouse Art Center, a nonprofit art gallery and community arts organization, emerged from the lobbying efforts of a group of artists who convinced the city of Norman to turn an old firehouse into an art center in 1971. Now run by Executive Director Danette Ward, who is an acrylics and mixed media artist, the gallery enriches the lives of the people of Norman by displaying quality artwork and offering art instruction and community events. The gallery covers the full range of artistic expression, from painting and sculpture to ceramics, stained glass and photography. The art displayed here represents artists from the Norman metropolitan area, other communities within Oklahoma and graduates of Oklahoma University. The center hosts several popular annual events, such as the Midsummer Nights' Fair in mid July, which features artist's booths, live entertainment and kid's art. The Chocolate Festival and Gala is an October fundraiser featuring outstanding food, plus live and silent art auctions. The center offers art instruction for budding artists of all ages, including one-night sampler classes, three-day workshops and nine-week sessions in a multitude of subjects. See how art can galvanize a community with a visit to Firehouse Art Center.

444 S Flood Avenue, Norman OK
(405) 329-4523
www.normanfirehouse.com

Melton Art Reference Library

Specializing in lesser-known artists of the 16th through 20th centuries, the Melton Art Reference Library attracts students, appraisers and aficionados from all over the country to its collection of fine art reproductions, auction catalogs, art books and biographies. Its adjacent gallery features themes within the collection. This reservoir of art education in the heart of Oklahoma promotes art awareness in the community and introduces Oklahoma artists to the world. Director Suzanne Silvester has been particularly eager to support Oklahoma artists. The library has added works from nearly 100 Oklahoma artists to the collection, published a directory and sent a special exhibit on a national tour. Suzanne is the daughter of lifelong art collectors Howard and Merle Melton, who established the nonprofit in 1989. To carry on their mission, Suzanne also organizes educational programs for elementary schools and scholarships for study abroad. In 2001, the Melton Art Reference Library donated a collection to the University of Central Oklahoma (UCO), where it is well-placed to inspire the community. UCO's composer-in-residence, Dr. Sam Magrill, wrote an orchestral piece inspired by three of the artists in the collection. Find your inspiration at the Melton Art Reference Library.

4300 Sewell Avenue, Oklahoma City OK
(405) 525-3603

Galleries & Fine Art • 25

Avondale Galleries

Avondale Galleries has been one of Oklahoma's leading fine art galleries since 1983 and is one of the most established international fine art galleries in Oklahoma. Avondale Galleries specializes in fine art restoration and appraisals, plus exquisite custom framing. The gallery also carries hundreds of American and European original oils, bronze sculptures and unusual gifts. The expert staff at the gallery can assist you with fine art placement, including gallery groupings and single placement in your home or office. At Avondale Galleries, you can choose from among hundreds of frames, including American, French and Italian mouldings, as well as custom designs and hand-carved custom frames in metal leaf and leaf finishes of up to 23.5 karat gold. Appraisals include photo-art and insurance. Avondale Galleries is located in the Nichols Hills Plaza in northwest Oklahoma City. Visit Avondale Galleries, and let the staff show you the real value that art can bring into your life.

**6463 Avondale Drive,
Oklahoma City OK
(405) 840-5614**
www.avondalegalleries.com

26 • Galleries & Fine Art

Cross Bar Gallery

Oklahomans know the Cross Bar Gallery for its stunning collection of Western art, much of it exclusive, and the handcrafted, one-of-a-kind Western furniture. The gallery was first opened by Oklahoma artist Bill Jaxon, voted one of America's 25 most popular artists in 1995. Jaxon set up his easel in the back corner of the Gallery. Many of his originals and limited edition prints are showcased on the walls today. In 2005, local horse owners Terry and Jo Wiens purchased the Gallery, and since then, have opened it to other local and regional Western artists. You'll see the J.F. Policky giclee *Wild Oats* as you walk through the door. Bronzes by renowned Western sculptor C.R. Morrison are on display. Other represented artists include G. Harvey, Jason Rich, Martin Grelle and Bill Anton, among many others. A visit to Cross Bar Gallery is like a trip back to the Old West. Museum quality displays of art, accessories and Western furniture make a visit to the Gallery time well spent. Cross Bar Gallery's talented furniture craftsmen can create a perfect leather sofa, cowhide chaise lounge or built-ins to your specifications for your custom kitchen. Select your own materials from the Gallery's extensive collection of only the highest quality leathers and cowhides. You'll also find a huge selection of Western chandeliers, table and floor lamps, wall sconces and lighting. Lampshades of high-quality skins, leathers and rawhides are in stock. Western chairs, tables and ottomans adorned with polished longhorns are ever popular items and are always in supply at the Gallery. Come see the Cross Bar Gallery, where you'll find everything for the ranch and Western home.

4312 W Reno,
Oklahoma City OK
(405) 943-5600
www.crossbargallery.com

Dean-Lively Gallery & Frame

Proprietors Greg and Elaine Dean established Dean-Lively Gallery & Frame in 1992. The gallery is located in the historical district of downtown Edmond. Oklahoma City newspapers have voted it one of the city's top galleries. Dean-Lively offers original art from local artists as well as the opportunity to special order art from national artists and publishers. Dean-Lively carries a broad selection of Giclée prints, canvas transfers, photography and many other types of art media. Recognized for its style, creativity and quality custom framing, Dean-Lively it has the largest selection of custom framing in the metro area. Other services include shadow boxing, custom mirrors, art restoration, hanging and delivery. All of these services are available to both residential and commercial clients. The main focus is on customer service. The friendly staff at Dean-Lively Gallery & Frame strive to make an enjoyable experience for anyone who may walk through their doors.

16 S Broadway (1½ blocks N of 2nd Street), Edmond OK
(405) 341-2143
www.deanlivelygallery2.com

Galleries & Fine Art • 29

One of the many public artworks in Bricktown

30 • Museums, History & Culture

Oklahoma History Center

Treasures from Oklahoma's past moved to a new home in 2005 with the completion of the $59 million, 215,000-square-foot Oklahoma History Center. The architectural triumph, described as "Oklahoma's temple to history" by Bob Blackburn, executive director of the Oklahoma Historical Society, gives visitors the opportunity to explore Oklahoma's adventurous past. Bob estimates that it would take most people five to seven days to view every exhibit, film and photo clip housed here. A soaring glass atrium features a replica of the Winnie Mae airplane that Wiley Post flew around the world in eight days. You'll find an 1830s-era Red River riverboat, a covered wagon from the Oklahoma Land Run and the Gemini 6 space capsule. The center includes four permanent galleries, including the Oneok Gallery of the American Indian. Exhibits change, but gallery themes remain constant. A fifth gallery is devoted to special exhibitions and events. One outdoor exhibit takes visitors on a walking tour that simulates the Red River Valley; another features drilling derricks and oil exploration equipment. Still another outdoor exhibit, 14 Flags over Oklahoma, describes the nations and people who lived here. As an official affiliate of the Smithsonian Institution, the Oklahoma History Center uses considerable space on the premises for research efforts. The center has an enviable newspaper collection and relies on its extensive Indian records, manuscripts and photographs to tell its dramatic tales. For entertainment that evokes real life adventure, visit the Oklahoma History Center.

**2401 N Laird Avenue,
Oklahoma City OK
(405) 522-5248 or (405) 522-5204**
www.okhistorycenter.org

Museum of Special Interest Autos

Since its opening in 1975 by owner Clifton Hill, the Museum of Special Interest Autos has delighted visitors of all ages. It is now Oklahoma's oldest automobile display open to the public. He bought his first antique car at the age of 14, a 1928 Chevrolet Touring Car, and from this auspicious beginning went on to acquire a proud collection. This is not a spit-and-polish type of display, it does, however, feature several rare and seldom-seen vehicles in addition to other collectible cars of the 1920s through the 1950s, plus motorcycles and automobile memorabilia. Among the rarest of the vehicles on display are a 1948 Playboy (one of 97), a 1950 Muntz (one of 29) and a 1942 Chrysler New Yorker convertible (one of four). You'll also see a 1928 Falcon-Knight and a 1953 Muntz with serial number one. One of the newest cars in the collection is a 1962 Lincoln convertible, a parade car that once carried astronaut Gordon Cooper. Visitors will find Clifton a relaxed and genial tour guide, glad to go into the historical background of his cars. The museum also offers surplus vehicles for sale. All ages are welcome at the museum for a modest fee, though hours of operation vary, so it is best to call ahead. If you appreciate cars, plan a visit to the Museum of Special Interest Autos.

1½ miles S of I-40 on U.S. 177, Shawnee OK
(405) 878-9775 or (405) 275-5877

National Wrestling Hall of Fame and Museum

Wrestling, humanity's oldest and most basic form of recreational combat, continues to appeal to cultures and societies around the world. America's shrine to the sport, the National Wrestling Hall of Fame and Museum, aims to preserve the heritage of the sport, honor new achievements and encourage youth to aspire to lofty goals. The Hall of Fame offers a glimpse of folkstyle and Olympic wrestling in America and beyond. Founded in 1976 and located on the northeast side of the Oklahoma State University (OSU) campus, the Hall of Fame and Museum are located in the shadow of one of the most historic wrestling arenas in the world, Gallagher-Iba Arena. Named after OSU's Hall of Fame wrestling coach Edward Clark Gallagher, this venue is where OSU wrestlers earned an unprecedented 34 NCAA championship team titles. In the Paul K. Scott Museum of Wrestling History, you'll feel the heat, smell the sweat and experience the excitement of wrestling from ancient to modern times. The John T. Vaughan Hall of Honors profiles those Americans who built the sport, as well as the young stars of tomorrow. Other facilities include the FILA (Fédération Internationale des Luttes Associées) International Hall of Fame, the Cliff Keen Theater and the William S. Heins Jr. Library. Come pay a thrilling visit to the National Wrestling Hall of Fame and Museum.

405 W Hall of Fame Avenue, Stillwater OK
(405) 377-5243
www.wrestlinghalloffame.org

Red Earth, Inc.

For over 25 years Red Earth, Inc. has promoted the rich traditions of American Indian arts and cultures through education, a premier festival, a museum and fine art markets. The Red Earth Festival is a three-day celebration held the first weekend of June at the Cox Convention Center in downtown Oklahoma City. For three exciting days, members representing over 100 tribes from throughout North America gather to share in the richness and diversity of their heritage with the world. The festival has grown into the largest and most comprehensive Native American arts and cultural event of its type, including a parade, juried fine art competition, art market, dance competition, cultural activities, pow-wow and run/walk-a-thon. Red Earth Festival has garnered awards including recognition as one of North America's Top 100 Events by the American Bus Association, and Oklahoma's Outstanding Event by the Oklahoma Tourism & Recreation Department. Red Earth Museum's permanent collection has more than 1,400 items of fine art, pottery, basketry, textiles and beadwork, including the renowned Deupree Cradleboard Collection and the only collection of totem poles in the area. The museum also hosts diverse traveling exhibits. Located in Omniplex near the Zoo in Oklahoma City, the Red Earth Museum is open 362 days a year.

2100 NE 52nd Street, Oklahoma City OK
(405) 427-5228
www.redearth.org

Oklahoma City Museum of Art

In 2002, the Oklahoma City Museum of Art opened in its new home in the heart of downtown Oklahoma City. The three-story, 110,000-square-foot facility, in the Donald W. Reynolds Visual Arts Center, features 15 galleries, three education rooms, a resource center and the 252-seat Noble Theater. The museum of art has been a part of the Oklahoma City scene since 1909, when the forward thinking Art Renaissance Club first met to discuss the need for a permanent art center in the city. Today the museum houses an extensive, permanent collection of European, Asian, and American art, including works by Renoir, Courbet, Mary Cassatt, Alexander Calder and Henry Moore. The museum also owns the most comprehensive collection of Dale Chihuly glass in the world, which consists of 18 vibrant installations and a specially commissioned 55-foot tower in the atrium. National and international traveling exhibitions fill the Special Exhibitions Gallery. The Noble Theater screens independent, foreign and classic films every weekend throughout the year. Many classes and a summer art camps for children are popular activities. The Museum Store carries merchandise relevant to the permanent and special exhibitions, and the Museum Café serves French fusion cuisine. The Oklahoma City Museum of Art invites you to join the 100,000 visitors who come to this beautiful space each year for enrichment, inspiration and understanding. You may want to join the many new members here that support a swelling staff and new acquisitions.

415 Couch Drive, Oklahoma City OK
(405) 236-3100
www.okcmoa.com

34 • Museums, History & Culture

World Organization of China Painters Museum

The World Organization of China Painters Museum celebrates the delicate art of painting on porcelain. The museum contains one of the finest collections of hand-painted porcelain in the United States, organized in several exhibitions. Enter through the Reception Room, which displays porcelain painted by a variety of noted artists. The State Room shows work by World Organization of China Painters (WOCP) members. These are prize-winning pieces from state and local shows and conventions. First-place winners are encouraged to donate their pieces to the permanent collection. The antique furnishings of the Victorian Room enhance the Old World elegance of the china on display. Hand-painted porcelain with holiday themes is on view in the Holiday Room. The Blue Room exhibits an outstanding collection of antique porcelain and winners of the Hall of Fame award. The Oriental Room, the newest addition to the museum, presents Eastern-style work, such as pastry dishes from Paris and many other items. The WOCP Museum supports a library, where additional pieces are on display. Visitors to the gift shop can purchase hand-painted china and supplies. Founded by Pauline A. Salyer in 1967, WOCP is a non-profit group dedicated to the fine art of china painting. The organization represents local clubs all over the world and publishes a bimonthly magazine, *The China Painter*. Visit the World Organization of China Painters Museum soon. You'll marvel at the beauty on display.

2641 NW 10th Street, Oklahoma City OK
(405) 521-1234
www.theshop.net/wocporg

Oklahoma Sports Museum

The Oklahoma Sports Museum (OSM), the state's official sports museum, recognizes more than 500 Oklahoma athletes, sponsors youth activities and sponsors a variety of awards. When you visit OSM, you'll learn about Mickey Mantle, Warren Spahn and many other baseball greats. Football displays celebrate Oklahoma's five Heisman Trophy winners and its many pro stars. See displays that cover all things basketball. Exhibits on Olympic champions line one wall, and another showcases Native American athletes, including Jim Thorpe and Johnny Bench. OSM is home to the Oklahoma High School Baseball Coaches Hall of Fame. Every year, OSM presents the Warren Spahn Award to the best left-handed pitcher in major league baseball. Johan Santana won in 2006 for the second time, and Randy Johnson has won four times. OSM has established the Bill Teegins award for outstanding Oklahoma sports broadcaster and the Ferguson Jenkins award for outstanding student-athlete. In 2004, OSM itself won an award, the Redbud from the State Tourism Department, for the Oklahoma Black Baseball Reunion, now an annual event. OSM provides a batting cage, baseball camps and activities to encourage youth to stay drug free and live positively. Groups can lease a group activity area. Come join the winners at the Oklahoma Sports Museum. The OSM is a 501c3 non-profit; donations and sponsors are needed and appreciated.

315 W Oklahoma Avenue, Guthrie OK
(405) 260-1342
www.oklahomasportsmuseum.org

Grady County Historical Society

In 1985, the Grady County Historical Society purchased the Dixie Department Store building. Once a major shopping destination for residents of Southwestern Oklahoma, the Dixie occupied a white brick building constructed in the early 1900s. The Historical Society's museum now shares the building with a gift and embroidery shop, an antique store and the popular Crazy 8 Café. In the museum, you'll find exhibits that interpret the social and natural history of Grady County. A key exhibit is the Geronimo Hotel murals painted by E.C. Peyraud, which greet you as you enter the museum. The murals depict Geronimo's family, Indian scenes and the awesome Oklahoma prairie. The Geronimo Hotel was one of Chickasha's show places in the early 20th century. The murals were lost when the hotel was torn down. Years later, they were found in a barn. The Historical Society is raising the funds needed to completely restore the murals. Photos, newspapers and scrapbooks help tell the Grady County story, as do furniture, china and clothing. You'll see transportation items, military uniforms and memorabilia, and medical and embalming equipment. Schoolbooks, tax rolls and business machines are also on display. Stop in and let the volunteer docents of the Grady County Historical Society help you explore the past.

415 W Chickasha Avenue, Chickasha OK
(405) 224-6480

Museums, History & Culture • 37

National Cowboy & Western Heritage Museum

The National Cowboy & Western Heritage Museum tells the multifaceted story of America's expansion into the West. This complex and romantic tale springs to life, thanks to a collection of more than 28,000 Western paintings, sculptures and artifacts, including the most extensive collection of rodeo photographs and trophies, barbed wire and saddlery in the world. In 1994, the Museum tripled in size, adding additional galleries and banquet facilities. A large art gallery contains work by early artists, such as Charles Russell and Frederic Remington as well as Prix de West pieces created in the past 30 years. One gallery explores the lifestyle of the American cowboy, and another looks at America's indigenous sport, the rodeo. Still other galleries describe firearms, sports hunting, trappers and traders, the military presence in the early West and the embellishments Western Indian tribes made to everyday objects. The newest gallery space pays tribute to Hollywood cowboys and the development of Western films. Exhibits explore Wild West shows, silent movies, singing cowboys and the stars of big budget films and television shows. At Prosperity Junction, visitors walk through a turn of the century prairie town. Charming gardens, an excellent dining experience and a calendar full of special events await the visitor. Look for the summer Prix de West art exhibition and sale, the Memorial weekend Chuck Wagon Gathering & Children's Cowboy Festival and the family-oriented Michael Martin Murphey's Cowboy Christmas Ball. Visit the National Cowboy & Western Heritage Museum for an inspiring look at America's western heritage.

1700 NE 63rd Street, Oklahoma City OK
(405) 478-2250
www.nationalcowboymuseum.org

38 • Museums, History & Culture

Museums, History & Culture • 39

Omniplex Science Museum

Omniplex Science Museum, a Smithsonian affiliate in Oklahoma City, aspires to enrich people's lives by revealing the wonder and relevance of science by valuing fun, creativity and learning. It satisfies your brain's hunger for knowledge and allows you to chomp down on interactive and entertaining science delicacies and much more. From hands-on activities to busy railroad cars and World War II airplanes to a relaxing walk in the gardens, visitors of all ages will find something to enjoy at Omniplex. Standing nearly seven stories tall, OmniDome Theater—Oklahoma's only giant dome-screen theater—houses a 70-foot diameter dome screen virtually encompassing each moviegoer's entire field of vision. Omniplex Planetarium, Oklahoma's first public-access planetarium since 1958, takes you to the farthest reaches of the universe and beyond. The aviation and space artifacts are one of the nation's premier collections, taking you through the history of aviation and space. Omniplex has over 350 hands-on exhibits and an array of educational programs designed to enlighten, entertain and educate the entire family. Indulge your creative genius and travel the globe with Omniplex's extensive collection of art and artifacts from around the world. The Omniplex Museum Store is a shopper's haven for unique items for all ages. There is no need to leave the museum for lunch. Stop at the Garden Café for a refreshing beverage, meal or quick snack. Omniplex is located in the heart of Oklahoma City's Adventure District.

2100 NE 52nd Street, Oklahoma City OK (405) 602-OMNI (6664)

Indian Trading Post and Art Gallery

The Indian Trading Post and Art Gallery is furnished like a traditional trading post, with a silver-tipped grizzly against one wall, two standing black bears and a rich collection of Native American art. The store represents the many artists of Oklahoma, but it also carries work by artists from other areas. You can find prized beadwork such as moccasins, jewelry, baskets, pottery and music as well as art. The fully beaded moccasins are one of the items purchased by customer Whoopi Goldberg. While she was shopping, a Baptist group in the store asked to have their picture taken with her. Goldberg laughed, said that the Baptists usually didn't want much to do with her and good-naturedly complied with their request. Authentic beadwork is a dying art and many of the artists who once supplied their work have passed on. As a result, it has become rare and in high demand by collectors. Owner Linda Wheeler is descended from a full blooded Cherokee who's family hid in the mountains of North Carolina during the Trail of Tears. Several of her family members own trading posts, including locations in Florida, Tennessee, Pennsylvania and West Virginia. Wheeler opened her own Indian Trading Post in Oklahoma more than 20 years ago. Indian Trading Post and Art Gallery is a beautiful reflection of her spirit and is well worth regular visits.

825 S Walbaum Road, Calumet OK
(I-40 and Spur 281 S, exit 108)
(405) 884-5599

Santa Fe Depot Museum

The Santa Fe Depot Museum provides a glimpse into the rich history of the diverse and colorful people who settled Pottawatomie County. The depot's Romanesque style resembles a castle and provides a memorable backdrop for photos. The building is constructed of limestone from Indiana. Each stone was numbered and shipped to Shawnee, where workers assembled the depot like a jigsaw puzzle. Inside, you'll find exhibits produced by the Historical Society of Pottawatomie County. *Prairie Life* invites you to walk through an early settler's daily life in a rustic cabin, and then the ornate splendor of later homes and businesses. Learn about household chores and entertaining guests with the piano. The fully furnished Beard Cabin, on the grounds outside the museum, was the first building built in Shawnee after the land run of 1891. The Native American exhibit has artifacts from Mary Bourbonnais, a member of the Citizen Potawatomi Nation, and Thomas "Wildcat" Alford of the Shawnee people. Railroad memorabilia and a display on Pottawatomie County's *Century of Progress* are also on view. Throughout the year, the Depot plays host to a variety of special events including the Quilt Show, Woodcarver's Festival and a Christmas Show. The museum offers tours and hands-on activities for students of all ages. For a true taste of Oklahoma history, visit the Santa Fe Depot Museum.

614 E Main Street, Shawnee OK
(405) 275-8412
www.santafedepotmuseum.org

Mabee-Gerrer Museum of Art

Founded in 1914, the Mabee-Gerrer Museum of Art is one of the oldest museums in Oklahoma. It was the project of Father Gregory Gerrer, an artist, Benedictine monk and member of St. Gregory's Abbey. Fr. Gerrer collected objects of artistic and anthropologic value during his travels throughout Europe, Africa and South America. Today, the Mabee-Gerrer Museum collects, preserves, exhibits and interprets outstanding works of art that nourish the human spirit. The Mabee-Gerrer has more than 3,500 artworks. A diverse collection of the art of ancient cultures including Mesopotamia, Greece and Rome, and paintings from the Medieval, Renaissance and Baroque eras are on permanent display, as are their noteworthy collections of Native American, pre-Columbian, African/Oceanic and Asian artifacts. The museum holds one of the region's most extensive Egyptian exhibitions and is home to Oklahoma's only mummies. Mabee-Gerrer Museum of Art is a beautiful setting for incomparable world art. It's worth making regular visits. Be sure to stop in the renovated gift shop for gifts and mementos. The museum is located on the campus of St. Gregory's University.

1900 W MacArthur Drive, Shawnee OK
(405) 878-5300
www.mgmoa.org

42 • Museums, History & Culture

Photos by G. Jill Evans

Museums, History & Culture • 43

Photo by Linda Cavanaugh

Oklahoma City National Memorial & Museum

Oklahoma City and the United States changed forever on April 19, 1995, when the Alfred P. Murrah Federal Building was attacked and destroyed by a blast that killed 168 people. In the time since that horrific day, much has been said about the tragedy, but healing began when the Memorial was dedicated in 2000, five years after the attack. The physical presence of a monument on the site of that awful event, and the Memorial Museum that was dedicated nine months later, provide a place for visitors to gather and remember. They remember those whose lives were lost, the many who survived and the large number of Americans whose lives were changed forever. A visit to the site of this event is, of course, a somber occasion, but gazing out over the reflecting pool or pondering the meaning of the Field of Empty Chairs allows a catharsis for those who recall the event. Stop at the feet of the Survivor Tree, a 90-year-old American elm that stands as a symbol of resilience, for a chance to reflect on the strength of those who came through that terrible time and made this city and nation stronger through adversity. Visit the Memorial Museum and experience that fateful day through the eyes of those most impacted—the survivors, family members and rescue workers. See the hope and resilience born of tragedy. For a glimpse into a tragic day that showed both the best and worst of America, make this historic site a stop on your itinerary.

620 N Harvey, Oklahoma City OK
(405) 235-3313
www.oklahomacitynationalmemorial.org

The Harn Homestead

A trip to the Harn Homestead and 1889ers Museum is an excellent way to learn more about the history of territorial Oklahoma. Only a few blocks from the State Capitol Building, the homestead encompasses more than nine acres and contains seven turn of the century buildings, including the 1890 Shepherd Family House, the 1897 Stoney Point Schoolhouse and the 1904 Harn House. Groups can schedule guided tours, and individuals can tour the buildings and grounds by themselves. Harn Homestead offers a dozen different programs for young students that introduce them to life on the farm a century ago. The hands-on sessions teach students about chores, such as tub laundry and chopping wood. Children can learn what school was like in the McGuffey Reader days. Holiday events include Victorian Valentines, Territorial Christmas and the Harvest Time program. William Harn was a Federal claims adjuster, who settled land disputes resulting from the great Land Run of 1889. The state capitol sits partly on land he donated to the state. The Victorian, Queen Anne-style home he erected for his wife in 1904 was actually selected from the Sears catalogue and shipped, unassembled, from Chicago. Individuals, houses of worship and corporations rent the homestead for special weekend events. Harn Homestead is a popular venue for weddings, which often use the barn for the reception and the Jane Van Cleef Gazebo for the ceremony. If you really want to see the past come alive, visit the Harn Homestead.

313 NE 16th Street, Oklahoma City OK
(405) 235-4058
www.harnhomestead.com

Citizen Potawatomi Nation Cultural Heritage Center

The Citizen Potawatomi Nation Cultural Heritage Center houses the nation's museum, library, veteran's memorial and much else. The museum's facilities, a source of pride, are absolutely state-of-the-art. As a result, the museum will be able to accept exhibitions from everywhere. The Citizen Potawatomi are a dynamic people with a bright future, and the museum emphasizes the connection between the nation's ancestors and the people of today. The theme is not Who We Were, but Who We Are. The permanent collection features Potawatomi artifacts drawn from the museum's collections, along with interpretive displays. Revolving exhibits in the Long Room consist of thematically grouped displays, for example, everyday textiles and how they changed over the years. The museum is digitally capturing its entire collection, and the results in time will be available over the Internet. The Long Room, a meeting hall that can seat up to 1,000, is also the site of the veteran's memorial, the Wall of Honor. This moving display of photos, framed letters, awards and decorations pays homage to the warriors who stepped forward when called. The center also houses offices, a genealogical research facility, a language classroom and a recording site for the Tribal Heritage project. Come see the Citizen Potawatomi Nation Cultural Heritage Center, one of the most impressive museum complexes in Oklahoma.

1899 S Gordon Cooper Drive, Shawnee OK
(405) 275-3121 or (800) 880-9880
www.potawatomi.org/Culture/default.aspx

Washington Irving Trail Museum

You'll be pleasantly surprised when you discover the Washington Irving Trail Museum, one of Oklahoma's best-kept secrets. This off-the-beaten path museum has received the prestigious American Association for State and Local History Award of Merit. The writer Washington Irving visited Oklahoma in 1832, when it was considered the Far West, and wrote of the trip in *A Tour on the Prairies*, a book that is still in print. The museum is near the site of one of Irving's encampments. The exhibits tell the stories of a dramatic past. The first battle of the Civil War in Indian Territory, the Battle of Round Mountains, took place nine miles northeast of the museum. Learn about the gunfight at nearby Ingalls that marked the beginning of the end for the Doolin-Dalton gang. In Ripley, just a few miles to the southeast, Billy McGinty and Otto Gray organized the Oklahoma Cowboy Band, the first western band to tour the country and draw national attention. Displays of songbooks, recordings and photographs bring back the early days of radio and country music. Other exhibits highlight the Boomer movement, pioneer days and much more. See History's Forgotten Treasures, rare and unusual historical artifacts that are sure to interest history buffs and collectors. An outstanding collection of Native American artifacts in the Gerald Johnson wing rivals those in much larger museums. In addition, a commercial gallery features western-related antiques and memorabilia for sale. You will be amazed at what you find at the Washington Irving Trail Museum. Come visit soon.

3918 S Mehan Road, Ripley OK
(405) 624-9130
www.cowboy.net/non-profit/irving

Oklahoma State Firefighters Museum

The Oklahoma State Firefighters Museum is more than a state treasure—it is of national importance. Owned by the Oklahoma State Firefighters Association, the museum has one of the nation's leading collections of antique fire fighting equipment. This remarkable collection dates back to the mid-1700s, and many items are on display from the nation's first fire company, commanded by Benjamin Franklin. Other exhibits include the first fire station built in the Oklahoma Territory, in 1864, and the world's largest collection of firefighters' patches. Especially valued items in the fire truck collection include a 1928 Ahrens-Fox front-mount piston pumper from New Orleans, which many consider the best fire engine ever made. A popular Virginia classic is the mint-condition 1920 Stutz with a brass block, one of only 100 made. The Last Alarm, a 59-foot mural painted on-site by artist Lynn Campbell, shows 38 historical machines. The Old Fire Station exhibit shows how city alarm systems worked a century ago. A protective clothing exhibit shows how such gear has improved over the years. The museum building, completed in 1969, also houses the offices of the Oklahoma State Firefighters Association, Fire Chiefs Association and Retired Firefighters Association. The Oklahoma Fallen and Living Firefighters Memorial is dramatically situated on a hillside next to the museum. Whether you are an Oklahoma City resident or visitor, be sure to see the Oklahoma State Firefighters Museum.

2716 NE 50th Street, Oklahoma City OK
(405) 424-1452 or (800) 308-5336
www.osfa.info/muse.html

Museums, History & Culture • 47

Oklahoma City

48 • Restaurants, Bakeries & Cafés

Nonna's Euro-American Ristorante & Bar

According to *Oklahoma City Downtown Monthly* magazine, Nonna's "unquestionably vies for the top spot among the metro's gourmet restaurants." *MetroFamily Magazine* gives it four out of four forks. Avis Scaramucci keeps the mood at her restaurant warm and upbeat while Executive Chef Shawn Davidson creates magic with pastas, meats and seafood. Two premier dishes include the Nested Sea Scallops, which are pan seared with spinach and mushrooms and topped with citrus beurre blanc, and Mango BBQ Shrimp, which is wrapped in bacon and served with mango salsa. Blackberry Duck and USDA-graded prime tenderloin are some top choices from the meat menu. Nonna's received the Wine Spectator Award of Excellence in 2006, offering 200 selections on the wine list so that diners will find a special complement for every meal. First time visitors may be unaware of the owner's prolonged effort to build a home for Nonna's in the city's Bricktown, an endeavor which *The Oklahoman* chronicled in a series of feature articles. Indeed, the more one knows about Avis' enterprising spirit, the more fascinating Nonna's becomes. The restaurant is just one of her Bricktown enterprises, which include the Purple Bar, a bakery, a Streetside Café and the Painted Door gift shop. Newly opened in 2007, the Painted Door gift boutique is also located in the beautiful Skirvin Hilton Hotel in downtown Oklahoma City. Avis and her husband also own Cedar Spring Farms, where most of Nonna's herbs, edible flowers and vegetables are grown. The insalata *Caprese* and tomato bisque provide a great way to get acquainted with the harvest. Nonna's, located in a 90-plus year old warehouse, is three floors of part art gallery, bakery, fine dining and pure fun. Valet parking available.

1 Mickey Mantle Drive, Oklahoma City OK
(405) 235-4410
www.nonnas.com

Cattlemen's Steakhouse

The year was 1945, and the place was called Cattlemen's Café, when lucky Gene Wade rolled the dice, looking for a hard six or two threes, and won the restaurant from Hank Fry. That's just one chapter in the colorful history of Cattlemen's Steakhouse, which has been serving hungry cowboys, ranchers and cattle haulers since 1910. Eventually, movie stars, rodeo greats and politicians began coming here. Today, Cattlemen's is a main attraction at the Stockyards, second only to the cattle themselves. Big helpings of biscuits and gravy have always been a favorite at breakfast, along with the grits, hash browns and eggs cooked every conceivable way. The doors open at six, right after the first crow of the rooster. Before they close each night, the staff will have served buckets of gravy, a mess of catfish and burgers and, of course, a ton of steaks. The perfect steak at Cattlemen's starts as corn-fed beef, is cut in the restaurant's own butcher shop and is never frozen. The beef is slowly aged according to a process that is one of the best-kept secrets in Oklahoma. Cattlemen's features a banquet room above the restaurant that can handle 100 and an event center next door that can hold 150. Got a big appetite for great rib-sticking grub? Give in to your cravings at Cattlemen's Steakhouse.

1309 S Agnew Avenue, Oklahoma City OK
(405) 236-0416
www.cattlemensrestaurant.com

The Mantel Wine Bar & Bistro

After undergoing a thorough review by members of Cornell University's school of hotel administration, the Mantel joins such classic American restaurants as Tavern on the Green in New York, Emiril's in New Orleans and the Ritz Carlton in San Francisco as one of the country's best gourmet restaurants. Patrons always knew that the steaks and seafood at this stylish bistro in the Bricktown district of Oklahoma City were something special. It's just good to have it confirmed by industry experts. The review was exhaustive, based not only on sampling the restaurant's menu, but on observing the presentation of the food and on interviewing the chef and staff. It lasted for several days to test the consistency of the Mantel's performance. For the final challenge, you could say that the Mantel went to college and came home with straight A's. Two Mantel representatives flew to Cornell's Ithaca, New York campus to take part in the Cross Country Gourmet Extravaganza. Was it the shrimp, beef and wild mushroom pastries known as the Wellington Trio that persuaded the judges to award the Mantel top honors? Perhaps it was the Chicken Brochette, grilled chicken breast prepared with artichoke hearts, bacon and chipotle remoulade, that won the day. For dining that is at the head of its class, go to Mantel Wine Bar & Bistro.

201 E Sheridan, Oklahoma City OK
(405) 236-8040
www.themantelokc.com

Trattoria il Centro

Your troubles melt away when you step into Trattoria il Centro, where Chef and Owner Christine Dowd prepares traditional Italian comfort foods with contemporary style. At Trattoria il Centro, presentation is almost as important as the authentic Italian cuisine. You can enjoy the scents from the wood burning pizza oven, view the bright tile decorations and feel the supple leather seats as you dine with a diverse clientele in downtown Oklahoma City. Trattoria il Centro offers authentic antipasti, fresh house-made pastas and oven roasted fish and meats. The wine list is extensive. You could start with the three-grain risotto that combines wild and Arborio rice, barley, white wine, seasonal vegetables and Parmesan cheese. Chef Christine fashions chicken *paillard* with cremini mushrooms, spinach and roasted tomatoes in a red wine sauce on top of angel hair pasta. Groups can dine in the Tuscan Suite, which features two picture windows opening directly into the bustling kitchen. A group can choose to watch the chefs at work or close the shades to focus on a meeting. Christine studied at the Culinary Institute of America and has 15 years of cooking experience in fine restaurants in New York, Paris, Portland and Chicago. Owner and partner Maggie Howell has years of experience as a restaurant general manager. Both Christine and Maggie are passionate about their business. Come to Trattoria il Centro to experience positive energy and great food.

**500 W Main Street, Suite 100,
Oklahoma City OK
(405) 601-5858**
www.trattoriailcentro.com

52 • Restaurants, Bakeries & Cafés

Sweet Basil Thai Cuisine

Sweet Basil Thai Cuisine offers a satisfying dining experience. Whether you already love Asian food or are new to these flavors, the freshness of Sweet Basil's ingredients and the delightful sauces are sure to please. The extensive menu, which ranges from the Evil Jungle Curry to pineapple fried rice, will satisfy many tastes and keep you amused on many a return visit. Nestled in downtown Norman, the restaurant has a warm and sophisticated ambience. A huge saltwater aquarium entertains customers. Sweet Basil is the perfect place for a date or for conversation with close friends. A staff of friendly professionals will certainly put you at ease. Sweet Basil is locally famous for its *Padthai*, a combination of bright colors, multiple textures and contrasting temperatures. The secret is in the sauce. You can pick your style of noodle and choose your favorite main ingredient from such selections as chicken, shrimp and tofu. The results are dazzling. Other beloved entrées include *pad ga-prow*, a lively combination of sautéed bell peppers, chili, garlic, onion and fresh basil with your choice of meat. The spring rolls, *po-pia tod*, are definitely worth a try. Call in a take-out order or sit down to catch the latest buzz at this reasonably priced restaurant. For good food at lunch or dinner, come to Sweet Basil Thai Cuisine, a restaurant in a class by itself.

211 W Main Street, Norman OK
(405) 217-THAI (8424)

Deep Deuce Grill

Located on historic Second Street in the heart of the Deep Deuce Jazz District, the Deep Deuce Grill is leading the development boom that is bringing the community back to life. The area was once an important incubator of African American culture. Here, jazz legends Jimmy Rushing and Charlie Christian grew up listening to the music emanating from the restaurants and dance halls. Second Street today bears few physical reminders of its heyday in the 1940s and 1950s, but the Haywood Building, home of the Deep Deuce Grill, still stands. Renovated in 2003, the grill retains the building's exposed brick walls. Hanging gas lanterns warm the space and the original red front door greets the guests. The grill's tables are made from the wood floor panels of the upstairs offices, and the countertop of the bar comes from converted pews salvaged from a nearby church that was destroyed by fire. The Deep Deuce Grill offers a classic Deep South menu of spicy half pound burgers, ribs and chicken wraps, along with a large selection of cigars, wines and imported Scotches. Guests can enjoy live music Thursday through Saturday and relax on the outside patio by an open fire pit. Experience the history of the Deep Deuce neighborhood and participate in its future at the Deep Deuce Grill.

307 NE 2nd Street, Oklahoma City, OK
(405) 235-9100

Restaurants, Bakeries & Cafés • 53

Brown's Bakery

Brown's Bakery is an Oklahoma City legend. The baked goods are some of the best in town, and it supplies many of the city's leading restaurants. This bakery reminds you of olden days. At Brown's, you'll find an enormous selection of mouthwatering cakes, pies and donuts, all made with the finest ingredients. Cookies are another major item. The shop offers a chocolate éclair that is to die for. It's a fresh pastry with a vanilla custard filling, topped with chocolate icing. You'll love the caramel-covered brownies, and the cheesecake bites with cherry or blueberry topping are addictive. Additional treats include twists, pecan stickies and devil dogs. Whatever your sweet tooth craves, you'll find something for it. Are you searching for the perfect wedding cake? The staff members at Brown's are experts in the art of making dreamy wedding cakes. They'll be delighted to listen to your ideas and show you their suggestions. Brown's also makes fresh breads. Try the three-seed wheat bread with honey. The shop recently opened a lunchtime deli service, where you can pick up soup, salads or sandwiches made with the bakery's own bread. Brown's Bakery, a family enterprise, has been in business for a long time. Michael Brown is the manager. His brothers, William and Randy, also work at the bakery, as do his father, Bill, and mother, Miss Katie. Michael's grandfather, also named Bill, opened the bakery back in 1946. Come to Brown's Bakery and let the Brown family tempt you with their amazing assortment of wonderful goodies.

**1100 N Walker Avenue,
Oklahoma City OK
(405) 232-0363**
www.brownsbakery.net

Photo by Jennifer Klotz

Castle Falls
Fine Dining and Event Center

Castle Falls is Oklahoma City's one and only castle. Once a private home, Castle Falls is now a special-events center that hosts weddings and other gatherings. A cascading waterfall, towering pines and oaks and the Royal Garden make this elegant structure, modeled after a Normandy castle, perfect for up to 200 guests. Construction manager Bill Blecha erected his dream castle in the years after World War II, modeling it on an architectural gem he discovered while serving heroically in World War I. The elaborate landscaping added in recent years provides Castle Falls with its current name. Castle Falls is also the site of Jutta's Keller at Castle Falls, Oklahoma City's finest German restaurant and, according to *Yahoo Travel,* one of the top five restaurants in town regardless of cuisine. Chef Jutta Scheider honed her exceptional culinary skills in the kitchens of fine European establishments. Her charming and intimate *keller* (cellar) comprises level one of the castle. Try a ribeye or the *Wiener schnitzel* (breaded pork cutlet) with a rich hunter sauce of mushrooms, onion and pepper. The pork loin roast is a house specialty. Jutta is also the catering chef for Castle Falls' special events. For your next event or night out, proprietors Amy and Ralph Rollins invite you to celebrate at Castle Falls.

820 N MacArthur Boulevard, Oklahoma City OK
(405) 942-6133
www.castlefalls.com

Hastings Entertainment–Yukon
Retail

Serving the eastern suburbs of Oklahoma City, Hastings Entertainment in Yukon takes its entertainment role seriously. "Nobody comes to us out of necessity," said manager Darrel Balenseifen. "They come to us to have fun, so it's our job to make sure that they do." A leading multimedia entertainment retailer since 1968, Hastings Entertainment is dedicated to providing its customers with a substantial selection of books, music, movies and games. In the Yukon area, the 21,000 square foot Hastings shop offers one of the only significant sources of books and music while giving video stores some healthy competition. Customers can rent as well as buy movies and video games. They can sample CDs at listening stations throughout the music department. The bookstore hosts frequent book signing events to promote awareness of literature. Darrel emphasizes customer service and an upbeat, happy atmosphere in his store. Associates greet customers as friends and fans of the entertainment industry while keeping an eye on the length of checkout lines to ensure a hassle-free shopping experience. Their training allows them to move freely between the departments, addressing questions and discussing the products of each. Visit Hastings Entertainment to discover the wide world of music, literature, gaming and film.

1105 Garth Brooks Boulevard, Yukon OK
(405) 350-1803
www.hastings-ent.com

Balliet's
Fashion

When Fred and Edna Balliet started their business in 1936, little did they know that it would still be around more than 70 years later. Women's high-end fashions might have changed over the years, but the clientele seeking these luxury goods continues to come to Balliet's to find the quality and service they prize. Current owners Bob and DeDe Benham and their staff pride themselves on the focus they place on their relationships with their customers. They will do anything they can to make sure that every customer is satisfied. Bob, DeDe and their staff offer friendly assistance to every customer who enters the store. The fine apparel choices and many accoutrements are just part of Balliet's mystique. This shop overflows with complimentary services, including gift wrapping, local delivery, refreshments and reserved parking. Many regular customers take advantage of the house charge account. Come see why Balliet's has been one of Oklahoma City's finest clothing options for nearly three quarters of a century, and make it your own personal fashion destination.

50 Penn Place, Oklahoma City OK
(405) 848-7811 or (877) 841-8078
www.balliets.com

Hastings Entertainment–Norman
Retail

With its large inventory of books, movies, music and games, Hastings Entertainment gives the community a great selection of divertissements, but it doesn't stop there. You can also find blank DVDs and CDs to store your own material, memory sticks and cards to transfer it, DVD players to play it, cases to personalize your iPod and guitar packs so that you can create your own sound. Hastings stands apart in its selections, as well. All CDs and DVDs are the unedited versions. The store has classic and foreign films you can't seem to find anywhere else. You can find entertaining t-shirts and board games at Hastings. Hastings stocks some unusual models, such as a Kurt Cobain doll and a series of Ghostrider figures. In the true spirit of entertainment, the shop provides rentals, buys, sells and trades, which results in an unusually varied collection of new and used stock. The Norman Hastings location, one of the company's top stores, has many places to sit and stay awhile. The Hardback Book Café features a nook with a two-sided fireplace, a big flat-screen television and a pastry display. The staff members are friendly and love their work. Stop by and say hello.

2300 W Main Street, Norman OK
(405) 329-5529
www.hastings-ent.com

Country Cottage Primitives
Retail

Lavender provides the theme for Country Cottage Primitives, a gift store in a quiet country setting. Debi Seaton and her husband, Lucky, came upon a lavender farm while visiting Sequim, Washington, and decided to try to raise the herb in Oklahoma. They were told that it would be difficult, but the lavender farm, located behind the shop, proved to be a great success. Come cut your own lavender bundle for $5. Lucky and Debi built the cream-colored cottage that houses the gift store by themselves in just eight months. Inside the cottage, the world and its responsibilities drift away. Lavender hangs from the wood beams, perfuming the air as it dries. You can learn about the lavender, its history and its special properties while you sip lavender lemonade in the summer months. Fresh lavender and floral arrangements are shop specialties. You'll also find handcrafted gifts, including primitive dolls, pillows and other special items. The shop offers handmade Shaker furniture. Debi designs much of the furniture herself, and Lucky builds it. Relax and sit a spell in the old-fashioned ambience at Country Cottage Primitives.

17206 Walker Road, Shawnee OK
(405) 275-3238

S&J Marketplace
Antiques & Collectibles

The owners of S&J Marketplace Antique Mall, Sandy and Joe Wick, first built a solid marriage and then risked their livelihood on a business venture founded on their love for sharing old and unusual things with others. They rented a building in Norman known as The Olde Town Market Place, changed its name to S&J Marketplace and rented out spaces to 30 antiques dealers who sell their own wares and carry consignment merchandise contributed by local antiques enthusiasts. The decision to open the antique mall was not easy to make. Joe left his 17-year position at the U.S. Postal Service, giving up the prospect of a guaranteed retirement income. He and Sandy sold their home on five acres and bought a smaller property. They pooled some of the money from the home sale with Joe's retirement funds to come up with enough cash to close the business deal and located their new business on Gray Street in downtown Norman. S&J's offerings include primitives, antique furniture, depression glass, vintage clothing, jewelry and Victorian items. A visit here is likely to turn up such unusual items as round Oklahoma milk bottles, aged trunks and many one-of-a-kind items. Come see what dreams are made of with a visit to S&J Marketplace. It is open seven days a week with 6,000 square feet and plenty of parking for your shopping pleasure.

219 E Gray Street, Norman OK
(405) 321-1242

The Webb
Fashion

Once only a shoe store, The Webb has expanded its merchandise since opening in 1951 but retained much of its old-fashioned charm. Lawrence and Edna Earle Webb first opened the business near Norman's Campus Corner, the area of shops near the University of Oklahoma, and relocated it to its present location in 1984. Although they are still partners in the business, their daughter, Lee Ann Looman is currently at the helm. In its original incarnation the business carried only shoes, but it now sells shoes, handbags and other accessories, plus pants, shirts and dresses in dressy, casual and fun styles. Lee Ann's merchandise is youthful, but her outlook is decidedly retro; she believes in one-on-one customer service and fills a niche not addressed by large stores. As proof of her commitment, the Webb will make home deliveries. Lee Ann also calls her customers with recommendations when she encounters new merchandise she believes will fit their individual tastes and lifestyles. For comfort and good looks, starting at the feet, look for prestigious shoe brands, such as Anne Klein, Cole Haan and Mephisto. Other shoe brands include Donald J. Pliner, Stuart Weitzman and Van Eli. Among the clothing lines, look for casual wear by Cambio, dressy fashions by Laundry and outfits that are chic and fun by BCBG. For glamorous women's adornments and refreshing service, shop at The Webb.

2101 W Main, Norman OK
(405) 321-8289
www.shopthewebb.com

Hastings Entertainment–Stillwater
Retail

When Hastings Entertainment opened in Stillwater in 1993, the small university-town was on the verge of a population boom fueled by the University of Oklahoma at Stillwater. A burgeoning contingent of students and university employees needed something to do on a Saturday night. Hastings had the answer. With new and used music, books and magazines, and renting as well as selling DVDs, video games and related electronics, Hastings was Borders, Blockbuster and Best Buy all in one. It was the beginning of a beautiful friendship. As Stillwater's entertainment center, Hastings grew hand-in-hand with the town into the full fledged superstore it is today. Now occupying 28,000 square feet, the store includes a café, mounted big screen televisions, reading areas and music listening stations. "We're kind of like the town mall," says manager Steven Spear. "People come over just to browse, meet each other, listen to music or have a conversation at the café." The store also hosts special events such as acoustic music performances, readings and book signings. Located just across from the university football field, Hastings is a tower of community recreation in Stillwater. Come and see Hastings Entertainment, where it's all happening.

316 N Main Street, Stillwater OK
(405) 377-0753
www.hastings-ent.com

Taylor's News Stand
Retail

Founded in 1913, Taylor's News Stand is the oldest surviving retail business in Oklahoma City and one of the last remaining newsstands in the state. It has been in the hands of the Priddy family for the last 60 years, and it has grown from 1,500 to 5,500 square feet. Largely dependant on walk-by traffic, Taylor's has made a business of responding to customer requests, accumulating some 3,000 different magazine in the process. "We have probably 150 automobile magazines and about 50 just on tattoos," current owner Hal Pridy says. Hal works with many wholesalers to gather his collection. The newsstand stocks not only local and foreign newspapers but hardback and paperback books, souvenirs, CDs and DVDs. Customers at Taylor's routinely wind up buying much more than they had planned, and you can expect to spot at least one or two fascinating magazines you've never seen before. Enjoy your time browsing and reading with an espresso or an ice cream from the in-house coffee bar. Visit Taylor's News Stand to experience an old world staple at the largest newsstand in the southwest.

133 W Main Street, Oklahoma City OK
(405) 239-6111

E. J. Provence
Retail

Folks in Edmond rely on E.J. Provence for a host of shopping needs. They know to check here for something decorative for the home, a gift for a loved one or a special outfit to wear to an event. Owners Tab Byrum and Michael Bates take pride in keeping the name E.J. Provence synonymous with variety and quality. You will find separate areas of the store devoted to home accessories and furniture, gourmet foods and bath and body items. Grandparents love to shop here for cuddly baby gifts and stimulating children's toys. E.J. Provence added fine women's apparel to the mix in Spring 2006. Linda Barker heads the clothing area, Lady of Provence, with a fine eye for style and a feel for comfort. E.J. Provence is a busy shopping destination around the holidays, not only for its abundance of gift ideas but for its delightful selection of ornaments and other decorative items. For diversity in fine merchandise, Tab and Michael invite you to try E.J. Provence.

3337 S Boulevard, Edmond OK
(405) 715-3652
www.ejprovence.com

Antique Garden
Antiques & Collectibles

Visitors to Antique Garden in Norman enjoy the creativity and good taste of the entire Fite family. The Fites have used the individual talents of family members to create a handsome shop that combines Old World antiques with new home accessories. Barbara Fite is the driving force behind the enterprise, and her daughter Mariah Pinkerton, a decorator and merchandiser, designed the store's layout. Immediately after purchasing the Spanish Mission-style building, the mother and daughter team embarked on an enormous renovation that required 80-hour weeks for two months. Barbara's son Nathan helped lay out and finish the pine plank floor. Her husband, Dennis, grows the orchids that decorate the shop and are also available for sale. Much of the furniture collection is antique, picked up by Barbara on her buying trips to Belgium and France. Most of the home accessories are new, and some have been built especially for the Antique Garden. A collection of outdoor items includes a large selection of topiaries, iron furniture and antique benches. You never know just what you might find among the antiques. The shop has carried old ceiling tins, chandeliers and a large, mirrored hall piece from the home of a former United States senator from Oklahoma. When you can't travel to Europe, travel to Antique Garden to adorn your home.

323 W Boyd, Norman OK
(405) 321-1772
www.antiquegardenstyle.com

60 • Shopping & Services

Shopping & Services • 61

Lorec Ranch
Home Décor

Eduardo Lopez designs high-end furniture with a rustic, Western style using natural woods and finishes, top grain leather, rust-aged metals and animal hides. Each piece is hand-crafted in the old-fashioned bench-made process. The same pair of hands and eyes supervises each piece from start to finish, preserving its individuality. Lopez's shop offers nearly 20 individual collections, including Hacienda, Texas Flower, Safari and Urban Cowboy. The styles range in personality from subtle to fashion-forward, yet most will harmonize with other styles for mixing and matching. Whether you're looking to furnish a whole room, pick up a missing piece or simply throw something new into your mix, you will find much to fire the imagination. The showroom is warm and inviting with studio lighting, painted floors, old pine planks and textured walls. In addition to living room and bedroom sets, Lorec Ranch offers a variety of desks, bookcases and credenzas for the office, and butcher boards and bar stools for the kitchen. A charming old cabin bench for the hallway or a red leather rocker with an antique painting of a cowgirl may be the piece you never realized you needed. You'll find decorations and accessories to help complete your home, including coverlets and duvets manufactured in-house by Lorec Ranch, animal hide lampshades and lamps made of twisted metal, horseshoes or antlers. Lopez hand-picks appropriate antiques to complete the showroom, including rare Western items such as lassos and spurs brought from his native Mexico. If you're looking for something truly original, stop by Lorec Ranch.

11702 N I-35 Service Road, Oklahoma City OK
(405) 478-2023 or (866) 877-4195
1400 S Agnew Avenue, Oklahoma City OK
(405) 488-1165 or (866) 517-4471
www.lorecranch.com

Painted Door
Retail

The term *gift shop* does not quite capture the Painted Door in Oklahoma City. *Emporium* might be more descriptive. Shoppers will find plenty of ideas for all of their gift giving needs and perhaps even that special gift for themselves. Clothing, rugs and hand-crafted pottery vie for attention. There are also delicious jams and soups, kitchenware, fragrances and slippers, just to name a few. Popular tableware items include the Vera Bradley collection, delightful toile Barnyard Babies from Sadek and elegant glassware that is featured in the restaurant. Also, Painted Door proudly carries a large selection of made-in-Oklahoma food and gift items. Take your time when you visit the Painted Door because there is so much to see. In 2005, after 14 years on Western Avenue, owner Avis Scaramucci moved the Painted Door to its current location in Bricktown. Avis owns a group of businesses in Bricktown that reflect her many interests and moods. The Purple Bar mixes martinis, while Nonna's Bakery features such temptations as butterscotch cream pie. You can grab a Nathan's hot dog at the Streetside Café or enjoy casual yet elegant dining at Nonna's Euro-American Ristorante. Newly opened in 2007, the Painted Door gift boutique is also located in the beautiful Skirvin Hilton Hotel in downtown Oklahoma City. Come and enjoy a wonderful shopping experience at Painted Door. Complimentary gift wrap provided. Valet parking available.

124 E Sheridan, Oklahoma City OK (Bricktown)

One Park Avenue, Oklahoma City OK (Skirvin)

(405) 235-4410

www.painteddoor.com

Panaderia La Herradura

Panaderia La Herradura, Oklahoma City's leading Mexican bakery, serves more than 100 varieties of specialty Mexican pastries. Panaderia La Herradura (The Horseshoe Bakery) is in the National Historic Stockyards District of Oklahoma City. A national tourist destination for its pioneer western heritage, the district is also home to many Hispanic Americans. Panaderia La Herradura provides them with the traditional treats they can't find elsewhere, while converting pastry fans of other backgrounds. "A lot of people find they prefer Mexican pastries to the European-style because they are less sweet and sticky," explains Kathy Montoya, who co-owns the bakery with her husband Sotero. Popular pastries include *cuernitos*, which are similar to croissants filled with cream cheese, and *conchas*, individual loaves of sweet bread that are topped with a shell shaped sweet topping. During the holidays the bakery sells hundreds of loaves of *rosca de reyes*, the bread of kings. Named in honor of the three kings of the nativity story, the bread is baked with one to five plastic babies inside, representing the baby Jesus. Whoever gets a baby in his slice must throw the next party. Co-owner Sotero Montoya, originally from Mexico, was a chef for 15 years before opening his own restaurant and four years later opening the Panaderia with his wife. In addition to baked goods, the Panaderia includes a small store of imported Mexican food products. Discover the enticing flavors of Mexico and Central America at the Panaderia La Herradura.

2235 SW 14th Street, Oklahoma City OK
(405) 232-3502

Parsons Vineyard and Winery

After years of hard work and education, Joyce and Joe Parsons finally realized their dream of opening a winery on their family land. Now, through Parsons Vineyard and Winery, the Parsons hope to help everyone learn to enjoy wine and to develop an appreciation for the processes of grape growing and wine making. Joyce, a biology teacher for 23 years, went back to school to learn the business. She began by taking courses at Oklahoma State University's wine program and finished her education with a prestigious course for vintners offered by the University of California at Davis. She and Joe oversaw the first planting of grapes in 2001 and produced their first wines in 2004 and 2005. The Parsons produce such well known varieties as Chardonnay, Cabernet Sauvignon and Pinot Noir. However, some of their greatest successes have been with less well known varieties, such as the red Villard Noir and the white Seyval Blanc. Other uncommon but notable varieties are the white Vignoles and the red Malbec. The tasting room is open every afternoon except Sunday. Visit Parsons Vineyard and Winery to enjoy special wines in a pleasant atmosphere.

15401 Gaddy Road, Shawnee OK
(405) 395-9178 or (405) 878-6588

The Winery at Greenfield Vineyard

In the Winery at Greenfield Vineyard, you can enjoy the luxurious tasting room with its beautiful oak tasting-bar, soft jazz and warm conversational seating. The winery makes its wines from its own premier Lincoln County grapes. Lincoln County has been Oklahoma's wine country for more than a century, and years of careful planning and experience go into every bottle. Savor a glass of one of Greenfield's premium estate wines at a table on the balcony overlooking the lush seven-acre vineyard. Panoramic windows let guests view the operating winery from above, an unusual opportunity. You can catch a concert, special event dinner or show in the amphitheater located at the winery. Greenfield Vineyard offers a family-friendly atmosphere with walking trails and picnic areas. Your hosts are two brothers, Gary and Mike Greenfield, and their spouses, Annette and Toni. The winery is sure to make your wedding or special event extraordinary. Whatever the occasion, create memories with a visit to the Winery at Greenfield Vineyard.

Route 2 Box 877, Chandler OK
(405) 258-0525
www.greenfieldvineyard.com

Wines & Specialty Foods • 65

Super Cao Nguyen

At Super Cao Nguyen, the largest Asian market in the Midwest, you'll discover aisles filled with exotic fruits, vegetables, meat and seafood from around the world. Ba Luong and Hai Luong, brothers who are taking over the family business from their parents, keep the market brimming with fresh foods. They purchase entire sides of beef and pork and cut it themselves to stock the giant meat service counter. Fresh fish, flown in once a week, comes from the coasts, Canada or as far away as New Zealand. The produce market is restocked with fresh vegetables and fruits three times a week, with Latin and South American fruits being exceptionally popular. Ba Luong, who is a frequent guest on *Gorilla Gourmet*, a local radio show, often conducts tours through the produce aisles for local chefs to explain what different fruits and vegetables are and to offer suggestions for preparing them. Other aisles teem with international sauces, teas, noodles and such household items as knives, dishes and plants. In the bakery, chefs offer several hot dishes to carry out as well as spring rolls and breads baked from scratch daily. On Fridays and Saturdays the market features hot foods for vegan diets. All foods are fresh and preservative-free. For exotic foods, check out the many departments at Super Cao Nguyen.

2668 N Military, Oklahoma City OK
(405) 525-7650
www.supercaonguyen.com

Moonfeathers Winery

Moonfeathers Winery uses fruits from all over Oklahoma to create its colorful wines. It offers fruity blends such as Blackberry Merlot and native Oklahoma Sand Plum in addition to classic reds and whites. The winery's signature honey wine, Moonlight, is Oklahoma's only native mead. This charming family-owned and operated winery was the dream of Bill and Teri Stovall, who became interested in winemaking while visiting the small wineries of northern California on their honeymoon. They appropriated the Moonfeathers name and logo from their wedding program, which Teri, a former art teacher, had designed. Bill, a medical technologist by day, was intrigued by the chemistry of winemaking and became the sole winemaker at Moonfeathers. The Stovalls opened Moonfeathers in April 2001, the year after their first child was born. Today, daughter Kali greets visitors to the winery and helps with stocking and bottling. In addition to tastings and tours, Moonfeathers Winery courts visitors with a summer Moonlight Concert series, featuring everything from rock to Celtic music. Guests can bring a picnic basket, buy a glass and enjoy a romantic evening on the front lawn. Taste the sweet life at Moonfeathers Winery.

**724 N Midwest Boulevard, Guthrie OK
(405) 282-8463
www.moonfeatherswinery.com**

Canadian River Vineyard & Winery

One of Oklahoma's premier wineries, the Canadian River Vineyard & Winery produces 12 original wines and fresh Concord, Maiden and Golden Muscat grape juices from grapes grown locally and throughout the Southwest. Enjoy a fruity Sangria, delicate Noble Blush or crisp Chardonnay on their scenic deck overlooking the vineyards. The beautiful grounds are open for tours and are also available for winery weddings. Ask about the wedding packages and let the friendly folks at the winery help you plan your special day. The Canadian River Vineyard & Winery is dedicated to promoting, educating and supporting local grape growers. Owner Gene Clifton holds frequent classes and seminars on the proper care of vineyards in Oklahoma. The winery also celebrates local wine and winemaking through an annual Spring Wine Festival. The festival offers wine tasting, quality food and craft vendors, plus live music and classes in basic winemaking and in wine and food pairing. Celebrate Oklahoma wine at the Canadian River Vineyard & Winery.

**7050 Slaughterville Road, Lexington OK
(405) 872-5565
www.canadianriverwinery.com**

Wines & Specialty Foods • 67

Wild Turkey—Oklahoma State Game Bird

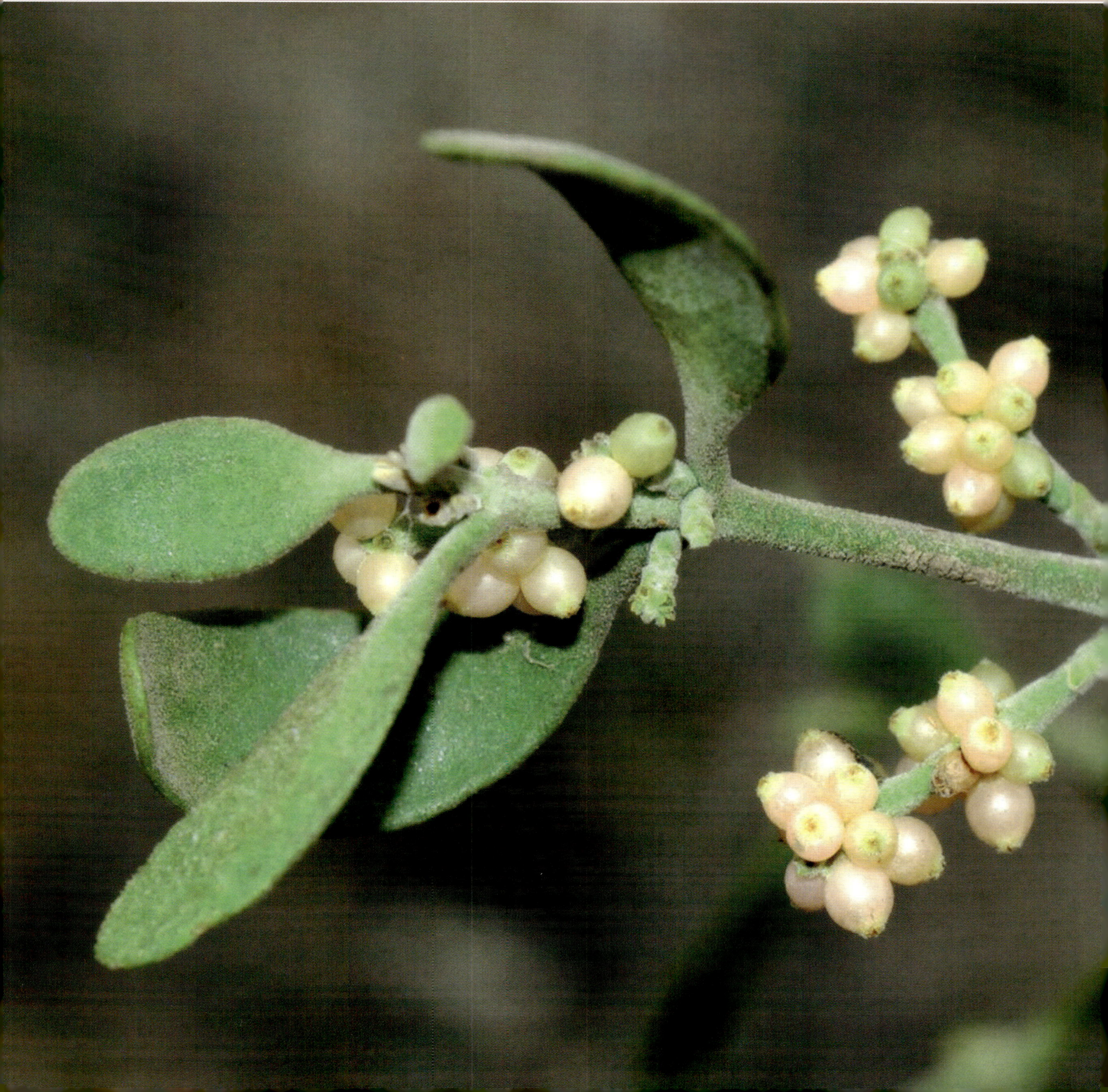

Western • 69

Western Oklahoma
Red Carpet Country
Great Plains Country

Mistletoe—Oklahoma State Floral Emblem

The Willows Inn

The Willows Inn Bed & Breakfast sits on four park-like acres just east of Guymon. Country quiet is one of the first things you notice when approaching the 5,000-square-foot home. Cherry wood and leather furniture mark the public spaces. In the great room you can visit or relax next to the bay window. In the dining room, guests enjoy a gourmet breakfast beneath a gorgeous chandelier. Romantic dinners can be arranged in advance. Innkeepers David and Marketta Kidwell grow their own herbs and maintain a greenhouse, so vegetables are always fresh and flavorful. The couple took possession of their dream home in 1998, a spacious 1970s ranch-style home that was state of the art in all its details. David ran a furniture store for 20 years and was well prepared to fill the empty house. Marketta is a registered nurse. The inn offers four guest accommodations, all with private baths and top-quality foam mattresses. The Dawn Room has French Country appeal, while the Kedwallen Suite features an elaborate cherry four-poster bed with a cream duvet, a sofa and reading chair. Soothing golds, tans and burgundies set off the sleigh bed and wicker furniture of the Floyd Room, which overlooks tall Austrian pines. For a media room with a sofa, chair and fireplace along with a romantic king canopy bed draped in tulle, consider the Heartland Room. A Tuscan-style garden mural surrounds the Jacuzzi. If you seek a quiet place to unwind, plan a visit to the Willows Inn.

E Highway 3, Mile Marker 32, Guymon OK
(580) 338-1303
www.thewillowsinn.net

Flying W Guest Ranch

The Old West truly comes alive at the Flying W Guest Ranch, a working ranch with Texas Longhorns, horses and buffalo. The W stands for Whinery, which is to say, Don Whinery and his dad A.L., who own the 2,300-acre prairie spread. You can tour a frontier Main Street at your leisure. Historical guides walk you through an authentic 1880s general store. The Flying W Museum displays one of the finest personal collections of early Western artifacts anywhere, including saddles, beautiful horsehair bridles and Indian arrowheads. The museum also showcases classic transportation, from horse-drawn buggies to hearses. Just off Main Street, you can see a rodeo where cowboys ride 1,500-pound angry bulls—briefly. Then get ready for a trail ride past the livestock into the country where you can spot deer, quail and armadillos. The two-hour trail ride includes a visit to the second largest buffalo kill site on the southern plains. University of Oklahoma archeologists are excavating bones, tools and spear points from a 2,300-year-old cliff kill site used by early plains Indians. At suppertime, you can chow down on steak or buffalo burger at Sassy's Café. There's so much to do at the ranch that you'll be ready for a restful night spent in a tepee or an air-conditioned cabin. The Flying W has RV hookups, too. For an experience you'll always remember, come to Flying W Guest Ranch.

10874 N 1920 Road, Sayre OK
(580) 225-5545 or (888) 928-8864
www.flyingwonline.com

Indian Creek Village

Set in the secluded Cross Timbers of Oklahoma, Indian Creek Village is an all-purpose getaway. This tract of ancient oak and cedar historically served as a natural barrier to both buffalo and human migration. Here, a multi-faceted retreat center features a winery, a bed-and-breakfast and a wedding chapel. Jenny and Terry Lewis began developing the village in 1997 when Terry, a physician, decided to take up winemaking and planted the first vineyards. Shortly after, the Lewis's rescued two local historic buildings and brought them to the site. One of the two, a 1910 cedar-wood house that would become the Village Inn, was built in the traditional Amish style for the first World Mennonite Conference. Today, guests can stay in one of six bedrooms at the Inn, each with its own bathroom, thermostat and high speed Internet access. All rooms are dressed in period decor. The swimming pool overlooking the vineyard is a peaceful spot to relax, cool off and enjoy the view. The Inn also serves as a site for specialized weekend retreats, where arts and crafts lovers can learn to quilt, scrap or take watercolor lessons with Jenny under a redbud tree. The second vintage building is now the wedding chapel. With its adjacent garden and gazebo, it is available for special events. Visitors to the winery's tasting room and gift shop can enjoy free live chamber music on Sundays, with complimentary *hors d'oeuvres* and samples of the winery's specialty grape juices. To make an evening of it, guests can stay for dinner at the Village Inn restaurant. Enjoy your favorite quiet pleasures at Indian Creek Village.

Off U.S. Highway 412 W, Ringwood OK
(580) 883-4919
www.indiancreekvillage.com

Mangum White House Bed & Breakfast

Return to Oklahoma's beginning to experience history, nature and romance. Come celebrate Oklahoma's centennial in Mangum's White House Bed & Breakfast, a 1907 Victorian historic home. Mangum is located just two hours from Oklahoma City and Amarillo, Texas, nestled in the great rolling plains of Southwestern Oklahoma. Whether you're in town for business or you just need to get away, your stay at this comfortable and beautiful home is sure to satisfy. Four guest rooms are available with the first floor Music Room featuring elaborate woodwork, stained glass and oak antique furnishings. Second floor rooms include the light and cheery Rose Room with white washed hardwood floors and a rose motif throughout. The Family Rooms are a two-bedroom suite, ideal for the traveling family. The third floor Loft Room is the largest room with a refrigerator, microwave and coffeemaker included. All accommodations have private baths. During your stay, choose from a host of activities to make your visit a memorable experience. Well-behaved children and well-mannered small pets are welcome. Your hosts, Ben and Evette Whisenant, invite you to step back, rest and relax at the Mangum White House Bed & Breakfast.

503 N Louis Tittle, Mangum OK
(580) 782-5100 or (877) 232-5259
www.mangumwhitehouse.com

The Standifer House

Luxury and elegance mark the Standifer House Bed & Breakfast on Route 66. Ten exquisitely appointed accommodations provide ambiance, romance and relaxation. Massive double doors lead to the Honeymoon Suite, filled with fabulous antiques and a bed of black cherry fabric. The Jungle Room, a favorite, sports an enormous jungle mural and is furnished to match. The Medieval Room is like the bedchamber of a great feudal king. The clean lines and geometric patterns of the Modern Room remind you of Frank Lloyd Wright. The décor of the other rooms is equally creative. Many rooms come with Jacuzzis and several offer fireplaces. The Standifer House makes a breathtaking backdrop for your wedding, party, meeting, reunion or other special event. The inn caters, and it can prepare special-request dinners for groups. A gift shop offers locally crafted items as well as antiques. Your hosts, Joe and Ann Smith, live on-site and are eager to meet your needs. In 1996, two sisters and their husbands bought the wonderful old Victorian building, then abandoned and forsaken. The result of extensive renovations is today's elegant inn. A thousand people, including many local dignitaries, gathered in 2002 for the grand opening. Come stay at the Standifer House, the perfect setting for romance or relaxation.

1030 W 7th, Elk City OK
(580) 225-3048 or (866) 723-3048
www.standiferhouse.com

Attractions & Recreation • 73

Route 66 Thunderbirds

Route 66 Thunderbirds buys and sells 1956 to 1966 Thunderbirds and other special interest and collector cars. You can list your Thunderbird, Mustang or other collector car in an extended inventory for maximum exposure at a modest cost. The listing remains until you sell the car or ask Route 66 Thunderbirds to remove it. The mission of Route 66 Thunderbirds is to secure a buyer for your vehicle and put the buyer in contact with you, the seller. You perform the balance of negotiations with the buyer, unless you want Route 66 Thunderbirds to be involved. Any additional fee is a good-faith amount. Route 66 Thunderbirds wants to build a satisfied customer base, so if you are not satisfied with the service or you did not sell the vehicle to the buyer in question, you pay nothing additional. On-site consignment in Weatherford is another option that may be appropriate for some sellers. If room is available, the company can store your vehicle in its climate-controlled building that fronts Route 66 and Interstate 40. Marion Davidson, a retired Ford-Lincoln-Mercury dealer with more than 48 years of experience serving Oklahoma customers, owns and operates Route 66 Thunderbirds. Whether you have a classic you need to sell or are looking for a thrilling car to own, check in with Marion at Route 66 Thunderbirds.

Leslie Powell Foundation and Gallery

Artist Leslie Powell, whose generous bequest created the Leslie Powell Foundation and Gallery, traveled widely but always maintained ties to his native Lawton. Today, the foundation supports the arts and humanities in Southwestern Oklahoma and in the broader region. Architecture, dance, literature, music, performance and the visual arts have all benefited from the foundation's support. In 2000, the gallery, one of the foundation's most important programs, moved into a renovated 1920s art deco building in downtown Lawton. One example of the many shows the gallery has sponsored is Oklahoma: Centerfold, a juried art show that over the years has grown into a nationally recognized event. To decipher the title of the show, flip open an atlas to the map of the United States. Oklahoma is on the centerfold. Lawton area residents can fight dull lunch hours with a visit to the gallery's Lunch Bag. These fascinating sessions examine art, customs of other societies, music, humanities and much else. Additional foundation activities include a grants program, which funds projects of cultural nonprofits in Southwestern Oklahoma and neighboring areas. The foundation also awards scholarships to art students at Cameron University. Come see the striking exhibits presented by the Leslie Powell Foundation and Gallery.

620 SW D Avenue, Lawton OK
(580) 357-9526
www.lpgallery.org

Museums, History & Culture • 75

Gateway to the Panhandle Museum

The little town of Gate is scarce on people now but has loads of public spirit. The Gateway to the Panhandle Museum is evidence of that. The museum, which has grown considerably since it opened in 1976, houses its core collection in the old Wichita Falls & Northwestern Railway depot. The town's old school and grocery store buildings also contain artifacts. Murals on buildings throughout the town depict life as it was a century ago. For example, the mural on the depot shows a train pulling into town. Exhibits at the depot include Civil War memorabilia and an original Oklahoma covered wagon. Farm and home items include an old threshing machine, a 19th century kitchen, antique cradles and quilts. You'll see Indian antiquities such as grinding stones for grain. A prehistoric elephant tusk and petrified turtles are fossils found locally. Newspapers and photographs illustrate past events such as the Dirty Thirties. School items are on display at the school and business items at the store. The museum is open afternoons. Entrance is free but donations are encouraged. Back in 1975, Postmaster Ernestine Maphet and the town's mayor, Ray Tillery, organized a museum committee. Though hard work, the board created an award-winning institution on a shoestring budget. Stop at the Gateway to the Panhandle Museum for a marvelous look at days gone by.

U.S. Highway 64, Gate OK
(580) 934-2004

The Pioneer Woman Museum and Statue

The timeless architecture of the Pioneer Woman Museum and Statue is a reflection of the strong spirit of pioneer women, which was the intent when construction began in 1957. The Museum expanded in 1998 to a total of 10,000 square feet of floor space, all of it dedicated to honoring the pioneer women of Oklahoma. The copper-lined entrance was fashioned to resemble the sunbonnets common in the early days. A motto—I See No Boundaries—is punched out in 12-inch letters at the top of the bonnet. At the entrance, glass doors reflect an image of the Pioneer Woman statue created by Bryant Baker. Exhibits present the lives of pioneering women from the early days of settlement through the present. A major display tells the story of daily life among the Cherokee Strip homesteaders. In the Heart of the Home exhibit, guests can try their hand at knitting, quilting and spinning. Craft demonstrations showcase traditions such as quilting and working the loom. Games and educational activities capture the interest of visitors of all ages. The museum offers special events for the public throughout the year. Call or scan the website to plan your visit to the Pioneer Woman Museum and Statue. You might choose to come when it has an event scheduled that intrigues you.

701 Monument Road, Ponca City OK
(580) 765-6108
www.pioneerwomanmuseum.com

Museum of the Great Plains

For over 50 years, the Museum of the Great Plains has told the story of prehistoric and historic times on the Great Plains. Once known as the Great American Desert, the plains are a unique environment that has challenged a diverse group of people over many centuries. Exhibits tell about nationally recognized prehistoric sites. Native American objects include clothing, dance regalia and instruments, and beaded jewelry. Displays celebrate the pioneers who ventured onto the land and tried to tame it. The outdoor compound comes to life with a Red River trading post and a historic one-room schoolhouse. The trading post is based on a written description of an actual fur trade station that operated along Red River in about 1840. The 1901 Elgin depot, moved to the museum in 1961, houses a new transportation exhibit. Sitting beside it on a line of railroad tracks is a Baldwin steam locomotive. Complete your outdoor journey and visit with the prairie dogs, which live wild in the adjacent Elmer Thomas Park. Back at the museum, the gift shop boasts locally handmade items, a large assortment of books for the history buff, toys for all ages and novelty items. An extensive research facility is available to scholars by appointment. For an educational and entertaining visit, come to the Museum of the Great Plains in Lawton.

601 NW Ferris Avenue, Lawton OK
(580) 581-3460
www.museumgreatplains.org

Stafford Air & Space Center

An attraction of national importance, the Stafford Air & Space Center will thrill even the most seen-it-all space enthusiast. It contains an outstanding collection of artifacts and replicas from every phase of air and space flight, along with General Thomas P. Stafford's personal memorabilia from four space missions. Displayed inside the museum, you'll find a Titan II missile, complete with (disarmed) nuclear warhead and Gemini capsule, plus a used solid rocket fuel segment and main engine from the Space Shuttle. The museum has almost every rocket engine ever built including the F-1 from the 36-story Saturn rocket. See replicas of the Lunar Lander and Apollo capsule and an actual console from NASA's mission control room. The museum boasts space suits from the Gemini through Space Shuttle eras. A Moon rock stars in a special exhibit. You'll find full-scale replicas of a 1903 Wright Flyer and the Spirit of St. Louis. Parked in the museum are an F-16, a MiG 21 and other aircraft. From a modest beginning of two display cabinets in 1983, the museum has expanded to 45,000 square feet. The Stafford Air & Space Center is an absolute must-see attraction for anyone visiting Oklahoma.

3000 E Logan Road, Weatherford OK
(580) 772-5871
www.staffordspacecenter.com

Museums, History & Culture • 77

Pioneer Heritage Townsite Center

The Pioneer Heritage Townsite Center contains 10 historic structures that tell the story of farming experience from 1900 to 1920 in Tillman County. Visitors learn of a time without running water or electricity, when farm labor was back-breaking. The complex got its start in 1977 when the Rotary Club and the Tillman County Historical Society teamed up to save the 1902 Horse Creek School building. In time, the center added a 1902 Frisco railway depot, a 1924 A.M.E. Church and the 1907 one-room Nill House that once served a family of eight. The Tillman County Historical Museum on the site offers revolving exhibits that recall territorial days, the world wars and the Great Depression. The center is transforming a barn into the new Abernathy Museum that highlights the adventures of the boys. The center regularly offers educational programs such as the Seed to Sew program that teaches elementary students about picking, ginning, spinning, weaving and sewing cotton. Other Frederick attractions include Centennial Park, Hamm's Sportsman Oasis and the Crawford Collection of trophy mount animals. Fans of early-day architecture will enjoy the Ramona Theater and the Grand Hotel, both from 1929, and the 1915 Carnegie Library. The area's Hackberry Flat is one of the most important wetland restorations in North America. The WWII Airborne Demo Team sponsors a museum and a parachute jump school.

201 N 9th Street, Frederick OK
(580) 335-5844
www.frederickokchamber.org/museums.htm

78 • Museums, History & Culture

Museums, History & Culture • 79

National Route 66 Museum

Located in Elk City's Old Town Museum complex on Old Route 66, the National Route 66 Museum offers a walking tour of the road's journey through the eight states between Chicago and California. The museum tells the story of the people who lived, worked and traveled on Route 66 through realistic murals, documents and exhibits. As you travel along, you can listen to recorded histories and personal accounts of the road from overhead audio kiosks. The museum curator is Wanda Queenan, who along with her husband Reece owned and operated the famous Queenan Trading Post on Route 66 on the west edge of Elk City. Wanda has been inducted into the Route 66 Association Hall of Fame for her extensive knowledge of the history of the Mother Road and she has plenty of interesting stories to share. The two Kachina dolls that once stood guard outside the Queenan Trading Post have moved with Wanda to the National Route 66 Museum. The museum's gift shop offers a wide range of memorabilia, from inexpensive trinkets and bumper stickers to jackets and glass collectibles. Those interested in further education can browse a large stock of books, audio and video tapes about Route 66. As a starting point for a deeper historical tour, the National Route 66 Museum can orient you to Elk City and the Oklahoma in general with maps, travel brochures and advice. Don't miss this monument of American folk history, the National Route 66 Museum. Call ahead for summer or winter hours.

2717 W Highway 66, Elk City OK
(580) 225-6266
www.visitelkcity.com

Plains Indians & Pioneers Museum

The Oklahoma Historical Society has named the Plains Indians and Pioneers Museum the best local history museum in the state. As you enter, you'll see Pat "Kemoha" Patterson's mural depicting Northwest Oklahoma Native Americans and Paul Laune's mural tracing the settlement of the pioneers. Further inside, you'll find exhibits such as Like My Fathers Before Me, which features hunters and farmers from prehistoric times through the Cheyenne and Arapaho era. The museum shows the growth of Woodward, a provisioning point for Fort Supply even before the government opened the area to non-Indian settlers. A log cabin, located outside, may date to 1869. Turn-of-the-century exhibits include the bank, the sheriff's office and jail, and a dance hall. The office of lawyer and gunfighter Temple Houston is of special interest. He was Sam Houston's youngest offspring and Woodward's favorite son. By 1902, crops replaced cowponies, and artifacts, photographs and murals by artists Fred Olds and Jana Sol tell the story of agricultural development. You'll learn about the 1947 tornado that destroyed much of the town and killed more than 100 people. Exhibits tell how Woodward began a new adventure in 1956—the roller coaster ride of oil and gas production. The Anna Lorry Williams Art Center features monthly art exhibits by local and out-of-area artists. Come see the Plains Indians and Pioneers Museum, one of the best small museums in the nation.

2009 Williams Avenue, Woodward OK (580) 256-6136 www.pipm1.org

It's All About Moi! At Miss Trudy's
Retail

It's All About Moi! At Miss Trudy's is an antique and designer mall featuring antiques, new merchandise and gifts. The mall has over 7,000 square feet with collections supplied by the shop's owners, Terre Nickels and Tamara Garrison, and items by other vendors as well. The store boasts a great variety of items, mixing about 60 percent antiques and 40 percent new goods. Booths include vintage clothing, jewelry, home accents, kitchen items, glassware, food items, western decor and furniture. Vendors work hard keeping the inventory fresh by bringing in new items on a daily basis. Tamara's section has a great variety including luggage, clothing, jewelry, pet accessories, home décor and European antiques. Terre hosts an area which includes antiques and a special section featuring hand-smocked children's clothes, embroidered specialty items and delightful baby gifts. Tamara and Terre have years of experience in antiques and gifts and decided to join hands in 2006. Terre had opened Miss Trudy's, an antique and gift shop named after her Mom, in 2004. Tamara has run her own design business, It's All About Moi! Designs by Tamara, since 2003. They created this one-of-a-kind shopping experience in one of the historical buildings on Main Street that was built in the early 1920s. Tamara's husband, Stan, purchased and renovated the building in 2006. Come visit It's All About Moi! At Miss Trudy's, where you can find the best of the old and new.

209 W Main Street, Weatherford OK
(580) 774-2088

Hastings Entertainment–Ponca City
Retail

Life in a modestly sized heartland municipality such as Ponca City has many advantages. It's easily to get to know your neighbors. But what about entertainment? That's where Hastings Entertainment comes in. A leading multimedia entertainment retailer since 1968, Hastings is dedicated to providing small to medium sized cities with a substantial selection of movies, music, books and games. Offering both rentals and sales of DVDs, CDs and video games, the store is an oasis of city-quality entertainment. Grateful crowds pour in, especially on hot summer days. In Ponca City, Hastings is the discerning viewer's choice in movie selection. "People come to us for the older and harder-to-find videos that they know they can't get elsewhere," manager Gerald Rhodes explained. "If you're looking for a boxed set of the first season of Gilligan's Island, it's here." The music and book departments are equally broad. Customers are welcome to browse at leisure in quiet reading and listening areas. Realizing its importance as a local nexus of entertainment, Hastings at Ponca City continues to look for new ways of fostering that culture. In 2007, Rhodes inaugurated concerts in the parking lot to feature local bands. The store also hosts local author readings and signings. Find local and world-class entertainment at Ponca City's Hastings Entertainment.

2900 N 14th Street, Ponca City OK
(580) 767-1455
www.hastings-ent.com

82 • Shopping & Services

Hastings Entertainment–Altus
Retail

In the age of big box stores, there is nothing quite like Hastings Entertainment, a multimedia retailer and rental store that is much like a brick-and-mortar Amazon.com. In Altus, Hastings spans 20,000 square feet, considered small for the chain but ample for a population of about the same number. Its many departments offer movies, books and music with all the trimmings. Customers can rent or buy DVDs from the movie department and video games from the game department. The game department also offers computer software and novelty gifts, such as character action figures, rock band clocks or celebrity t-shirts. In contrast to the often mind-numbing experience of online browsing, Hastings is an easy place to linger and explore. Customers can sample the CDs at music listening stations or cozy up with a book or magazine in the quiet reading area. Hastings also interacts with its community, buying and selling used CDs, DVDs and hardback books and consigning media from local authors, musicians and film makers. The corporation is dedicated to improving literacy by donating to nonprofit literacy programs and sponsoring reading clubs and children's story hours. Hastings is a place where individuals or whole families can come and spend an afternoon or stock up for the evening at home. Find true value at Hastings Entertainment in Altus.

1700 N Main Street #2, Altus OK
(580) 477-4140
www.hastings-ent.com

Hastings Entertainment–Enid
Retail

Enid's thriving musical scene includes many well-known bands, including Philosopher Stone, Infamous and the Roustabouts, and frequent concerts in the downtown historical district. With the arrival of Hastings Entertainment, Enid also has the deep music inventory it deserves. Hastings, which opened in Enid in 1990, is unchallenged in its repertoire of CDs, DVDs, video games and books. Those who prefer uncensored music and who want to both rent and buy movies flock to Hastings from miles around. Customers can spend hours browsing each department, trying out video games at the gaming station, paging through books in comfy chairs or sampling music at the listening stations. They'll also find extras such as musical instruments, computer gadgets, media players and media storage. Hastings recently remodeled the 22,000 square foot store in Enid to include a coffee bar and to better organize the abundant stock. The sharp design, bright colors and spaciousness created by the remodeling have impressed long-time customers. Hastings is also committed to community support. It offers local educator discounts and a special military discount to those who serve at the Vance Air Force Base, the largest employer in Enid. Donation jars at the checkout counters collect funds for the Enid Literacy Council. Join the community of media lovers in Enid and find what you want at Hastings Entertainment.

104 Sunset Plaza, Enid OK
(580) 242-6838
www.hastings-ent.com

Granny Annie's Amish Furniture
Home Décor

Rather than a style, the name Amish furniture denotes a standard of excellence. The only place in Oklahoma that you can find this outstanding furniture is Granny Annie's Amish Furniture. Here you'll find pieces made with America's richest hardwoods, hand-finished in a thousand different styles. While Granny Annie's keeps a number of items in stock through a quick-ship program, you'll normally special-order your furniture, choosing among thousands of designs, hundreds of woods and finishes and countless fabrics. Amish craftsmen working on one of more than 50 family farms across the Midwest then build your furniture. Seasoned hands cut, shape, sand and stain each piece of lumber. Solid drawers contain dovetail joints front and back and use the smoothest, most durable hardware available. The furniture is distributed by Simply Amish, which guarantees each piece for the life of the customer. Kevin Kaufman and his uncle, John Mast, were raised Amish, and they founded Simply Amish in 1989 to connect Amish craftsmen to the world. Carol Ann Janning opened Granny Annie's in part so that the Jannings themselves could buy Amish furniture. The shop is named after Carol's late mother, and Carol has now brought her daughter, Kathie Thomas, into the business. For the best custom furniture anywhere, come to Granny Annie's Amish Furniture.

912 North Van Buren Avenue, Elk City OK   (580) 225-5693   www.simplyamish.com

Hastings Entertainment–Lawton
Retail

A leading multimedia retailer, Hastings Entertainment is Lawton's one-stop shop for movies, books, music and games. Its many departments allow customers to browse books and magazines in peace, sample CDs at listening stations and even try out video games on large flat screen TVs. The movie department offers both rental and retail versions of its extensive stock. You'll find foreign and independent films and complete television box sets. Customers depend on Hastings's selection and service, which together guarantee that they will find they are seeking. "If we don't have it, we'll track it down and special-order it, even from a competitor," manager Jeremy said. "We don't call it customer service, we call it guest service, because we want to treat everyone the same whether they are buying something from us or not." Guests can attend regular book and CD signings at the store and supplement their fandom in the novelty department, which offers thematic gifts like action figures, lava lamps and posters. Hastings even supplies music and video electronics equipment for enjoying its multimedia. Have a good time and find what you're looking for at Hastings Entertainment.

616 NW Sheridan Road, Lawton OK
(580) 248-0392

Hastings Entertainment–Duncan
Retail

With something for everyone, Hastings Entertainment is a haven for families, friends and anyone looking for fun and relaxation in Duncan. Hastings is a major entertainment retailer that supplies books, music, movies and games for purchase or for sampling. Guests can read in a quiet reading area, play video games on big screen televisions or listen to CDs at listening stations throughout the music department. Hastings's vast stock of movies is available for purchase or rent. "You see teenagers heading for the music department, whole families going into the movie department, groups of students meeting in the book department," says Janice, the assistant manager. "The students take their shoes off to study. Parents grab a coffee to browse. Children break off to go play games. It feels good to see them. People come here for comfort, and they find it." The store trains its associates to treat customers like family. Remarkably for a large chain store, customers know the staff members by name. Hastings hosts regular children's story hours and book signing events. Dedicated to promoting literacy, the store collects donations by the cash registers to give to local literacy foundations. Discover a world of entertainment at Hastings Entertainment in Duncan.

1225 N Highway 81, Duncan OK
(580) 252-0980

Plain View Winery

The Pekrul family farm, the original home of Plain View Winery, lies out in the Oklahoma plains where the view runs for 25 miles. Facing a bumper crop of strawberries, the Pekruls decided to attempt strawberry wine. After several years of experiments, they had a colorful line of 20 fruit wines in every flavor from apricot to crabapple. Hart Pekrul didn't let his 78 years stop him from turning the family hobby into a business, and he moved Plain View Winery to a convenient in-town location. He recruited his son, Con, from the restaurant business to help make the wine and purchase specialty foods for the tasting room and gift shop. When you visit Plain View Winery, you'll find Hart and Con running every angle of the business together. Ask for the grand tour and they will show you where they make and bottle the wine. Talk to Con about food and wine pairing and you'll likely bring a few recipes home with your groceries. Have you ever sautéed your mushrooms in blackberry wine? Would you like a sausage to go with that? Let Plain View Winery equip you with whatever you need to experiment with fine food and wine.

231 W Lahoma Road, Lahoma OK
(580) 796-2902
www.plainviewwinery.com

Plymouth Valley Cellars

In 2006, the Oklahoma Farm Bureau named Dennis and Elaine Flaming the Farm Family of the Year. That same year, the couple opened Plymouth Valley Cellars. The Flamings have been a farm family since they were married in 1966, raising livestock, wheat and alfalfa. In 2001, they planted a vineyard, Plymouth Valley Vineyard, which eventually led to the winery. Plymouth Valley Cellars produces a worthy Oklahoma Riesling, a varietal that has been enjoying a renaissance of late due to its flavor and its excellent adaptability when paired with many foods. The winery is also developing a reputation for its aromatic Gewürztraminer, tenacious Cabernet Sauvignon and rich Zinfandel. It also has a first-rate Cabernet Doux, Kiwi Strawberry and Flaming Ice, an ice wine specialty. Non-alcoholic grape juices and Oklahoma-made products are available at the winery gift shop, which is open for tours, wine tastings and visits that give the guests a chance to enjoy the beautiful location. Plymouth Valley Cellars is surrounded by the Gloss Mountains and colorful gypsum formations, in a town that has existed since the late 1800s. The Flamings extend their invitation to wander the vineyards and taste the bottled fruits of their labor. Located five miles south and one mile east of Fairview.

N2550 Road, Fairview OK
(580) 227-3207 or (580) 227-0348
www.plymouthvalleycellars.com

Woods & Waters Winery and Vineyards

The Woods & Waters Winery is Caddo County's first and largest commercial winery and Woods & Waters Vineyards is one of the largest winery-owned vineyards in the state. This family-owned and operated winery was established in 1998 by Dale Pound, vintner and viticulturalist, and his wife, Lena Voznesenskaya Pound. Woods & Waters is located on a 600-acre ranch of rolling hills, trees and ponds, where the abundance of sunshine and the dry summers are ideal for the production of true vinifera wine grapes. Dale and Lena have planted eight varieties of grapes on 20 acres. They produce wines using Oklahoma-grown grapes exclusively, and most of the grapes are from their personal vineyard. When you sample wine from Woods & Waters, you'll understand the wonderful taste that Oklahoma has to offer. A house specialty is the Rose of Caddo, a light, sweet red wine with a dry finish. This wine is delicious for all occasions and is best served chilled. Another award-winner is the Gewürztraminer, voted the states best wine made from Oklahoma grapes. It has an interesting spicy taste that is excellent with Tai and Mexican foods. Oklahoma Sparkle is a Champagne-style sweet bubbly. It is one of the newest productions and one of the only sparkling wines in the state. The winery also showcases gorgeous Russian Orthodox icons painted by Lena. Dale and Lena invite you to visit Woods & Waters Winery and Vineyards soon for a warm welcome, beautiful art and great wine.

17153 County Road E1380, Anadarko OK
(580) 588-2515
www.woodsandwaterswinery.com

Wines & Specialty Foods • 87

Raccoon—Oklahoma State Furbearer

88 • Northeast

Northeast • 89

Northeast Oklahoma
Green Country

Redbud—Oklahoma State Tree

90 • Sapulpa—the Heart of Route 66

Sapulpa Photos by Kathleen Curran

Sapulpa
The Heart of Route 66

Sapulpa, the county seat of Creek County, is located in northeastern Oklahoma's Green Country. This is an area where six nations have flown their flags—Spain, France, England, Mexico, the Choctaw Indian Nation and the United States. Sapulpa's character has been shaped by three historic factors: Indians, railroads and oil.

Chief Sapulpa, the area's first permanent settler, was a full-blooded Lower Creek Indian of the Kasihta Tribe in Osocheetown, Alabama. He arrived in Indian Territory around the year 1850 and established a trading post near the confluence of Polecat and Rock Creeks, about one mile southeast of present-day downtown Sapulpa. When the Atlantic and Pacific railroad line was extended to the area in 1886, it was called Sapulpa Station in honor of the chief, who had befriended the railway workers.

The treaty of 1866 between the Creek Nation and the United States provided for the establishment of post offices in the territory. In 1889, the Federal government opened the Sapulpa Post Office. In 1898, citizens incorporated the town. In 1905, the discovery of Glenn Pool oilfield six miles southeast of Sapulpa ushered in the community's greatest period of growth.

The oil boom, the Frisco railroad, two brick plants and four glass plants combined to transform Sapulpa from a sleepy little village in Indian Territory into a bustling community of 20,000 by the mid-1920s. Most of the buildings in downtown Sapulpa were erected in the boom period. This collection of buildings led to the placement of Sapulpa's downtown on the National Register of Historic Places in 2003. The city center is bisected by old Route 66, which once carried Okies and others west to greener pastures. Throughout the year, Sapulpa plays host to visitors reliving the myth of Route 66, the Mother Road.

101 E Dewey, Sapulpa OK
(918) 224-0170 (Chamber of Commerce)
www.sapulpachamber.com

Downtown Sapulpa

The downtown historic district is filled with unique shops. There is much to be said for a business whose owner is the one waiting on you. You will receive that special one-on-one attention that big stores don't offer. Whether you are looking for antiques, home accessories or just a gift for yourself, Sapulpa has it all.

Sapulpa—the Heart of Route 66 • 93

Treasures of Sapulpa

Every small community has its hidden treasures, and Sapulpa is no different. More than $26 million has been spent in the historic downtown area over the past 17 years. Route 66 is filled with treasures of the past and present. Frankoma Pottery is one of those unique finds. Frankoma is nationally known for their pottery made from the red clay of Sapulpa. A few other Route 66 treasures include the Sapulpa Trolley and the Sapulpa Historical Museum. Both locations are a great source of information about the history of the community. Be sure to make time to take in an evening or matinee performance at Sapulpa Community Theatre.

Left Page, clockwise from top: Downtown Sapulpa; Downtown Holiday Lights; Ghost Sign; Martha's Corner.
Right Page, clockwise from top: Historic Route 66 Bridge; Sapulpa General Store; Community Theatre; Frankoma Pottery; Sapulpa Trolley.

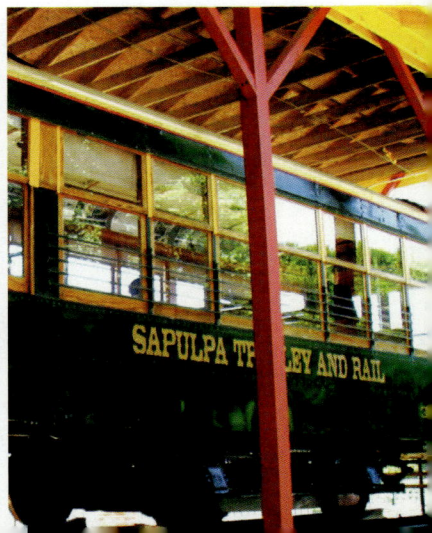

Events in Sapulpa

The fun never ends in Sapulpa. From January to December, the calendar is filled with family events throughout the year. Pretty Water Lake is a spring-fed lake that is stocked with trout in October and pan fish in the early spring. The Route 66 Blowout is one of the most popular events of the year. More than 15,000 people attend this one-day festival, enjoying crafts, art, food and one of the largest car shows in Oklahoma.

Sapulpa Parks

Sapulpa boasts 20 parks and recreation areas within the Sapulpa Parks System totaling 539 acres of land and 413 surface acres of water. These parks include sports fields, trails, golf, fishing, a splash pad and playgrounds. The newest facility, Heritage Park, was built by 1,700 community volunteers in nine days. Sapulpa Main Street received three awards from Oklahoma Main Street in 2006 for this community project. This is a must-see when visiting Sapulpa.

Left Page, clockwise from top: Downtown Parade; Route 66 Blowout; Fishing Derby; Route 66 Blowout

Right Page, counter clockwise from top: Davis Park; Rotary Splash Pad; Heritage Park; Sahoma Lake.

Sapulpa

Southern Oaks Resort & Spa

Nestled among 30 acres of lush woodlands, Southern Oaks Resort & Spa is the only resort on the secluded southern end of Grand Lake o' the Cherokees. Its five cozy cottages accommodate parties of between two and eight in comfort with fully stocked kitchens, satellite television, DVD players and open-air covered decks. Special cottages, such as the honeymoon suite, include hot tubs and fireplaces. Partners Brad Scott and Thomas Bogle bought the resort from other members of the family three years ago and added several new facilities, notably a day spa. Guests can embellish their weekend getaways with a range of massage options and therapeutic mud treatments. Southern Oaks also offers an outdoor family pavilion and a clubhouse for special events. The pavilion in the resort's park-like setting includes outdoor grills and picnic tables that are perfect for a cookout. You might just see some deer grazing in the back part of the property. The clubhouse seats up to 60 people and includes its own full-size kitchen. To keep the whole family entertained, the resort offers a full size basketball court, sand volleyball court and swimming pool. Water sports and boat rides, a tempting selection of small restaurants, and the Pensacola Dam are nearby. Discover the beauties of southern Grand Lake at the Southern Oaks Resort & Spa.

Langley OK (918) 782-9346 *www.southernoakscottages.com*

Tenkiller Lodge

Tenkiller Lodge, situated at the gateway to the popular Lake Tenkiller, offers vacationers and business travelers a tranquil and welcoming stay for nearby fishing, hiking and enjoying the area's sensational views. The lodge, perched atop historic Park Hill, opened in 1997 and is owned by Don and Nancy Matuska and managed by David and Michelle Ferguson and their small children, making this an ideal vacation destination for the whole family. The stunning log lodge offers 25 comfortable rooms that feature hand carved four-poster beds fitted with quilts, as well as televisions, coffeemakers and complimentary wireless high speed internet. Additional features of this year-round lodge include a swimming pool and a lovely pavilion with a barbecue grill, along with a homey gathering room enhanced by a grand fireplace. Visitors to the lodge can also enjoy the in-house gallery of local artists and the work of Cherokee artists who remain in touch with their native heritage. Tenkiller Lodge is conveniently located just minutes from historic downtown Tahlequah, the Illinois River and the Trail of Tears Drama at the Cherokee Heritage Center. Historic sites, shopping venues and recreational opportunities abound. Whether you are traveling the area for business or pleasure, treat yourself to a rustic getaway highlighted by modern amenities at the superb Tenkiller Lodge.

26247 Highway 82, Park Hill OK
(918) 453-9000
www.tenkillerlodge.com

Holiday Inn Express Hotel & Suites

Relax and enjoy luxurious accommodations and top-notch service with a stay at the Holiday Inn Express Hotel & Suites, ideally situated adjacent to the sensational Oklahoma Aquarium with its 200 exhilarating underwater exhibits. This beautifully designed, state-of-the-art facility offers 76 comfortably appointed guest rooms, 19 elegant suites and six rooms that have been specially designed and equipped for those with special needs. Cable television, microwaves and refrigerators are available in each room, along with comfortable workstations and free high-speed wireless Internet service. Holiday Inn Express Hotel & Suites is a family-friendly, nonsmoking hotel that offers a heated indoor pool, sauna, hot tub and outdoor tanning deck, along with an exercise room and many terrific amenities for your enjoyment and convenience. The hotel also offers a large conference room and a 24-hour business center, making this the ideal place to hold corporate events and conferences.

The welcoming atmosphere and sublime service available at the Holiday Inn Express Hotel & Suites, accommodating groups of up to 300, make it a great locale for family reunions, weddings and other special occasions. Discover your new home away from home with amenities fit for a king at the Holiday Inn Express Hotel & Suites.

150 Aquarium Drive, Jenks OK
(918) 296-7300

Fin and Feather Resort

Nestled among the rolling hills of Oklahoma's Green Country, near the clear waters of beautiful Lake Tenkiller, is the Fin and Feather Resort. Family-owned and operated since 1960, The Fin has grown from a small resort with 20 cabins and a small café to a favorite family getaway that offers 83 lodging units, banquet facilities, a gift shop, on-site recreational activities and dining options to suit every taste. Although many things have changed over the years, The Fin has retained the warmth and charm of its earliest days. Guests to the resort are treated like family and the successive generations of owners wouldn't have it any other way. With its scenic backdrop, family-friendly atmosphere, wide selection of cabins and houses and exceptional dining facilities, The Fin is a popular destination for reunions, church and corporate retreats and other large group gatherings. No trip to the area would be complete without stopping by The Fin's spacious dining room to enjoy the all-you-can-eat evening theme buffets and weekend break*feast* buffet, both of which regularly draw crowds from all over eastern Oklahoma and western Arkansas. You can also enjoy The Fin's more casual eatery, Soda Steve's, known for its famous cheese fries, cold mugs of homemade root beer and specialty entrées. Opened in 2006, Soda Steve's is the creation of Head Chef Steve Pool, a self-described culinary tourist whose travel souvenirs are the all-time favorite recipes he has brought back to The Fin for the enjoyment of all his guests. With so much to do, visit Fin and Feather Resort today.

N of town on Highway 10A, Gore OK (918) 487-5148
www.finandfeatherresort.com

Paradise Cove Marine Resort

Located on the Grand Lake o' the Cherokees, the crown jewel of northeast Oklahoma's chain of lakes, the Paradise Cove Marine Resort is a collection of premium waterfront homes and condominiums designed to accommodate the water-loving vacationer. Condominiums for parties of 2 to 10 include fully equipped kitchens, fireplaces and private decks overlooking the lake. A honeymoon suite sports a king size bed and hot tub. For large family gatherings or longer stays, guests can rent one of two fully furnished three-bedroom houses. The newly completed houses boast 12-foot ceilings, granite countertops, stone fireplaces and hot tubs. Paradise Cove is the brainchild of Ray and Katherine Maloney, who realized that Oklahoma lake country was an untapped paradise. To make the most of the location, Paradise Cove provides a 24-hour automated gas dock and boat rentals for their guests. Spend an afternoon exploring the lake on a waverunner or plan a picnic luncheon on the 13-person pontoon, and enjoy some of the best fishing in Oklahoma. Family reunions love the swimming pool, children's playground and party deck with barbeque, which complete the facilities. Plan the perfect waterfront vacation at the Paradise Cove Marine Resort.

30736 S 4539 Road, Afton OK
(918) 782-3767
www.paradisecoveresort.com

TeraMiranda Marina and Resort

TeraMiranda Marina and Resort is ideally situated for fully enjoying the 66 mile long Grand Lake o' the Cherokees, and is accessible by water, land or sod airstrip. Recreational opportunities abound with a swimming pool, fenced playground, tennis court, volleyball and water sports. The marina features 117 covered boat slips in two coves plus a 50-ton marine travel lift. Each all-electric air-conditioned cottage can sleep six to 12 people, and many have kitchenettes. Everything you need is close at hand, from a store equipped with groceries, sporting goods and marine supplies, to a restaurant overlooking the lake.
The marina is prepared to handle the service and repair of your boat with a team of master mechanics and a 12,000-square-foot climate controlled service facility. It is authorized to service many brand name generators, stern drives, outboards, marine inboard engines and air conditioning systems. TeraMiranda is also a pre-owned, consignment and brokerage dealer for all types of boats and yachts from 16 to 60 feet. It can handle everything from sales, service and storage to financing and insurance. The Grand Lake o' the Cherokees is well worth your visit, and TeraMiranda can make your outing here everything you hoped it could be. The Gregg family purchased the existing resort in 1961 and remains actively involved in management and operations today. They invite you to start your outing to Grand Lake from TeraMiranda Marina and Resort.

28251 South 561 Road, Monkey Island OK
(918) 257-4274
www.teramiranda.com

Hilton Garden Inn Tulsa South

Discover for yourself why the elegant Hilton Garden Inn Tulsa South earned one of Hilton World Wide Regional's Top 10 spots for customer satisfaction. This favored inn boasts 104 guestrooms, including six sumptuous suites, and features everything you need to host a presentation, wine and dine colleagues or just relax with the family. The 24-hour fitness center and heated pool and Jacuzzi is just the beginning of what this inn has to offer. An 80-person conference room and a smaller boardroom are available for a variety of events, complete with audiovisual equipment and catering packages. The guest room amenities surpass expectations with the Garden Sleep Systems by VSS Sleep System in select rooms, work desks with Mirra desk chairs from Herman Miller and complimentary accessibility to the hotel's high-speed internet, including wireless. Start your day with a hearty breakfast in the Great American Grill, Hilton Garden Inn's on-site restaurant, or unwind with dinner in the restaurant or in the comfort of your room. The choice is yours. The cozy Pavilion Lounge offers beverages and spirits in a welcoming atmosphere, complete with a fireplace, comfortable seating and a high-definition flat-screen television. If you forgot a necessity or need a midnight snack, an assortment of food and personal items can be found in the Pavilion Pantry, the inn's concenience mart. While visiting Tulsa, take advantage of the inn's centralized location by checking out the sights and sounds of Tulsa and surrounding area. Enjoy an optimal lodging experience with a stay at the Hilton Garden Inn Tulsa South.

8202 S 100th East Avenue, Tulsa OK
(918) 392-2000
www.tulsasouth.gardeninn.com

Tivoli Inn & The Glass Hall

Tivoli Inn looks like an Italian villa from the hillside town of Tivoli, Italy. In actuality, this charming inn was built specifically as a bed-and-breakfast, named in honor of the Tivoli Gardens of Copenhagen, Denmark. The Copenhagen gardens are the inspiration behind each of the six tastefully appointed bedrooms in this grand establishment, located in a woods overlooking a winding creek in Broken Arrow, not far from Tulsa. Tivoli Inn is a masterpiece of comfort and convenience. Amenities include wireless Internet, plus television, VCR and DVD. The inn serves satisfying breakfasts and bedtime snacks, while the Tea Room takes care of light lunches along with afternoon or high tea by appointment. The Glass Hall is an impressive location for such special events as showers, a bridesmaids' tea or lunch, a ladies luncheons or a rehearsal dinner. The inn has also hosted corporate meetings and many birthday and Christmas parties. The Tarp Chapel and Gardens is in demand for weddings. A visit to Tivoli Inn is an opportunity to experience comfortable seclusion from within the city. Kathleen Tarp, her daughter Kristina, and Anna Slater invite visitors and residents to share their peaceful home and grounds at Tivoli Inn & the Glass Hall.

1401 W Washington Avenue, Broken Arrow OK
(918) 449-8648
www.tarpchapelandgardens.com

The Country Inn Bed and Breakfast

For a quiet, restful and romantic getaway, the Country Inn Bed and Breakfast is ideal. The inn sits on five acres of beautiful landscaping, with lawns, wooded hills and shade trees. Guests enjoy an outdoor swimming pool, a gazebo and many intimate places to lie or sit. An outdoor hot tub is also available. The inn itself is a rustic, two-story converted barn that has four guest rooms decorated with country antiques. All rooms have private baths, and the honeymoon loft has a jetted spa tub for two and a California king bed.

Hosts and Owners Linda and Dennis Coons provide warm hospitality. Linda is the chef and has a degree from the famous Sclafani Cooking School in Metairie, Louisiana. Linda's skill guarantees an outstanding breakfast for the bed-and-breakfast's guests, but the Country Inn also offers custom catering for corporate functions, weddings and other special occasions. Linda's specialties are Mediterranean and Cajun dishes. Come visit the Country Inn. It is located northeast of Tulsa in rural Rogers County in the charming town of Claremore.

20530 East 430 Road, Claremore OK
(918) 342-1894
www.countryinnbandb.com

Accommodations & Resorts • 103

Pine Lodge Resort

Your dream of getting close to nature in a log cabin comes true at Pine Lodge Resort. The resort was honored by the Grand Lake Association for "Most Outstanding Visitor's Accommodations." Pine Lodge Resort, located on Grand Lake of the Cherokees, offers waterfront and secluded log cabins, a clubhouse and swimming pool. Each cabin provides everything you need for a rustic, yet comfortable romantic experience with a wood-burning fireplace and a private hot tub on each deck. The resort comes alive in December with its Winter Wonderland light tour. Owners Art and June Box go all out with their decorations and illuminations, which draw many visitors each year from the four-state area. Pine Lodge is located next to Duck Creek, where the largest firework display in Oklahoma took place in July, 2006. In celebration of the state centennial, the 2007 fireworks show is likely to be equally impressive. For boating, fishing and watersports, Grand Lake beckons. Pine Lodge offers a quiet getaway, surrounding you with the sounds of birds and nature. When you need a break from every day life, your cabin in the woods is waiting for you at Pine Lodge Resort.

**Highway 85 N
(2.5 miles east of Ketchum) OK
(918) 782-1400 or (800) 640-3173**
www.pinelodgeresort.com

Elk Creek Resort

If you're searching for a great vacation spot that is fun for the whole family, head for Elk Creek Resort, where owners Ernie and Kathy Son and their family have been helping to create happy memories for vacationers since 1999. Elk Creek offers a full range of services and amenities, including dry storage for your boat and both pontoon and wave runner rentals. The staff is happy to take your boat out of dry-dock for you and get it ready to go so you can hit the water as soon as you arrive. The resort offers several cozy, well-appointed cabins and generously sized campsites that come complete with water and electric hookups, along with a swimming area, snack bar and gas dock. Elk Creek Resort is famous for its delicious hand-dipped ice cream cones, malts and shakes and also sells convenience items like suntan oil and t-shirts; however, it does not offer alcohol or tobacco products, because the Sons want to maintain the resort's family-friendly atmosphere, a quality which makes Elk Creek an ideal place for visitors of all ages. The Sons, along with daughters Amy, Kari and Beth, son-in-law Brian and their grandsons, are dedicated to providing a safe and exciting getaway for the entire family and look forward to meeting you when you come for a visit to Elk Creek Resort.

22911 W 877 Road, Park Hill OK
(918) 457-5142

Terrapin Peak Bed, Breakfast & Beyond

Go where wildlife viewing is an all-day event and the stars are so close at night you can almost touch them; go to Terrapin Peak Bed, Breakfast & Beyond. This welcoming inn features modern rooms and exudes a comfortable, country atmosphere that is ideal for vacationers of all ages. Owner and founder Genny Maiden, who has more than 25 years of experience in the food service industry, opened Terrapin Peak early in 2006 and has quickly earned a reputation for excellence, based on her attention to detail and dedication to personalized service. Chef Gregg, who does double duty as the inn's concierge, plans his breakfast menus around each guest and happily accommodates all dietary needs, including vegetarian and diabetic diets, as well as dairy or gluten-free meals. Each cozy room features a wall-sized photograph of a picturesque Lake Tenkiller scene along with comfortable beds and homey amenities, such as a television and DVD player, self-controlled heating and air conditioning, a microwave and a small refrigerator. The rooms additionally offer coffeemakers, first aid kits, private grills and boat trailer parking with water and electric hookups. Terrapin Peak is conveniently located near numerous area attractions, including SixShooter Resort & Marina, Tenkiller State Park and Ft. Gibson Military Park. Enjoy a backwoods vacation with all the comforts of home at Terrapin Peak Bed, Breakfast & Beyond.

20965 W 921st Road, Cookson OK
(918) 457-4906
www.terrapinpeakbbb.com

Eagle Bluff Resort

Eagle Bluff Resort provides more than just a place to stay while you enjoy the Illinois River. Its trained, friendly staff provides everything you need for a fun and safe canoe, raft or kayak trip. That means all the gear you need, plus transportation and free instruction. The stretch of river accessible from the resort offers plenty of beautiful scenery while flowing at a pace that even a novice canoeist can handle. As one writer puts it, "The Illinois River meanders through the Ozarks of Oklahoma like a Sunday driver out to enjoy the scenery—and not in any big hurry to get where he's going." Overall, the waters run leisurely with some easy rapids. A person can typically cover around 12 miles in four to six hours. Eagle Bluff Resort is a family-oriented campground with spaces to pitch your tent or hook up your RV. The campgrounds are rated three diamonds by Woodall's. Cabins with kitchens are also available, plus two group lodges with cooking and meeting areas. When not having fun on the river, guests play on the sand volleyball court and at the children's playground. Miss Ellie's Café, which overlooks the river, offers a sandwich and snack menu and catering services. Be sure to stay at Eagle Bluff Resort when you visit the Illinois River.

9800 Highway 10, Tahlequah OK
(918) 456-3031 or (800)-OK-RIVER (657-4837)
www.eaglebluffresort.com

Room at the Top of the World

Imagine yourself tucked into a secret hideaway surrounded by the sights and sounds of nature, luxuriating in a hot tub with champagne at hand or lounging by the fire with that special someone. Turn your daydreams into reality with a trip to the Room at the Top of the World, where you can enjoy 10 private acres with views of the crystalline waters of Barren Fork Creek and a wealth of recreational activities, like bass fishing, swimming, floating and hiking. Owners David and Pam Weaver opened the welcoming and graciously designed Room at the Top of the World in 2004 as a place where people could experience a rejuvenating getaway. The retreat features two peaceful bedrooms and two comfortable living areas, along with a large private deck and a country bathroom with a vintage claw foot tub. Amenities include satellite television and entertainment components, such as a DVD player and stereo system, as well as a regulation pool table, a built-in bar and a fully equipped kitchen stocked with beverages, popcorn and pantry staples. Outside visitors will find inviting patio furniture and a cozy hammock, along with an outdoor cooker and a fire pit that is perfect for roasting marshmallows and hot dogs. Reserve the Room at the Top of the World for memories that will last a lifetime.

19001 S 580 Road, Stilwell OK
(918) 456-6883
www.roomatthetopoftheworld.com

Doubletree Hotel at Warren Place

The Doubletree Hotel at Warren Place is a full-service luxury hotel that exudes both elegance and comfort. With a recent $11 million dollar renovation, the Doubletree's 370 stylish guest rooms and executive suites provide all the comforts of home along with amenities like spacious work areas and wireless high speed Internet access. Guests can enjoy the sparkling new indoor pool, whirlpool, sauna and fully equipped fitness center. Though it's centrally located, the Doubletree is set in a beautifully landscaped, park-like environment, with scenic walking and jogging trails for guests to enjoy. For an elegant evening or business lunch, the Warren Duck Club has been an award winning, four-star restaurant of choice for 21 years, and if it's a more casual meal you're looking for, Starbuck's Café is on-site too. The Doubletree also offers almost 20,000 square feet of versatile meeting spaces that will guarantee any event will be a smashing success. There's a state-of-the-art amphitheatre with tiered seating that can accommodate workshops or seminars. The Doubletree's creative team of meeting and catering specialists will provide complete support and take care of all the details, so you can just relax and enjoy yourself. Whether you're traveling for business or pleasure, the Doubletree's friendly and professional hotel staff will give you a warm Tulsa welcome and one of their world-famous chocolate chip cookies when you check in.

6110 S Yale Avenue, Tulsa OK
(918) 495-1000
www.doubletreehotelwarrenplace.com

Holiday Inn Express

The Holiday Inn Express in Locust Grove offers big-city accommodations in a little town. The hotel features 28 standard rooms and 22 suites that are sure to meet your lodging needs. If you're looking for a romantic getaway, check out one of the four whirlpool suites with a Jacuzzi in each one. Those with children will enjoy one of two KidSuites with an adult area and a separate portion for kids with a Disney theme, television, video player and Sony PlayStation video game system. Business travelers will find the 16 Executive Suites comfortable and well outfitted with two-line phones with dataport capability, refrigerator and microwave. Travelers will also want to take advantage of the hotel's free high-speed Internet service. Those looking to hold business meetings at the Holiday Inn Express can take advantage of the hotel's meeting rooms. The hotel has a pool, spa and fitness area for those looking to keep in shape as they travel. The Holiday Inn Express offers a Continental breakfast and is conveniently located near several local restaurants. Those looking for local culture can find plenty to do at the nearby Salina Speedway, the Mid America Industrial Park and the Willard Stone Museum. For great service and accommodations, business and vacation travelers should check into the Holiday Inn Express.

**106 Holiday Lane, Locust Grove OK
(918) 479-8082
www.hiexpress.com/locustgroveok**

The Hotel Savoy

The Hotel Savoy offers guests the opportunity to stay in a charming luxury suite at a very affordable price. The hotel retains many of its beautiful original features from the 1930s, and after an extensive renovation in 2001, provides all of the modern conveniences you would expect in a first-class establishment. Each of the seven suites is furnished with beautiful French antiques and offers the comforts of home, including a separate bedroom and living room, air conditioning and on-site laundry facilities. The spacious accommodations and full kitchen, stocked with snacks and drinks, make the hotel an ideal family getaway. Business travelers will appreciate the desk and complimentary high-speed Internet access as well as the convenient location less than a mile from downtown Tulsa and minutes from the Tulsa Convention Center. Special touches, such as silk bedcovers, feather pillows and fine linens, make you feel pampered and ensure your stay is relaxing. Each morning, start the day off right with the hotel's Continental breakfast as you contemplate the day's activities. Stay at the Hotel Savoy on your next visit to Tulsa and experience top-notch amenities with value pricing.

**631 S Peoria Avenue, Tulsa OK
(918) 34-SAVOY (72869) or (866) 34-SAVOY (72869)
www.tulsasavoy.com**

Terri's Sixshooter Bed & Breakfast

Luxuriate in a bed and breakfast experience that exceeds usual expectations at Terri's Sixshooter Bed & Breakfast, overlooking the glorious Lake Tenkiller. Terri Ussery opened this popular hideaway in 2001 to provide a lodging experience for those visiting what many consider the prettiest lake in the state. Terri's Sixshooter offers four inviting and elegantly furnished rooms and suites designed for optimal comfort, including the Honeymoon Suite, which includes both a hot tub and a generously sized bathroom, featuring a whirlpool tub made from imported Italian marble. Each morning Terri treats guests to a delicious Continental-style breakfast that comes complete with freshly made treats like Persimmon muffins, orange cream crepes and homemade cinnamon rolls, along with a variety of cereals, yogurts and fresh fruit. In addition to offering some of the nicest rooms at the lake, the inn provides a game room with a full-sized pool table and a gorgeous polished stone floor. Guests of Terri's Sixshooter Bed & Breakfast, located just one block from Sixshooter Marina, can also take advantage of the inn's large houseboat, which is ideal for cruising the lake with family and friends. Enjoy a tranquil vacation highlighted by breathtaking views, exceptional hospitality and a gracious atmosphere with a stay at Terri's Sixshooter Bed & Breakfast.

20183 W Sixshooter Road, Cookson OK
(918) 457-7933
www.sixshooterBB.com

Diamondhead Resort

When it comes time to plan your family vacation, it can be hard to please the whole gang unless you head to Diamondhead Resort with its choice of a nine-hole disc golf course, volleyball and other games, along with canoes, rafts and kayaks for floating adventures. Kevin and Barbara Kelley took over this family friendly resort in 2002, and it has since become a favored vacation spot for anyone looking for fun on the Illinois River. In addition to running the camp, the Kelleys made the primary donation needed to fund an emergency airboat for the river, which in turn saved a young girl's life in 2003. Diamondhead Resort offers canoe and raft trips of varied lengths, including a two-day canoe excursion. You can also arrange transportation to your launch site and pickup at your destination. The resort meets lodging needs with several options, including a private campground with restrooms and electric hookups, two bunkhouses that sleep up to 60 people each, cabins that sleep 12 and a cozy motel with comfortable rooms that hold up to four guests. The 40-acre camp, open April 1 to the end of September, accommodates an air-conditioned game room, where you can beat the heat and enjoy pool or video games. Diamondhead Resort's large on-site store offers everything you need to make your trip perfect, including firewood, souvenirs, snacks and picnic supplies. Discover the vacation spot that's sure to become a family favorite with a stay at Diamondhead Resort.

12081 Highway 10, Tahlequah OK
(918) 456-4545 or (800) 722-2411
www.diamondresort.us

Skelly Lodge

Only minutes from Tulsa, the Skelly Lodge has overlooked the tranquil Verdigris River Valley and Oklahoma's wooded hills for decades. The lodge has given shelter to some larger-than-life historical figures over the years. Presidents Franklin Roosevelt, Harry Truman and Dwight Eisenhower have all spent time here, not to mention Britain's Winston Churchill. The lodge is a graceful eight-bedroom Swiss chalet in a peaceful setting, ideal for special events and restful escapes. It contains a fully functional kitchen, spacious dining room and comfortable living areas in its 8,000 square feet of living space. Outside, a romantic balcony and a covered veranda and porch give visitors a place to unwind and enjoy some serene viewing of the scenery and wildlife surrounding the lodge. The lodge was known as the Verdigris Club in the early years. A group of influential oil men, including Skelly Petroleum's William G. Skelly, incorporated the club and built a private hunting reserve and retreat. Skelly eventually purchased the property. After his death, it became the Diamond Bar D Ranch bed and breakfast and the Woods and Water hunting retreat. In 2000, Skelly Lodge was opened to the public for functions, events and overnight accommodations. Consider the popular 24-hour package for your next event, and take advantage of the catering or wedding cake services. Skelly Lodge makes any occasion a carefree time of celebration.

27795 S Skelly Road, Catoosa OK
(918) 266-3331
www.skellylodge.com

112 • Attractions & Recreation

Attractions & Recreation • 113

Catch the Fever Music Festivals

If you've got either country fever or heartland fever, Catch the Fever Music Festivals is sure to cure you. Country Fever is a four-day event featuring 25 of country music's finest entertainers at a 400-acre outdoor concert venue four miles north of Pryor. The first Country Fever, held in 2003, hosted more than 32,000 fans over the four days of the fest. Beyond showcasing Nashville's best, Country Fever features top local and regional artists, as well as great arts and craft vendors, camping and an incredible food and beverage lineup. The live music begins each day at 11 am and usually runs well past, 2:30 am, with time in between to enjoy great company and all the festivities. The Heartland Fever festival, held in August, hosts Christian music acts. The Rodeo Fever festival, slated for the fall, features PBR bull-riding events on top of music. The goal of Catch The Fever President Mark Nuessle and staff is to make these festivals the premier showcase for country music, Christian contemporary, classic rock and bluegrass acts in Oklahoma. For true western entertainment, check out the schedule of Catch the Fever Music Festivals. There's sure to be a major attraction you can't resist.

114 S Mill Street, Pryor OK
(918) 824-2288 or (866) 310-2288
www.feverfest.com
www.countryfeverfest.com

Tara Cottage

The quaint Tara Cottage just off Main Street in the heart of historic Broken Arrow can teach you things you never knew about Gone with the Wind. Schedule a tour to step back in history to the time of Scarlett O'Hara and take another look at Margaret Mitchell's Pulitzer Prize winning novel and the Academy Award wining movie it inspired. The décor and atmosphere of the cottage are romantic and period-correct. Tara Cottage offers Gone with the Wind themed rooms, fun facts, stories, costumes, ornaments and gifts. End your tour with a signature Gone with the Wind dessert, served on the Tara Terrace or in the Tara Tea Room, and pick up a treasure to take home from the gift shop. Choose from such specialty items as a line of signature dessert candles or bath products by Rhett and Scarlett—Nothing Modest Will Do. Tara Cottage may be far from Georgia, but it's close to the heart of one of America's most beloved novels and motion pictures. In addition to tours, Tara Cottage can host ladies' gatherings, small weddings and vow renewals upon request. Owner and proprietor Marcia Taylor invites you to stop by Tara Cottage soon. As Mammy says, "See ya'll at Tara, it's fitten, just fitten."

307 East Midway Street, Broken Arrow OK
(918) 853-3002
www.expressedesigns.com

LaFortune Park Golf Pro Shop

The Golf Pro Shop at LaFortune Park Golf Course is frequently listed among the top 100 golf shops in America, and *Urban Tulsa Weekly* has voted it the best golf shop in Tulsa. The shop offers an outstanding selection of golf accessories, from vintage to modern. The extensive clothing selection here is as practical as it is stylish and includes the largest selection of golf shoes in the area. Whether you are shopping for a new set of clubs, a stylish new golf shirt or some last-minute gift ideas, LaFortune's pro shop offers the brand names that golfers count on for quality, such as Cleveland, Ping and Mizuno. You'll find clubs and balls from Titleist, Callaway, Bridgestone and TaylorMade. Cobra clubs also have a strong following. The junior set benefits from the lighter club weight of clubs by U.S. Kids. The golf shop's professional staff provides free custom fittings with any purchase. LaFortune Park Golf Course itself is located in the heart of Tulsa. Renowned golf course architect Randy Heckenkemper recently renovated its layout, bringing it in line with some of the finest public courses anywhere. LaFortune Park offers two sets of 18 holes, one a championship course and the other a lighted par 3 that's great for evening play. The experts at LaFortune Park Golf Pro Shop invite you to stop in for golfing equipment and supplies every golfer will appreciate.

5501 S Yale Avenue, Tulsa OK
(918) 596-8627
www.LaFortuneParkGolf.com

Oxley Nature Center

The Oxley Nature Center is a preserve of 804 acres along the south bank of Tulsa's Bird Creek. Its diverse habitats—forests, fields and wetlands—support plants and animals that were once widespread across northeast Oklahoma. Naturalists have observed more than 200 species of birds and 50 species of butterflies at the center. Mammals such as deer, bobcat, mink, bats and coyote thrive here undisturbed. Designed for both protection and education, the center provides a variety of facilities and programs that let visitors view the wildlife safely. Eleven miles of the trails are largely flat, smooth and wheelchair accessible. First-time visitors may want to stop by the Oxley-Yetter Interpretive Building to pick up maps of the trails or educational brochures on the nature center's plants and animals. The Interpretive Building offers hands-on exhibits, a classroom and a wildlife viewing area. The Nature Store stocks books, games and souvenirs. Oxley offers several clubs and naturalist programs for children, as well as the award-winning Riddle of the Woods school tour. Families and nature lovers of all ages can participate in ongoing programs that include night walks, bird, butterfly and wildflower walks, and a regular schedule of classes. The result of dedicated citizen effort, the Oxley Nature Center is a legacy that everyone can enjoy. Experience the treasures of the Oklahoma wild at the Oxley Nature Center.

5701 E 36th Street N, Tulsa OK
(918) 669-6644
www.oxleynaturecenter.org

Duchess Creek Marina

For more than 31 years, many families have made an annual tradition of visiting the Duchess Creek Marina, where they enjoy great food, cozy cabins in a beautiful setting, and the friendly hospitality of the Cottrell family. Ed, Rusty, Leah and K.C. Cottrell invite guests to enjoy their property on scenic Lake Eufaula. Bring your RV and stay in one of the campsites, or relax in a comfortable cabin, complete with air conditioning, refrigerator and a lake view. Start your day off right with a hearty breakfast in the café, and then return later for a bacon cheeseburger basket or a steak sandwich. Some visitors call the marina's burgers the best on the lake. Duchess Creek offers boat rentals for a day of fun on the lake, or for unlimited adventures, check out the marina's sales department, including a selection of pontoon boats by Beachcomber Boats. The cool, clear waters of the lake offer recreation for every water sport enthusiast, from adventurous wake boarders to contemplative fishermen. Come to Duchess Creek Marina to create lasting memories and perhaps even start a new family tradition.

Route 1, Box 16900, Porum OK
(918) 484-5210

Oklahoma Aquarium

Deep in the heart of the Midwest is an underwater world that puts the creatures of the deep right at eye level. Opened in 2003, Oklahoma Aquarium is located on a 66-acre campus in the city of Jenks, near Tulsa. It contains 200 exhibits that showcase freshwater and saltwater animals in naturalistic settings. Look for exhibits that recreate the journey of the Arkansas River to the sea and others devoted to the fish of Oklahoma, including spotted gar and blue catfish. View a coral reef like you might find in the Caribbean Sea; marvel at octopi, seahorses and electric eels, or enter an underwater viewing tunnel with a 25-foot window for a face-to-face encounter with a giant bull shark. One gallery is devoted to such underappreciated invertebrates as sponges, sea urchins and sea stars. The aquarium partners with the Oklahoma Department of Wildlife Conservation and dedicates itself to conservation through education with factual explanations at each exhibit, special wetlab classrooms and a weeklong summer camp. It's also home to the Karl and Beverly White National Fish Tackle Museum, the world's largest collection of fishing regalia. The shimmering walls of fish in the Great Hall serve as a backdrop for many public events, including Mardi Gras, HallowMarine and the 12 Days of Fishmas. The Cape Cod style architecture, 10,000-square-foot sand beach and half-acre casting pond artfully transport the visitor to various watery realms. For a look at creatures that inhabit the most mysterious parts of the planet, visit Oklahoma Aquarium.

300 Aquarium Drive, Jenks OK
(918) 296-FISH (3474)
www.okaquarium.org

118 • Attractions & Recreation

The Little Prince, 2006

Soprano Ai-Lan Zhu
Giacomo Puccini's *Madama Butterfly*, 2004

Pamela Armstrong (Violetta) and Yeghishe Manucharyan (Alfredo)
Giuseppe Verdi's *La Traviata*, 2003

Tulsa Opera

Tulsa Opera ranks among the top 10 regional opera companies in the United States and draws its audiences from the immediate five state region and from across the country. The company's rich history includes performances by some of the most celebrated names in opera—Beverly Sills, Luciano Pavarotti, Sherrill Milnes, Samuel Ramey and many others. Under General Director Carol I. Crawford, the company produces three grand operas each season that feature internationally-known singers, a professional orchestra, full chorus, richly detailed sets and spectacular costumes and lighting. Tulsa Opera was founded in 1948, but Tulsa's love of the art form dates back to before statehood. In 1905, L. J. Martin, president of the Commercial Club, famously commented, "Of course, we did not have any sewers or street paving, but these were luxuries that could wait, whereas an opera house loomed as an immediate necessity." The civic pride of those who made Tulsa bloom also fostered a thriving cultural heritage, of which Tulsa Opera is a cornerstone. In addition to its mainstage operas, Tulsa Opera sponsors an extensive educational outreach program that provides opportunities for both adults and children statewide. Enjoy Tulsa Opera and support an Oklahoma cultural powerhouse.

1610 S Boulder Avenue, Tulsa OK
(918) 582-4035 (office)
 or (918) 587-4811 (tickets)
www.tulsaopera.com

Diamond Triple C Ranch at Grand Lake

Diamond Triple C Ranch at Grand Lake, established in 2001, concentrates on breeding prime alpaca bloodlines to produce genetically superior suri (straight, penciled fiber) and huacaya (thick, crimpy fiber) alpacas. Alpacas are originally from Peru. Alpacas from Chile and Bolivia have long been revered for their luxurious fleece, which is warmer, lighter and softer than wool. Ranch owners Stephen H. and Gwen Coltrin, along with their their son, Wilson, have their headquarters in Yardley, Pennsylvania. However, they carry out primary breeding and fleece processing at a ranch in Bath County, Virginia and another at Grand Lake in Afton. Mitchell and Brenda Ramsey manage the Oklahoma operation. On this 200 acre ranch they maintain DTC's reputation for quality care, originating with their love for these unique, beautiful animals. At Diamond Triple C Ranch, you can get a firsthand look at alpacas, then browse next door at their farm store, Echo Valley Fruit and Fiber, for beautiful products such as scarves, hats and jackets, made from alpaca fiber. Learn more about alpacas with a visit to Diamond Triple C Ranch at Grand Lake.

450358 S Highway 85, Afton OK
(918) 256-1993
www.diamondtriplecranch.com

Route 66 Harley-Davidson and the 5 & Diner

Get your motor running and experience the open road from a whole new point of view at Route 66 Harley-Davidson and the 5 & Diner, two American classics located along the country's most nostalgic highway. Pat and Larry Wofford, owners of the dual businesses, pride themselves on the fun and friendly atmosphere they have created since first opening in 1998. In 2006, Dealernews magazine named Route 66 Harley-Davidson grand prize winner in the 15th annual Top 100 awards for powersports dealers in North America. Route 66 Harley-Davidson features a choice array of quality clothing, gifts, and riding accessories, along with a full parts and service department that can assist you with everything from routine maintenance to the installation of performance parts and chrome. This destination Harley-Davidson shop also features an amazing collection of sculptures and paintings against the backdrop of a Route 66 themed décor. Visitors can also experience the Museum of the Road located in the upstairs event center where catering for up to 120 people is available for special events, meetings, and parties. Located just a few steps from the dealership is the fabulous 5 & Diner, a razzle-dazzle eatery that takes diners on a trip back in time to poodle skirts and soda fountains. Enjoy the music of the 1950s during breakfast, lunch or dinner, and choose from over 150 menu items, cooked to perfection and served with a smile. Heed the call of the wild and come get your kicks at Route 66 Harley-Davidson and the 5 & Diner.

3637 S Memorial Drive, Tulsa OK
(Route 66 Harley-Davidson)
(918) 622-1340 *www.route66hd.com*

3641 S Memorial Drive, Tulsa OK
(5 & Diner)
(918) 828-3467

Peyton's Place

Find everything you need to float the Illinois River in safety and style with a trip to Peyton's Place, the oldest privately owned and operated canoe and rafting trip camp on the river. Archie and Virginia Peyton opened this popular family hot spot in 1968, and today second and third generation Peytons operate the camp, which means you'll get plenty of service, thanks to Archie Jr. and his wife, Becky; their children, Archie III, Amy and Casey; and Amy's young son, Nicholas, who is already helping out around camp. Peyton's Place, which was the first canoe livery operating on the Illinois, is open from April 1st until October 1st; however, the Peytons are happy to make special arrangements all year long for float trips, as long as the weather permits. The Peytons have a full selection of quality rafts and canoes available and are happy to provide instruction to beginners upon request. The camp features several shaded campgrounds and RV sites, along with air-conditioned rental cottages and a lodge that can sleep 48, making it the ideal place for family reunions or corporate retreats. At the Peyton's Place general store you can find picnic supplies, souvenirs and t-shirts, as well as the camp's own hickory-smoked meats, used to make sensational barbecue sandwiches that feature Archie Sr.'s scrumptious secret recipe barbecue sauce. Create cherished family memories and leave only footprints behind at Peyton's Place.

10298 Highway 10, Tahlequah OK
(918) 456-3847 or (800) 359-0866
www.peytonsplace.com

Muskogee Parks & Recreation

For the beautiful city of Muskogee, parks have always been a priority. Ever since the Muskogee Parks & Recreation Department was founded in 1907, locals and visitors have had unparalleled access to the recreational opportunities offered by a well-maintained parks system. Honor Heights Park is known as the crown jewel of the Muskogee parks system, and offers visitors 132 beautifully landscaped acres with picnic areas, five lakes and ponds with fishing from the shores as well as easily accessible docks for boats, three tennis courts, play areas, a pavilion, a shelter, an aboretum, splash pad, a sand volleyball court and public restrooms. Honor Heights Park was purchased from the Creek Nation in 1919 and was renamed Honor Heights in honor of veterans of World War I. In 1935, the park received the More Beautiful America Achievement award from *Better Homes and Gardens*. Each year, the park plays host to the Azalea Festival, where locals get together to celebrate the success of the blooms in the park, even though they were told that no one could grow azaleas in Oklahoma. Another crown jewel of the Muskogee Parks & Recreation Department is the Love-Hatbox Sports Complex, which is home to softball, baseball, soccer and football fields, a skate park, five-kilometer trail, pavilion and the River Country Family Water Park. The complex was built on a historical airport site that was visited by such notables as Amelia Earhardt and Charles Lindbergh. Muskogee Parks & Recreation, a department managed by the City of Muskogee, is housed in the city's original Fire Station No. 4 and features its original Art Moderne Décor from the 1930s. Visit Muskogee Parks & Recreation, your gateway to recreation and relaxation in beautiful settings.

837 E Okmulgee, Muskogee OK
(918) 684-6302
www.muskogeeparks.com

War Paint Horse Ranch

Dedicated equestrians insist that the most beautiful countryside is seen between the ears of a horse, and Louis Dawson of War Paint Horse Ranch couldn't agree more. Dawson offers guided horseback rides through the lush pine forests, cool streams and rugged mountains near picturesque Lake Eufaula. A 10-mile trip takes about five hours, and guests appreciate the cool drinks and outhouse facilities that Dawson provides at rest stops. Riders ordinarily bring their own mounts, but Dawson has a few kid-friendly horses to rent. A horse hotel assures that you and your horse trailer or RV will have plenty of place to park, and your horse will have a stable for the night. Trail rides take place from March through September, although Dawson organizes rides for fundraising at other times. In June 2006, the Highway 9 East Merchants Association, of which Dawson is a member, put together the 10-Mile Yard Sale. The giant flea market also featured horse and pony rides, where kids could have their pictures taken with the horses. That evening folks relaxed after a long day of bargain hunting at the ranch. Dawson hosted a concert featuring country music singer and fiddle player, Pake McEntire, brother of Reba McEntire and an authentic cowboy. In 2007, Dawson is going to book Pake for two concerts, as well as 17-year-old singer and songwriter Sarah Louco, and her band. If you're looking to leisurely explore beautiful country that you can't see from the highway, call Louis Dawson at War Paint Horse Ranch and get ready to ride.

Highway 9, East of Eufaula OK
(918) 452-2587

Safari's Sanctuary

Safari's Sanctuary is a non-profit, 501c3 tax exempt, wildlife refuge that houses around 200 exotic animals. All of these animals were rescued. Some came from private people who attempted raise a tiger, monkey, or alligator as a household pet. Others came from zoo's that over-bred their big cats. Safari's Sanctuary is open to the public on the weekends year-round (Saturday & Sunday, from 12 noon to 5pm), plus weekday tours by appointment. They also have party areas to host picnic, birthdays and corporate parties. When you visit the sanctuary, a tour guide will take you on a journey of up close and personal experiences, tell the animal's personal stories, and show you how to pet lemurs, skunks, foxes, wolves, snakes, birds, or even alligators. You can also purchase treats to feed the big cats, bears, wolves, monkeys, birds and barnyard animals. Imagine closing your eyes to sleep while being serenaded by wolves and lions right outside your window. Such is the concert that overnight guests experience while staying in an 1890s log cabin, or camping out on the grounds of Safari's Sanctuary. If you can't make it to the park, they also have a Mobile Petting Zoo. For a nominal fee, they can bring any of their pettable critters to your door, school, event, or office. Come meet the animals, become a docent volunteer, or sponsor your favorite animal with your tax deductible donations. For the latest additions and events, check out their MySpace site or website. Safari's Sanctuary—for the love of the animals.

26881 E 58th Street, Broken Arrow OK (918) 357-LOVE (5683)
www.myspace.com/ladysafari   www.safarissanctuary.org

126 • Attractions & Recreation

Tulsa Zoo

Eastern Oklahoma's most popular family attraction is the Tulsa Zoo, named America's Favorite Zoo in an online contest by Microsoft. One of the oldest zoos in the nation, the Tulsa Zoo is also one of the most modern. It continuously updates its facilities, programs and exhibits to 21st century standards. The interactive *Elephant Encounter* is one of the jewels of the zoo's ongoing development plan. This 2½ acre exhibit includes a reserve yard where the elephants can roam freely and a demonstration yard with amphitheater seating where visitors can watch their vocal, exercise and enrichment routines. One of these happy elephants, Gunda, has been at the Tulsa Zoo since Asian elephants arrived in 1954 (she was four then). Another exciting program is the full-immersion program, which allows visitors to fully experience an animal habitat. At the *Tropical American Rain Forest* exhibit, visitors follow a winding footpath through an authentic rain forest environment controlled to appropriate humidity and temperature. Birds dart freely overhead in the canopy, which reaches up to 50 feet, and such exotic species as the black howler monkey, anaconda, piranha and jaguar range within. The zoo spans 86 acres, contains nearly 1,500 animals and represents every continent in the world. For an intimate animal experience, visit the Tulsa Zoo.

6421 E 36th Street N, Tulsa OK
(918) 669-6600
www.tulsazoo.org

All American Floats & Liquid Lightning Water Slide

Enjoy wet and wild fun in the sun with your friends and family at All American Floats & Liquid Lightning Water Slide, open for water recreation since 2002. This family-friendly water park, owned by Vechil and Tammy Eller, is located right on the Illinois River, so you can easily enjoy a full and relaxing day of fishing and swimming. The Liquid Lightning Water Slide is a giant, seven-story thrill ride that sends visitors on a fast and furious plunge down one of three slides that converge in a large pool at the bottom. Go-karts and a miniature golf course, which are ideal for visitors of all ages, add on-site pleasures for your group. You can stay a few days or longer in the beauty and comfort of riverside campsites with full bath and shower facilities and a concession stand filled with food staples, snacks and beverages. Campers often bring their own picnic and meal supplies to use while camping. All American Floats rents a wide variety of canoes, rafts and kayaks for daylong and overnight float trips that can range anywhere from four to 57 miles. The park is open seven days a week from May to September and offers special rates for groups, so grab the whole gang and head to All American Floats & Liquid Lightning Water Slide.

17170 Highway 10, Tahlequah OK
(918) 456-6949 or (877) 2FLOATS (235-6287)
www.allamericanfloats.com

Tulsa Ballet

For 50 years, the Tulsa Ballet has been setting the standard for dance in Oklahoma, offering interpretations of both timeless classics and cutting-edge works by the world's leading choreographers. 2006 was Tulsa Ballet's 50th Anniversary, and they celebrated in style, offering a season that included such classics as Swan Lake and Carmina Burana along with works by Twyla Tharp, George Balanchine and Agnes de Mille. Tulsa Ballet was founded in 1956 by the husband-and-wife dance team of Roman Jasinski and Moscelyne Larkin, and musician Rosalie Talbot. The artistic mission of the Company has remained constant: To combine the beauty and joy expressed by dance with the drama and entertainment of the theatre. The Company has toured in 30 states and throughout the world, receiving consistent critical acclaim. With four productions annually in addition to The Nutcracker, Tulsa Ballet reaches more than 48,000 people every season. For the last 11 seasons, under Marcello Angelini's leadership, Tulsa Ballet has undertaken an ambitious repertory building program, adding more then 60 new works to its repertory that were either Oklahoma, American or world premieres. In addition to the company, the Tulsa Ballet Center for Dance Education offers training for students from beginner through pre-professional levels. The curriculum emphasizes classical ballet technique based upon the Russian tradition of training, also known as the Vaganova method. Enjoy the best that Oklahoma has to offer. Make plans to attend a performance of the Tulsa Ballet.

4512 S Peoria Avenue, Tulsa OK
(918) 749-6006 (tickets) or (918) 749-6030
www.tulsaballet.org

Jana Jae's Gallery Southwest

If you loved Buck Owens and his Buckeroos, and if Hee-Haw was your favorite weekly television show, then you know Jana Jae as the world-class country fiddle virtuoso that she is! From the Tonight Show to the Grand Old Opry and Symphony Pops, Jana Jae has carved out a unique niche in the world of music as a fabulous entertainer. It's no surprise then that her powerhouse talent should extend to every enterprise she touches, and that includes her inspiring Jana Jae's Gallery Southwest. Jana Jae's Gallery specializes in original art that focuses on the Midwestern and Native American experience. Her gallery features both well-known and exciting newer artists working in a variety of media, as well as gorgeous gift items made by artisans from various tribes and regions. Gallery Southwest features powerful bronzes by sculptors like Willard and Jason Stone, paintings by such artists as Jerome Chris Tiger, Fred Beaver and Bill Rabbit, and fine Santa Clara, Acoma and Cherokee pottery. Here you'll also find authentic Southwestern furniture, handwoven rugs, kachinas, jewelry and beautiful Native American crafts. You can take in the wonderful camping, fishing, picnicking and swimming that Grove offers, enjoy one of the several fiddle festivals Jana Jae hosts and performs at every year and explore this wonderful gallery all at the same time. Jana Jae's heart and talent will welcome you as you discover the wonderful things she shares with the world.

920 S Main Street, Grove OK (918) 786-5780 *www.janajae.com*

Galleries & Fine Art • 131

Talisman Gallery

In a city known for its architectural landmarks and museums, Talisman Gallery draws plenty of traffic in its own right. Once the exclusive home of the works of world-famous artist Richard Schmid, Talisman Gallery still handles all of Schmid's early works in addition to an impressive collection of pieces by other artists. Born into a family of artists, owner Jody Kirberger originally met Schmid through her father, Charles Reynolds. He represented Schmid at the Reynolds Gallery until 1963, when the beloved gallery owner passed on. Though her father had always begged her to follow him into the art business, Jody, a mother of four, never gave it much thought. Then one day in 1964 she saw an empty building for rent. She borrowed $50 from her husband and rented it the same day, finally following in her father's footsteps. With its impeccable reputation, Talisman Gallery draws connoisseurs from everywhere. You will want to see the collection at Talisman Gallery.

115 E 12th Street, Bartlesville OK
(918) 336-1786
www.talismangal.com

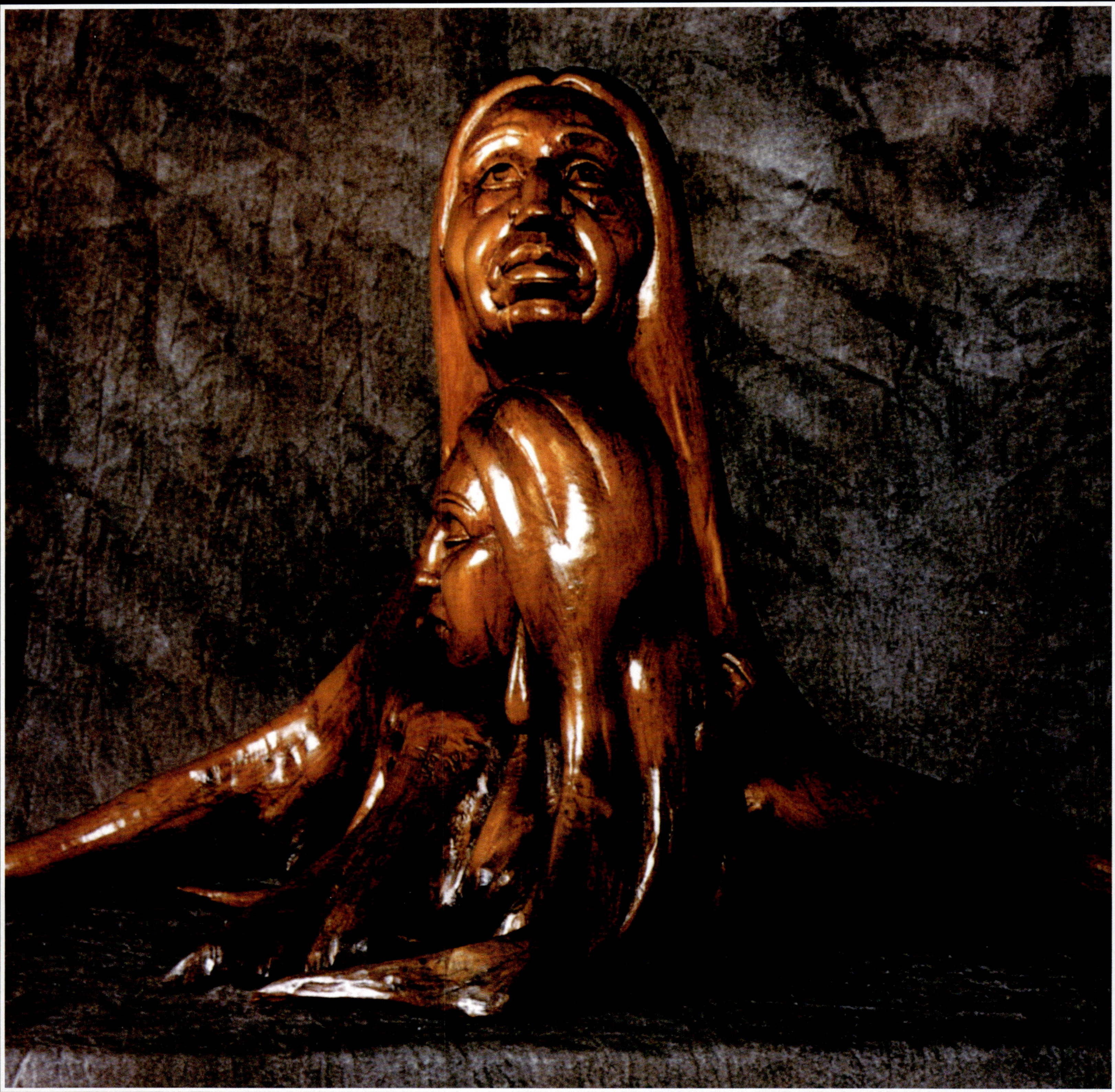

Willard Stone Museum & Gallery

The Willard Stone Museum houses a large collection of works by world-renowned wood sculptor Willard Stone. Willard was known as a humble man of warmth and vision. A dynamite cap explosion at the age of 13 caused Willard to lose two fingers and part of a thumb. The disability thwarted his interest in drawing, but he soon found a new outlet for his creativity. When not occupied in the cotton fields, he began modeling native clay into familiar forms. His carvings on a mailbox drew the attention of the Muskogee postmaster, who introduced Willard to Grant Foreman, an Oklahoma historian and author who encouraged the part-Cherokee boy to seek formal training. It was at Bacone Indian College that Willard first gained national recognition. He discovered wood sculpting and enjoyed searches for the right piece of wood to capture a particular subject, employing a style with Art Deco undertones. Because he could not support himself as an artist, Willard pursued other work. In the 1940s, he refined his art further with a three-year grant as artist-in-residence at the Gilcrease Institute of American History and Art. In 1961, he could finally afford to devote himself fulltime to his art. His compelling figures delight visitors to the Willard Stone Museum & Gallery, located at the Locust Grove home, where Willard lived until his death in 1985. Admission to the museum and gallery is free and by appointment only. Make arrangements to view Willard Stone's sculptures, and spend a few moments with the soul of a man who created poetic expression in wood.

7980 E Highway 412, Locust Grove OK
(918) 479-6481
www.willardstonemuseum.com

Tulsa Air and Space Museum & Planetarium

The Tulsa Air and Space Museum (TASM) is dedicated to preserving the very large part Tulsa has played in the field of aviation since its inception. Visitors can explore 19,000 square feet of exhibits and educational displays and marvel at Tulsa's first planetarium. You can examine everything from an F-14 Tomcat fighter jet and a Bell helicopter to the world's first amphibious ultra light in the Aircraft Museum, or let the Museum Exhibits take you on a tour of Tulsa's aerospace timeline, starting with the first brush with flight in 1897 to Tulsa's major contribution to President Kennedy's space program. Finally, interactive exhibits that involve everyone. You can experience how an F-16 reacts to the slipstream of a wind tunnel, sit in the cockpit of a T-37 or launch the Space Shuttle. The planetarium's ESky multimedia display creates a three-dimensional journey in a spectacular 50-foot diameter dome that will transport you to the outer limits of the universe. You won't sit in the audience and just watch the stars, you'll travel through a huge real-time simulation of the universe. Classes, tours and camps all provide opportunities for exploring America's exciting aerospace world and principles of flight. At TASM the mission is to prepare and educate our youth with the scientific skills and imagination needed for our technologically advanced century. Don't miss Tulsa's Air and Space Museum, where the past and future meet to inspire today.

3624 N 74th E Avenue, Tulsa OK
(918) 834-9900
www.tulsaairandspacemuseum.com

Ataloa Lodge Museum

The Ataloa Lodge Museum offers a collection of American Indian artifacts and the stories behind those artifacts. Museum Director John "Yafke" Timothy brings the culture and history of the Indian nations, including the Five Tribes of Oklahoma, alive for guests to the museum. You will hear how the museum's 88 kachina dolls, the largest collection in the Southwest, sometimes change their positions at night, when the rooms feel heavy with their souls. Timothy is a member of the Muskogee/Creek Nation and goes by his Creek tribal name, Yafke, meaning evening. He is a master fl ute maker and an accomplished fl utist, who often plays at the request of his guests. Guests here view a fascinating array of artifacts, including Hopi pottery, a Navajo loom, an Apache fi ddle and a ghost dance shirt. The museum was built in 1932 at the Indian University, later renamed Bacone University. Today, it is named after Mary Stone McClendon, an educator at Bacone, who called herself Ataloa, meaning little song in the Chickasaw language. Mary collected some of the fi rst art and artifacts for her dream American Indian museum. You can purchase authentic arts and crafts by Indian artisans at the museum shop or preview a selection online. Join Yafke at the Ataloa Lodge Museum for an experience that's bound to prove educational, entertaining and life enriching.

2299 Old Bacone Road, Muskogee OK
(918) 781-7283
www.bacone.edu/ataloa

Woolaroc

It takes a space as large as the 3,700-acre ranch called Woolaroc to celebrate oilman Frank Phillips' vision of America's past. Established in 1925 as a retreat in the Osage Hills for the Phillips family, today's Woolaroc preserves animals native to the region as well as the cultural record of the peoples who lived and, at times, clashed on the nation's western frontier. The original lodge is now a museum exhibiting the Phillips collection of paintings and sculpture by Frederic Remington, Charles M. Russell, Harry Jackson and many other masters of Western art. Crowning the gun room is a collection of Colt Patterson firearms, considered one of the finest in the world. Beginning with artifacts from prehistoric civilizations in Oklahoma, the Native American section of the museum displays regalia and practical crafts from 40 different tribes. The wildlife preserve, accessible via a two-mile drive, is home to elk, longhorn cattle and a bison herd with blood lines back to 1926. It also keeps exotic animals from around the world, including Japanese Sika deer and Sardinian donkeys and pygmy goats. In many ways, Frank Phillips preferred the rustic life at his Woolaroc ranch to the high style of his mansion in Bartlesville. He never viewed Woolaroc as "a dream about something," but, he said, as "a place where I can get back to nature and the fundamental things in life." For glimpses of the world that Frank loved, visit Woolaroc.

State Highway 123, Bartlesville OK
(918) 336-0307
www.woolaroc.org

The Sherwin Miller Museum of Jewish Art

In 2004, the largest collection of Judaica in the American Southwest moved to a new facility on the Zarrow campus of the Jewish Federation of Tulsa. The Sherwin Miller Museum of Jewish Art, formerly the Fenster Museum, began its collection of art and artifacts in 1966 under the leadership of Sherwin Miller; the collection lodged at the B'nai Emunah Synagogue for many years. Despite its name, the nonprofit museum operates as an educational resource rather than an art repository with more than 10,000 works that trace the 5,000-year history of the Jewish people from the pre-Canaanite era through the settling of the Jewish community of Tulsa and the Southwest. Visitors learn about Jewish life, history and ritual practice through archaeological pieces, ritual objects, costumes, synagogue textiles, historical documents and fine arts. The Sherwin Miller Museum of Jewish Art is located in the Fenster/Sanditen Cultural Center, which is also home to the Herman and Kate Kaiser Holocaust exhibition devoted to teaching about the Holocaust and its lessons for today's world. By taking a close look at the origins of Judaism, Christianity, and Islam as well as the state-sponsored discrimination that resulted in the Holocaust, The Sherwin Miller Museum seeks to not only preserve and present Jewish culture but to foster an understanding between people of all cultures through an appreciation of their common history and values. The Sherwin Miller Museum of Jewish Art is open to the public and hosts guided tours for school groups and clubs.

2021 East 71st Street, Tulsa OK
(918) 492-1818
www.jewishmuseum.net

Muskogee Parks & Recreation

For the beautiful city of Muskogee, parks have always been a priority. Ever since the Muskogee Parks & Recreation Department was founded in 1907, locals and visitors have had unparalleled access to the recreational opportunities offered by a well-maintained parks system. Honor Heights Park is known as the crown jewel of the Muskogee parks system, and offers visitors 132 beautifully landscaped acres with picnic areas, five lakes and ponds with fishing from the shores as well as easily accessible docks for boats, three tennis courts, play areas, a pavilion, a shelter, an aboretum, splash pad, a sand volleyball court and public restrooms. Honor Heights Park was purchased from the Creek Nation in 1919 and was renamed Honor Heights in honor of veterans of World War I. In 1935, the park received the More Beautiful America Achievement award from *Better Homes and Gardens*. Each year, the park plays host to the Azalea Festival, where locals get together to celebrate the success of the blooms in the park, even though they were told that no one could grow azaleas in Oklahoma. Another crown jewel of the Muskogee Parks & Recreation Department is the Love-Hatbox Sports Complex, which is home to softball, baseball, soccer and football fields, a skate park, five-kilometer trail, pavilion and the River Country Family Water Park. The complex was built on a historical airport site that was visited by such notables as Amelia Earhardt and Charles Lindbergh. Muskogee Parks & Recreation, a department managed by the City of Muskogee, is housed in the city's original Fire Station No. 4 and features its original Art Moderne Décor from the 1930s. Visit Muskogee Parks & Recreation, your gateway to recreation and relaxation in beautiful settings.

837 E Okmulgee, Muskogee OK
(918) 684-6302
www.muskogeeparks.com

Bartlesville Area History Museum

The Bartlesville Area History Museum is a 10,000 square foot facility located on the top floor of the city center, a historic building that was once home to the Hotel Maire during the Bartlesville oil boom. The community has a rich and colorful heritage with roots traced back to the Delaware, Cherokee and Osage peoples who lived in the region before the arrival of white settlers. Through photographs, artifacts and video, Bartlesville's heritage unfolds with stories of oilmen, Indian chiefs, ranchers and bankers. You can also learn about outlaws, school teachers, smelter workers, shop clerks and many others who helped to shape a tiny frontier settlement into a modern city. History unfolds with interactive displays, exceptional photography and intriguing artifacts. One of the museum's most popular attractions is a talking animated likeness of Frank Griggs, a pioneer photographer who spent seven decades documenting Bartlesville life. In November and April, area fourth grade students can experience a typical day of education and lifestyle of the early 1900s when they attend classes in the Nelson Carr one-room schoolhouse. There is no admission charge for a trip through more than 100 extraordinary years of history at the Bartlesville Area History Museum. Please call ahead for hours of operation.

401 S Johnstone Avenue, 5th floor, Bartlesville OK
(918) 338-4290
www.bartlesvillehistory.com

Oklahoma Music Hall of Fame

The Oklahoma Music Hall of Fame has plenty to celebrate. Oklahomans have always had a profound impact on music. Woodie Guthrie helped define folk. The Texas Playboys, pioneers of Western swing, were based in Tulsa for much of their career. Patti Page, who still performs today, was the first major crossover artist to bring country to the general public. "Okie from Muskogee" Merle Haggard almost single-handedly introduced country to the electric sound. In 1995, a group of Sooner citizens recognized the need to educate the public about the influence Oklahomans have had in the music industry, and the vision for the Oklahoma Music Hall of Fame was born. In 1997, the first Oklahoma Music Hall of Fame Induction Ceremony and Concert was held at the Muskogee Civic Center. Every year since, the Oklahoma Music Hall of Fame has honored some of the world's most notable talents at a gala event graced by top musicians. In 2003, the organization completed the initial renovation of the Frisco Depot in Muskogee, and in 2006 it opened phase one of the Oklahoma Music Hall of Fame Museum. You'll want to see the museum, and you can also attend one of Oklahoma's greatest annual concerts when the Oklahoma Music Hall of Fame inducts new honorees.

401 S 3rd Street, Muskogee OK
(918) 687-0800
www.omhof.com

Will Rogers Memorial Museums

Will Rogers got his show business start as a trick roper, but his patter was so funny that he quickly became a comedian. He hosted his own radio show, appeared in 71 movies and became an enormously popular newspaper columnist. The Will Rogers Memorial Museums provide intriguing exhibits on the man and his times. Part Cherokee Indian, Rogers was born into a successful ranching family when Oklahoma was still Indian Territory. His birthplace near the town of Oologah is now a living history ranch and one of the memorial museums. The log-walled Greek Revival house is authentically conserved. Historically dressed ranch hands work a herd of Texas Longhorns, and you can stroll among these and other farm animals to your heart's content. The ranch is open dawn to dusk year-round and offers RV hookups. The Will Rogers Memorial Museum, located in nearby Claremore, has nine galleries of memorabilia, including a saddle collection. Two theaters show a documentary on Rogers and a rotating selection of his Hollywood films. A children's museum features interactive computer exhibits. A promoter of early aviation, Rogers died in 1935 in a plane crash, and his death was a major national tragedy. The Memorial Museum frames the family tomb. The museum is also a research site, containing a library and archives. Museum Director Michelle Lefebvre Carter invites you to come and learn more about a great humanitarian, one of the most widely quoted writers in America. As Rogers said, "I never met a man I didn't like."

1720 West Will Rogers Boulevard, Claremore OK
(918) 341-0719 or (800) 342-9455
www.willrogers.com

140 • Museums, History & Culture

Price Tower Arts Center

In 1956, Frank Lloyd Wright saw his only skyscraper completed as a multi-use building housing the H.C. Price Company headquarters and many local businesses. On the National Register of Historic Places, this landmark again realizes its multi-use purpose and offers museum-goers an emersion experience in Wright's masterpiece, Price Tower. Price Tower Arts Center, a modern and contemporary museum inside the Tower, focuses on the intersection of art, architecture and design with fully restored 1956 interiors on the top three floors. It also houses a 21 room high-design hotel, Inn at Price Tower and Copper Restaurant + Bar, offering eclectic cuisine with a view unlike any other in the Osage Hills. Before you leave, be sure to stop by The Wright Place Museum Store for one-of-a-kind souvenirs and Frank Lloyd Wright items. The museum is open Tuesday through Sunday (call for regular and holiday hours). Historic tours are available daily. Price Tower Arts Center is 45 miles north of Tulsa on Highway 75. Turn west on Highway 60 and then right on Dewey Avenue. For more information or for reservations, call ahead or visit the website.

510 Dewey Avenue, Bartlesville OK
(918) 336-4949 (info) or (877) 424-2424 (reservations)
www.pricetower.org

Five Civilized Tribes Museum

The Five Civilized Tribes Museum in Muskogee gives the visitor a comprehensive history of five Indian nations who inhabited the southeastern United States. The stories of the Cherokee, Chickasaw, Choctaw, Creek and Seminole Indians, and their lives on their ancestral lands, come alive at this year-round museum. Visitors learn about their development as separate nations in Indian Territory and the trails they traveled on their removal to Oklahoma. Built in 1875, the Union Indian Agency has served many owners and purposes. In 1966, it became the home of the Five Civilized Tribes Museum, which is dedicated to preserving and encouraging the cultures and traditions of today's tribal members. The museum includes a gallery of traditional Indian art with sculpture and paintings by such noted artists as Willard Stone, Jerome Tiger, Solomon McCombs, Fred Beaver, Terry Saul and Joan Hill. The museum further promotes tribal art with competitive art shows and an annual outdoor Indian art market. Arts and crafts by today's tribal members are for sale in the museum store. Look for beadwork, baskets, pottery, jewelry and fine art, along with books and art prints. The museum also houses a research library, which holds rare documents written by or about members of the Five Civilized Tribes. A holiday market and events celebrating the traditions of separate tribes give visitors opportunities to meet members of the tribes. The Museum is open Monday through Saturday from ten to five and Sunday from one to five.

1101 Honor Heights Drive, Muskogee OK
(918) 683-1701 or (877) 587-4237
www.fivetribes.org

Greenwood Cultural Center

It is possible to trace the history of the Greenwood Avenue black business district back to the early days of Tulsa, before Oklahoma even became a state. Perhaps the most interesting place to do so is at the Greenwood Cultural Center, where in 1970, several Tulsa civic leaders, aided by Model Cities money, came together to reclaim and restore the neighborhood that had once played a key role in the city's Black experience. The Greenwood Cultural Center is now a gathering place for visitors of all cultural and ethnic backgrounds. It rents out its 10,000-square-foot meeting and banquet facilities and hosts the Oklahoma Jazz Hall of Fame. Even a brief visit here is enough to capture the essence of the people who are honored by the Greenwood Cultural Center, but if you can stay longer, you begin to get a sense of the unique partnerships that revolve around this center. Greenwood Cultural Center promotes several causes that work towards preserving aspects of African-American heritage and does so in engaging ways that help the local economy along the way. While you're visiting the Greenwood Cultural Center, make sure to stop by the charming Gift Boutique and browse through authentic African jewelry and an assortment of books by African-American authors. You will be certain to enjoy the experience and add to your knowledge of the business community created by Tulsa's first black citizens.

322 N Greenwood, Tulsa OK
918-596-1020
www.greenwoodculturalcenter.com

USS Batfish at the Muskogee War Memorial Museum and Park

It may look docile now sitting in a field, but the USS Batfish was a killer of the deep during World War II. The 312-foot submarine is open to the public at the Muskogee War Memorial. It once sunk three enemy submarines within 76 hours. During its seven patrols of duty, it sunk 14 vessels in all. Today, visitors gain an inside look at naval history as they tour the narrow passageways of the Batfish, which was commissioned on August 21, 1943. Peek inside the torpedo rooms, from which 71 torpedoes, 24 of them hits, were launched. Imagine being packed into the bunk compartment with dozens of your crewmates. View the guns on the submarine's bridge section. With the Batfish as its centerpiece, the Muskogee War Memorial Park honors the role that our service men played during the war. Especially poignant are the bronze reminders of the 52 submarines that never returned from their missions. A total of 3,505 sailors were lost on these vessels. A self-propelled artillery and other military machines and equipment rest upon the quiet grounds of the park. An indoor museum displays uniforms, documents and photographs to honor the triumphs and tragedies of the fight for freedom. Visit the USS Batfish at the Muskogee War Memorial Museum and Park.

3500 Batfish Road, Muskogee OK
(918) 682-6294
www.batfish.org

Three Rivers Museum and Thomas-Foreman Historical House

In the heart of Eastern Oklahoma at the juncture of the Arkansas, Grand and Verdigris Rivers, you'll come across one of the first settlements on the American frontier. Three Rivers Museum and the Thomas-Foreman Historical House are your windows onto the multi-ethnic history of this region. Three Rivers Museum opened in the restored Midland Valley Railroad Depot in downtown Muskogee in 2001. It houses a superb collection of historical artifacts and special exhibits throughout the year. Special events here include the annual Railroad Day. You can view the 14 flags that have flown over the Three Rivers region since the 14th century and get a great overview of local history that is sure to add rich detail to your Muskogee vacation. The museum's Whistlestop Gift Shop carries books on local history, railroad memorabilia, children's toys and souvenirs. The Thomas-Foreman Historical House sits nearby. This charming 1898 farmhouse was built by John R. Thomas, Sr., a federal judge in the Indian Territory. His two children, Carolyn and John R. Thomas, Jr., a celebrated Spanish American War hero with the Rough Riders, joined their father in Muskogee. Carolyn married Grant Foreman, and the couple lived out their lives in the house, writing more than 20 books on Oklahoma history. The house displays books and memorabilia from the couple's many trips abroad, along with rare photos, documents and Native American works of art. For insight into the Three Rivers region, visit the Three Rivers Museum and the Thomas-Foreman Historical House.

Three Rivers Museum
220 Elgin Street, Muskogee OK
(918) 686-6624
www.3riversmuseum.com

Thomas-Foreman Historical House
1419 W Okmulgee Avenue, Muskogee OK
(918) 682-6938

146 • Restaurants, Bakeries & Cafés

Gina & Guiseppe's Italian Ristorante

The walls of Gina & Guiseppe's Italian Ristorante in Jenks are lined with memorabilia telling the Macri family story. Jacquelyn Macri-Spraker and her son, Christopher Drover, are the proprietors of this popular, upscale Italian eatery, which is named in honor of Jacquelyn's parents, Mary Jean (Gina) and Joseph (Guiseppe). In 1924, after serving in the Italian Army during World War I, Guiseppe's father, Dominic, left his family behind and came to America. The family was reunited in 1927, when Guiseppe, his mother Maria, and the rest of the family traveled to America by steamship. In 1940, Guiseppe wed Mary Jean (Gina) Heiden. Being of German descent, Gina spent many hours at Maria's side learning the family recipes, which she then passed down to her four daughters. Keeping it in the family, Cynthia painted the murals in the Ristorante's full wine and spirit bar, giving a windows view of a Tuscany hillside. Throughout the restaurant, vintage family photographs create a warm, homey atmosphere, while aromas wafting from the kitchen tease the senses. Jacquelyn's daughter, Lauren, leads the service team, which takes great pleasure both in describing the unique Italian dishes and telling the family's story. The menu features 100-year-old Macri family recipes prepared by Executive Chef Walter Mullins and his staff. Customer favorites include five-layer lasagna, Gina's spaghetti with homemade sauce and meatballs, the chef's special ravioli of the day and hand-tossed brick oven pizzas. Chef's specials may include green lip mussels with lobster sauce or t-bone lamb chops with rosemary demi-glace. Finish your dining experience with a slice of tiramisu, Italian cream cake or a cannoli. In 2006, Gina and Guiseppe's was voted Best New Restaurant by the readers of *Tulsa People Magazine*. Savor the flavors at Gina and Guiseppe's Italian Ristorante, where you'll feel like part of the family.

400 Riverwalk Terrace (at Riverwalk Crossing), Jenks OK
(918) 296-0111
http://gngitalian.com

Backyard Deli & Galleria LLC

All great food enthusiasts will want to make a point of visiting Backyard Deli & Galleria LLC in Locust Grove. This eatery provides a unique ambiance coupled with a diverse range of foods. Owners Cil and Rick Boehmer hope to offer something for everyone through their menu selections and their eclectic assortment of gifts. If you're entertaining a large crowd, consider their five-pound pizza, the 16-inch-wide Deliverance. Cherokee artists Bill and Traci Rabbit's favorite pizza is the Rabbit Patch, with bell peppers, onions, tomatoes, mushrooms, artichoke hearts, green and black olives, pineapple and jalapeños. The Backyard Cheese Steak is said to be better than any cheese steak in Philly and the sandwich offerings at Backyard Deli range from BBQ pork to Rick's signature Grilled Cashew Chicken. For women enduring those special days of moodiness, there's the PMS dessert, a warm chocolate walnut brownie served with vanilla ice cream and topped with warm Hershey's chocolate cobbler. We don't know whether it works, but it sure can't hurt. The varied Art pieces in the gallery include such gems as the Evelyn Stone-Holland Exclusive Jewelry Collection, stained glass window panels featuring Native American themes, as well as other painters, bead works and more. This unique place is located in Rural Oklahoma on the upper finger of Fort Gibson Lake. If you're looking to stock your pantry at home, Backyard Deli can fill your needs with an eclectic assortment of grocery and specialty items. Whether you need an easy night out for dinner or are looking for a meaningful gift, come to the Backyard Deli & Galleria LLC, Your Deliberate Destination.

35894 E 650 Road, Locust Grove OK
(918) 386-2880

Mid American Grille

When you are hungry in Pryor, there's a special place to go called the Mid American Grille. This restaurant has everything from burgers to lobster. Owners Mark and Marty Marsh have been serving food to Pryor locals and their guests since 2001. They like to vary the menu and ask that you watch for Chalkboard specials. Filet mignon, grilled prime ribeye (ask to have it blackened suggests one loyal customer), rainbow trout, halibut and grouper are all fine choices to try. Baked potato soup is a must have and their bistro chips can't be beat. What do you want when you go out for a meal? Good food? Then visit the Mid American Grille.

101 Cobblestone Drive, Pryor OK
(918)824-7625

Restaurants, Bakeries & Cafés • 149

The Shebang—Wine, Dine, Dance, Sing, Shop

The Shebang by Larry and Joyce Duke is your number-one destination on Monkey Island. The Dukes offer four exciting spots: a restaurant, clothing and décor shop, a nightclub and a summer bar & grill. The Shebang, the flagship enterprise, is a fine dining establishment with a varied menu sure to satisfy the most sophisticated palate. The atmosphere is fun and inviting. Five rooms include the famous standing-room-only Shebang Bar and the Vaudeville room for comfortable family dining. The adults-only Burlesque room offers lingerie fashion shows, the Backstage room is for private parties and the outdoor Patio and Balcony Bar are great in season. You might start with Shebang's own cracker bread and salad. Whether you crave prime rib, Papa Duke's baby-back ribs or pizzas Chicago would howl for, the Shebang sends you home satisfied. A fine dessert tops off your night—French Silk Pie makes a romantic nightcap. In the mood to escape sameness? The Den of Uniquity next door sports the latest South Beach fashions and swimsuits hotter than the sun. The Den offers nouveau couture, one-of-a-kind accessories and home décor for every taste. Stride across the street to Big Shots, where you can collect your favorite drink and become a Monkey Island karaoke idol. You can dance behind the silhouette screen or in a cage suspended above the dance floor. Finally, from Memorial to Labor Day, Island Joe's Outdoor Bar & Grill at Shangri-La Marina has great food, cold drinks, hot music and cool views. Feed your face, feed the fish and feed your ego. Head for the Shebang on Monkey Island for the most fun you can have with your clothes on.

29975 S 566 Road, Monkey Island OK
(918) 257-5750

Clanton's Café

Dwelling under its giant EAT sign along the famous Route 66, Clanton's Café is legendary. The oldest restaurant on the route, it has been continuously family-owned since it was established by Sweet Tater Clanton in 1927. The Clantons' legacy is now in the hands of Melissa Clanton Patrick and her husband, Dennis. In addition to starting the café, Sweet Tater also began a tradition of community involvement which the Clanton family has fostered through the generations. Sweet Tater was famous for going outside and beating on a pot to lure customers into his café. He fed even those who couldn't afford a meal. When Sweet Tater's children grew up, they all owned cafés in Vinita and supported their community. They fed World War II soldiers and served with the American Legion. In 2006, the family was inducted into the Vinita Area Chamber of Commerce Hall of Fame, and at the ceremony, people tried in vain to recall a school, civic or philanthropic event from which the Clanton family had been absent. In February 2006, Gourmet magazine recognized Clanton's Café for serving the best chicken fried steak on Route 66 and acknowledged several of its other exceptional dishes, including the calf fries. Many of the café's clientele are truly regulars; some are fourth-generation customers who have been dining at Clanton's all of their lives. Make time for the best of Route 66 and EAT at Clanton's Café.

319 E Illinois, Vinita OK
(918) 256-9053
www.clantonscafe.com

Jazmo'z Bourbon Street Café

With the demise of New Orleans, it's a long way to anything but a memory of Bourbon Street. Luckily, Tulsa has its own version of a Bourbon Street jazz club with Jazmo'z Bourbon Street Café. Jazmo'z has two Tulsa locations. Its 15th Street joint has been serving up the blues and dishing out some of the best Cajun food this side of the Bayou for 10 years. They serve lunch and dinner daily, along with live jazz and blues music four times a week. The café books local talent, as well as acts from around the country, and has featured such legends as Earl Clark and Steve Pryor. The food is classic New Orleans and includes Chicken Bon Ton, Loyola Street oysters and Satchmo's Salmon (blackened salmon with a crab beurre blanc sauce). Jazmo'z offers a full bar and extensive wine list. This casual dining experience appeals to a diverse clientele, with jazz and blues posters on the walls and the soft touch of linen tablecloths. A private room can be reserved for meetings and parties with seating for up to 20. Banquet facilities are available at the South Tulsa location. The inspiration behind this good-looking, great-sounding and wonderful-tasting pair of restaurants are founding partners Ward Harrison, Dave Southard and Blake DeMent. Next time you want to recreate the excitement of the old New Orleans, visit Jazmo'z Bourbon Street Café.

1542 E 15th Street, Tulsa OK
(918) 583-5555
www.bourbonstreetcafe.com

Restaurants, Bakeries & Cafés • 151

Fin and Feather Resort

Nestled among the rolling hills of Oklahoma's Green Country, near the clear waters of beautiful Lake Tenkiller, is the Fin and Feather Resort. Family-owned and operated since 1960, The Fin has grown from a small resort with 20 cabins and a small café to a favorite family getaway that offers 83 lodging units, banquet facilities, a gift shop, on-site recreational activities and dining options to suit every taste. Although many things have changed over the years, The Fin has retained the warmth and charm of its earliest days. Guests to the resort are treated like family and the successive generations of owners wouldn't have it any other way. With its scenic backdrop, family-friendly atmosphere, wide selection of cabins and houses and exceptional dining facilities, The Fin is a popular destination for reunions, church and corporate retreats and other large group gatherings. No trip to the area would be complete without stopping by The Fin's spacious dining room to enjoy the all-you-can-eat evening theme buffets and weekend break*feast* buffet, both of which regularly draw crowds from all over eastern Oklahoma and western Arkansas. You can also enjoy The Fin's more casual eatery, Soda Steve's, known for its famous cheese fries, cold mugs of homemade root beer and specialty entrées. Opened in 2006, Soda Steve's is the creation of Head Chef Steve Pool, a self-described culinary tourist whose travel souvenirs are the all-time favorite recipes he has brought back to The Fin for the enjoyment of all his guests. With so much to do, visit Fin and Feather Resort today.

N of town on Highway 10A, Gore OK
(918) 487-5148
www.finandfeatherresort.com

Cookson Smokehouse Restaurant

Perched alongside scenic Highway 82 is the charming log cabin that houses Cookson Smokehouse Restaurant, a favorite of locals and visitors for more than 20 years. This delightful, family-friendly eatery is owned and operated by Garold and Janet Richardson, who use only fresh quality ingredients to create scrumptious down-home favorites that will appeal to the whole family. Cookson Smokehouse Restaurant has a full menu of classic American favorites, including hickory-smoked barbecue, jumbo shrimp and catfish, along with charbroiled steaks and chicken dishes. Other favorites include juicy burgers and tasty sandwiches, like the bacon and Swiss burger or smoked chopped beef sandwich, as well as Frito chili pie, hot links and Cookson's Old Smokie BBQ Combo, featuring ribs, sliced beef and a grilled hot link. Cookson Smokehouse offers a kids' menu and delicious homemade desserts, such as apple dumplings and cheesecake. Garold and Janet further provide a full catering and take-out menu, so that you can enjoy sensational barbecue at home, for your next special event or as a treat at your next office meeting. Enjoy the hearty meals, rustic surroundings and smiling servers at Cookson Smokehouse Restaurant.

Highway 82, Cookson OK
(918) 457-4134
www.tenkiller.net/smokehouse/home.htm

Katfish Kitchen

Katfish Kitchen offers diners tasty home-style cuisine served by welcoming staff members in a relaxed and casual atmosphere, making it the ideal place to enjoy a cozy meal with friends or family. This community favorite, located behind the Holiday Inn Express, first opened in 2000; however, the restaurant offered a limited menu and restrictive hours. John and De Ann Garrison purchased the struggling eatery in 2003 and have since turned it into one of the area's most popular gathering spots. Now open extended hours seven days a week, Katfish Kitchen features a full menu of choices that will delight even the pickiest of eaters, including all-you-can-eat steak or fried catfish. Other favored options include, smoked pork loin, five kinds of shrimp and chicken fried steak. All dinners come with the restaurant's famous Kitchen Set-up, which features slow cooked pinto beans, fresh coleslaw and hushpuppies, as well as a relish plate and strawberry dumplings for dessert. According to the Garrisons, their employees are more like family and include such diverse individuals as professional cooks, part-time working mothers and students, all dedicated to providing you with a memorable dining experience. The next time you dine out, head to Katfish Kitchen, where the Garrisons promise good food, good service and good value on each and every visit.

1095 E 4th Street, Tahlequah OK
(918) 453-2620

Restaurants, Bakeries & Cafés • 153

The Pits Barbecue

Nearly everyone has a theory on barbecue sauce. Some say it should be fiery hot, while others argue that a mild, sweet sauce is best; however theories are quickly cast aside in favor of the deliciously juicy and tender, falling-off-the-bones barbecued ribs from the Pits Barbecue. Buddy Robertson opened this favored community eatery in 1994, after converting an old crooked building on North J.M. Davis Boulevard back to its original purpose. The Pits Barbecue follows other purveyors of fine barbecue at a location known since 1929 as the Barbecue Corner of Claremore. The Pits Barbecue offers a wide range of down-home favorites, such as pulled pork, sliced beef and hearty Polish sausages, as well as traditional sides, like okra, coleslaw and honey carrots. Other popular menu items include sweetly smoked ham slices and perfectly prepared chicken-fried steaks served with tasty country gravy. The Pits Barbecue offers meat by the pound to-go, along with freshly made sauce and side dishes, so that you can feed your hungry crew fast on even the busiest of nights. Catering options here are ideal for parties of two to 600. A kids' menu offers a choice array of child-friendly delights, including chicken strips and corn dogs, which are served with French fries and a beverage. Be sure to save room for some of the scrumptious cobbler or a root beer float. Savor slow cooked barbecue at its best with a stop at the Pits Barbecue.

500 N JM Davis Boulevard, Claremore OK
(918) 341-6737

Big Daddy's Restaurant & Catering

Big Daddy's Restaurant & Catering at Lake Tenkiller has been a hit with locals and tourists since it opened its doors on the Dam Highway in 1968. Joe and April Hill purchased the eatery in 1982 and, throughout the years, expanded the building using Joe's admittedly limited construction talents and April's unlimited artistic ones. By 1999, the restaurant had improved both its seating and its hours, and the Hills' adult children, James and Autumn, were working there full-time and adding their personal touches to the place. Big Daddy's, named after a prominent bluff overlooking Lake Tenkiller, is known throughout the region for its welcoming ambience and fabulous food, which ranges from tasty hot dogs to succulent rib eye steaks. Additional menu favorites include the Frito chili pie, catfish and barbecue dishes, along with their juicy Big Daddy burger. Today Big Daddy's is open year-round and offers a great new deck that is ideal for summer dining along with a crow's nest featuring a sports bar atmosphere and a big screen television for watching your favorite game. The restaurant also has served as a first job opportunity for numerous area youth and now boasts employee alumni all the way to New York State. Enjoy a hearty and delicious meal with friends and family at Big Daddy's Restaurant & Catering, a Lake Tenkiller tradition that improves with age.

Highway 100 Tenkiller Dam, Lake Tenkiller OK
(918) 489-2201

Dutch Pantry

The Dutch Pantry in Chouteau is known for Amish-style home-cooked meals that are made from scratch. If second-generation owners Eugene and Louise Detweiler were to invite you to their home for dinner, you would find the same food at the family table as you would at the Dutch Pantry. Guests are served buffet style for breakfast, lunch and dinner six days a week. Each day features a different lunch and dinner special at the buffet. Monday is turkey and dressing, Tuesday has chicken fried steak, Wednesday brings fried chicken, Thursday means roast beef and Friday features catfish or meatloaf. On Saturday, you can enjoy barbecued pork ribs or fried chicken. The homemade rolls and breads are beyond impressive and are made daily, as are the pecan pies, cookies and other desserts. No one walks away hungry. The Dutch Pantry is truly a family operation. The original owners, Robert and Susan Detweiler, are still very involved in the business. Treat your family to breakfast, lunch or dinner at the Dutch Pantry.

10 W Main and Railroad, Chouteau OK
(918) 476-6441

The Artichoke Restaurant & Bar

The owners and management staff at the Artichoke Restaurant & Bar bring more than 130 years of combined experience in providing sophisticated dining to the Grand Lake area. The cuisine rivals that of restaurants in Tulsa or Oklahoma City and the old farmhouse that now houses the Artichoke offers an intimate and cozy atmosphere. The most requested dishes from a menu of creative steak, seafood and chicken choices are the Chicken Santa Fe, baked stuffed shrimp and Steak Oscar. If the vegetables and herbs taste particularly fresh, that's because Diana Sellers, who owns the Artichoke with her husband Jim, grows some of them in the greenhouse and the 1,600-square-foot garden behind the restaurant. Jim and Executive Chef Mike Allen have worked together for nearly 30 years, a relationship that began at a restaurant that had only one vegetable on the menu. Can you guess what it was? Jim and Mike do more than commemorate their shared past at the Artichoke. They run with it. The menu gives lyrical instructions on how to eat an artichoke and touts the health benefits of the artichoke. Artichokes appear on the menu as appetizers, served warm with dipping sauces. If you should fear that you have stumbled into the headquarters of some strange artichoke cult, the gourmet meal that Mike and his cooks prepare will assure you that the only agenda here is fine dining. For innovative cuisine in the Grand Lake area, visit the Artichoke Restaurant & Bar.

**35896 S Highway 82, Vinita OK
(918) 782-9855 or (866) 682-9855**

Chastain's Casual Cafe & Catering Co.

Located in the historic downtown district of Sand Springs and on historic Route 66 in downtown Sapulpa, Chastain's Casual Cafe & Catering Co. combines delicious lunch fare and a friendly, small town atmosphere. Open weekdays for lunch at both locations and Thursday for dinner at the Sand Springs location, the café is well known for its laid-back ambience, tasty tortilla soup and fabulous quesadillas. For the past ten years owner Laurie Rhodes has featured great sandwiches, while the soups and salads come in small and large portions to accommodate your appetite. Chastain's even offers a bottomless bowl of tortilla soup for those who can't get enough of it. Seriously hungry? You may want to order the one-half pound hamburger which is sure to satisfy the heartiest appetite. Appease you inner chocoholic with the hot fudge brownie served with ice cream and chocolate syrup. Chastain's To Go offers the restaurant's famous tortilla soup and chicken salad by the quart. You can also take home a bottle of Chastain's poppy seed dressing and a choice of whole pies. Call on Chastain's Catering to help out with your next event or special occasion. Whether it's a party, business meeting, banquet, or family reunion, Chastain's can take care of the food, either at a place of your choosing or in their new banquet facility. For big food choices and small town flavor, come on over to Chastain's Casual Cafe and Catering Co.

122 N Main, Sand Springs OK (918) 241-5855
126 E Dewey, Sapulpa OK (918) 224-3399
http://www.chastainscafe.com

Molly's Landing

Molly's Landing isn't just a five-star restaurant, it's a place that has thoroughly captured the hearts of Tulsa area residents. In 1982, Linda Powell moved to Catoosa from Arizona and erected a three-bedroom log home kit next to the Twin Bridges on the Verdigris River. She moved windows and walls around to create Molly's Landing. The restaurant is known for its fork-tender steaks and fine seafood, homemade bread and outstanding salad dressing. Herbs grown on-site flavor many of the dressings and sauces. Linda has added a couple of rooms to the log cabin over the years and an outdoor eating area. Customers enjoy a roaring fire, antique furnishings and a fun gift shop. Molly's is suitable for intimate dinners or large parties. Big groups often take advantage of a large, outdoor barbecue pit, strategically located under a canopy of trees beside the river. The property adjoins abandoned sections of old Highway 66 and accommodates a helicopter pad, available to the public, and an outdoor chess game. Molly's Landing is also the home of Chocolate Fountains of Tulsa. Be sure to ask about the Saturday murder mysteries, a crime solving entertainment that features a choice of signature dishes. This delightful venue draws loyal customers from miles around, thanks to the consistent quality of its food and service. Like the customer base, many of the restaurant's employees have been with Linda for a very long time. Next time you want a special lunch or dinner, visit Molly's Landing.

3700 N Highway 66, Catoosa OK
(918) 266-7853
www.mollyslanding.com

The Roadhouse Restaurant

The Roadhouse Restaurant on Grand Lake's Monkey Island offers patrons sensational food and a rousing good time. This fine dining restaurant is owned and operated by J.R. and Judy Harris, who are dedicated to giving their customers an elegant atmosphere, excellent service and unsurpassed cuisine. Favored menu items include fresh seafood, like grouper, walleye and mahi-mahi, along with succulent steaks that will rival the finest New York City restaurant. Additional favorites include the New Zealand lamb chops, farm-raised quail and scrumptious, homemade desserts. J.R. and Judy give all the credit for the restaurant's stellar cuisine and attentive service to their exceptional staff members, including Chefs John Johnson and Terry Miller, Bartender Donna Moore and Head Waitress Denise Whitson. The Harrises and the Roadhouse Restaurant are annual contributors to the national Toys for Tots program, overseen by the United States Marine Corps and strongly supported by the ABATE motorcycle organization, which gathers thousands of toys for needy children at the holidays. The Harrises begin collecting donations from friends, neighbors and customers in October. Then, they take a day to run through the toy aisles of an area chain store and fill up basket after basket with toys. Enjoy great food, welcoming ambiance and wonderful people when you dine at the Roadhouse Restaurant.

28730 S Highway 125, Monkey Island OK
(918) 257-8185

The Pink House

The rapidly growing community of Claremore offers visitors and residents a wide range of excellent recreational, shopping and dining venues, including the Pink House, a celebrated eatery that is a Claremore tradition. The luncheon and gift house opened in 1982 and has been owned by Julie McGoffin since 2002. The Pink House fare highlights their sumptuous homemade meals and from-scratch desserts. Julie, along with her mother, June Morose, and her sister-in-law and kitchen manager, Angie Morose, use only the freshest ingredients for their delicious entrées, which include sensational quiches and stuffed baked potatoes. All meals are served with both fruit and garden salads and the famous Pink House banana bread. Other menu favorites include homemade soups and gourmet sandwiches, served up on hearty slices of home baked bread. The Pink House caters in-house private parties for up to 120 people indoors or up to 400 people indoors and outdoors. The staff can also cater events at the location of your choice, an ideal arrangement for holiday parties, corporate events and weddings. The Pink House is located inside a gorgeous 1902 Victorian home. Treat yourself and others to a true Claremore tradition with lunch or catering from the Pink House.

210 W 4th Street, Claremore OK
(918) 342-2544
www.pinkhouseofclaremore.com

True Grits Restaurant

If you're looking for great home style cooking, reasonable prices and a family-friendly atmosphere, head on over to True Grits Restaurant in Claremore. Owners Randy and Toni Bucsok, who purchased the Western-themed restaurant in 2005, offer only fresh food made from scratch in their kitchen. Steak is an option for breakfast, lunch or dinner at True Grits, where really hungry hombres can start their day with the Rooster Cogburn Special, featuring three eggs and a charbroiled eight-ounce steak. Lunch and dinner choices include the steak sandwich, chicken fried steak or hamburger steak. Salad lovers can indulge in a blackened steak salad. Beyond steak, look for a variety of breakfast meats served alongside eggs, pancakes or a croissant sandwich. Grits as well as biscuits and gravy are popular. Burgers, a grilled ham and cheese sandwich, a BLT or a grilled chicken breast offer other meaty choices. Even a meat lover sometimes hankers for something different. That's where the hot paninis come in. The Spaghetti Western features pepperoni and salami, while the Lousy Hunter is a meatless creation with vegetables and mozzarella cheese. If you are still hungry after your meal or you opted for a salad, your server will be happy to describe today's desserts. For a taste of the Old West, try True Grits Restaurant, where you'll enjoy the John Wayne memorabilia almost as much as the fresh grub.

630 N J. M. Davis Boulevard, Claremore OK
(918) 343-2200

Restaurants, Bakeries & Cafés • 159

Zackary's Gourmet Grill

Zackary's Gourmet Grill brings great food, dancing and live music about as close to Lake Eufaula as you can get while still keeping your meal dry. The restaurant floats on the state's largest lake, offering diners an up-close view of the water while enjoying their food. Owner Zack Robinson founded the restaurant in 2003 and welcomes customers from April through November. Zackary's caters to a variety of clientele, from boaters out for a day of fun on the water to those in search of a fine dining experience. To get the evening started with some zing, try the hot wings, tossed in a spicy sauce and served with blue cheese dressing to take the edge off. The artichoke bake is a rich appetizer of artichoke hearts stuffed with crabmeat. For your entrée, Zackary's offers a range of options, including steak, seafood and pasta. The salmon, sautéed in a basil Cognac cream sauce, is sure to delight any seafood lover, and the rib eye steak is always grilled just the way you like it. On Saturday nights, get your groove on with live rhythm and blues from the outdoor patio, complete with a Caribbean-style tiki bar and dance floor. Head over to Zackary's Gourmet Grill for great food on Lake Eufaula.

**400 Lakeshore Drive, Eufaula OK
(918) 689-7535**

The Silver Flame

The story of the Silver Flame, a Tulsa steakhouse and seafood restaurant, is a story of a successful merging of two cultures, and what is possible in America. Owner Abdul Alhlou immigrated to the United States from Syria. In 1987, after graduating from the University of Tulsa, he opened the Silver Flame in Tulsa, giving such American favorites as steak and lobster a uniquely Middle Eastern twist. Lunch specials include broiled salmon, shrimp scampi and steak sandwiches. In the evening, you can enjoy live music from the piano bar as you dine on porterhouse steak, Alaskan king crab or pork tenderloin. A favorite of customers, the Silver Flame Steak is a filet mignon prepared with peppers, onions and seasonings. Each entrée comes with numerous side dishes, including tabouli, hummus and salad. The restaurant offers an impressive list of wines to accompany your meal. If you would like to bring the flavors of an authentic Syrian steakhouse to your next occasion, the Silver Flame accommodates parties of up to 600 people with its catering service. Come to the Silver Flame for an enticing blend of flavors and cultures.

6100 S Sheridan Road, Tulsa OK
(918) 496-3311
www.silverflamesteakhouse.com

ArabicaDabra's Coffee House

If you have a passion for coffee or tea and want the total experience that only the finest blends can provide, you will want to visit ArabicaDabra's Coffee House. This coffee house was established in December 2005 by David and Melissa Fell, and Dr. and Mrs. Tony Fell. A comfortable and friendly atmosphere greets you when you walk in the door, intertwining with the mixed aromas of specially blended coffees, teas and life. Specialty coffee is about the quality, not the method, and at ArabicaDabra's, quality is an essential part of this experience. David is fully qualified with a Barista Certification from the Coffee Academy of Portland, Oregon. With 13 blends of beans and 22 blends of teas from around the world, they offer something that will make you want to sit back and enjoy yourself. Your visit comes complete with a comfortable setting and Wi-Fi connection, so come to ArabicaDabra's Coffee House and try a cup of La-Minita Terrazu or Ethiopian Moka Harrar.

2524 E Kenosha, Broken Arrow OK
(918) 355-4361
www.arabicadabras.com

Krawdaddy's BBQ & Such at Snake Creek Marina

When you're out cruising the scenic Lake Tenkiller and hunger strikes, head to Krawdaddy's BBQ & Such at Snake Creek Marina, where serving great barbecue has been a tradition since 1965. Krawdaddy's is owned and operated by partners Dwight Beard and Justin Pollard, who delight in being part of the marina community and make a point of providing their customers with the best service possible, bar none. This welcoming waterside eatery is well known for its casual, laid-back atmosphere and cheerful staff members, who go out of their way to ensure that your dining experience is perfect. The restaurant offers a full menu of tasty options; however, Krawdaddy's real claim to fame is its succulent, hickory smoked barbecued meats and ribs, which the restaurant prepares with a dry rub and then allows to slowly cook until they reach tender, delicious perfection. Krawdaddy's uses only fresh, quality ingredients to prepare its meals, which include crisp salads and delicious stacked sandwiches, served on hearty, freshly made sourdough bread. On the weekends the popular hideaway kicks it up a notch by offering live music, which is a perfect backdrop for watching the sunset over the lake from the restaurant's patio seating area. Enjoy a tranquil meal, good company and barbecue nirvana with a visit to Krawdaddy's BBQ & Such at Snake Creek Marina.

18576 W Snake Creek Road, Cookson OK
(918) 457-5674
www.snakecreekmarina.com

Iguana Cafée

The clientele at the Iguana Cafée in Tahlequah form a friendly, eclectic community. The Iguana, located close to Northeastern State University, is a hang-out for students, professors, retirees, businesspeople and a mix of local residents. It's a great place to enjoy hot or cold classic espresso concoctions and an assortment of hearty deli sandwiches, with names like the Chameleon, the Gila Monster and, of course, the Iguana. The menu also includes pizza, bagels and New York cheesecake. If you stroll down Muskogee Avenue to visit galleries, boutiques and antique stores, the Iguana Cafée makes a nice change of pace. You can sit a spell on an outdoor deck, sample light fare and smoothies, or relax and enjoy a beer or glass of wine during a live music session. Owners Gordon and Christina Zabik and their friendly staff create a home away from home environment with such services as wireless Internet access. You can even find some special gifts here. Whether you are visiting or count yourself lucky to reside in Tahlequah, you are sure to feel at home in the easygoing atmosphere of the Iguana Cafée.

500 N Muskogee Avenue, Suite A, Tahlequah OK
(918) 458-0044

Saffron

On weekdays and Saturdays, Saffron buzzes with activity. The year and a half-old Tulsa coffeehouse and bistro has all the espresso specialties, like café latté, cappuccino and macchiato, and a full complement of flavored syrups. It also features some hot creations of its own, like Cup of Luv and Vanilla Gorilla. Add to that a full breakfast, lunch and dinner menu, live music and weekly special events, and Saffron becomes interesting to more and more people. This amusing coffeehouse is the brainchild of owner Jenna McQuigg with her sister Kella operating as store manager. Saffron features Topéka coffee from El Salvador. The beans for this full-bodied brew are grown on a Free Trade coffee plantation where growers share in the profits. Look also for a nice mix of teas and Italian sodas. Saffron is the perfect destination for a hot or cold sandwich or small appetizer, including several vegan specials. Customers can take advantage of free wireless Internet access or enjoy live music weekday afternoons and Friday and Saturday evenings. Another attraction at this bouncy new venue is a weekly open mike with music, poetry and other amusements for every age and interest. Saffron is nicely decorated with local artwork that is available for sale. Bring a friend or make a new friend at this peppy new hot spot where coffee, food and art make an unbeatable blend.

1148 S Harvard Avenue, Tulsa OK
(918) 599-8915
www.saffroncoffee.com

Restaurants, Bakeries & Cafés • 163

Jenks Restaurant & Amazing Clocks

You've never seen or heard anything like Jenks Restaurant. From the time you walk in you'll be entranced by the kaleidoscope of rhythms and colors, chimes and music of clocks. Lots of clocks. All kinds of Rhythm Clocks, from wall clocks to mantle clocks. It really is something to behold. What makes it so unusual is that this is both a clock store of Rhythm Small World clocks and a restaurant. Jenks Restaurant & Amazing Clocks is a darn good restaurant serving all-day breakfasts and family-style recipes that really hit the spot. Jim and Shin Copeland have been in the restaurant business for 40 years. They've owned Jenks Restaurant for a decade. They serve up amazing omelets, made-from-scratch pancakes, waffles, French toast and daily specials. The lunch and dinner menus are filled with down-home favorites ranging from chicken and seafood to steaks and pasta. The breakfast menu covers two giant pages that don't have much empty white space on them, covering everything from omelets and platters to grits and smoked ham. Located in the historic downtown shopping district, their intention is to provide a business where the community and travelers can enjoy good home cooking in a clean, friendly, affordable atmosphere. The next time you are within 100 miles of Jenks, figure out a way to get there. Jenks Restaurant & Amazing Clocks is a place you'll be talking about for years.

215 E Main Street, Jenks OK
(918) 296-4000

Ol'Dutchman Bakery

Savor the delicious aromas and comforting flavors of your favorite breads and pies with a visit to the Ol'Dutchman Bakery in Claremore. Owner Eddie Burkholder, who opened the bakery in 2001, prides himself on using only the freshest, highest quality ingredients to prepare traditional Amish baked goods and treats for you and your family. Eddie, a native of Jamesport, Missouri, learned baking from his mother in the mid-1990s and has since created a delicious array of favored recipes, including his signature cinnamon rolls and cookies. Ol'Dutchman Bakery further offers a tasty selection of freshly made yeast and nut breads as well as Eddie's own homemade jams. The bakery's melt-in-your-mouth, regular and sugar free pies are another reason why Ol'Dutchman has become a community favorite. During the holiday's you can preorder beloved baked goods and pick them up fresh and ready to go for your holiday table. For scrumptious goodies reminiscent of grandma's kitchen, visit Ol'Dutchman Bakery, where great taste is made fresh daily.

18435 S Highway 66, Claremore OK
(918) 341-7505

Mecca Coffee Company

Customers rave about the expertly brewed coffee at Mecca Coffee Company. You'll never realize how good coffee can be until you've come to this shop. Named for the city where the first coffee houses appeared as early as the 16th century, Mecca strives to serve the ultimate cup. There's much more to this comfortable coffee shop than coffee. Kitchen connoisseurs of all varieties swoon over the gourmet foods and gadgets at Mecca. Customers often stop by just to browse for these items. Top-of-the-line espresso machines, beer and wine brewing kits are just the beginning. Fancy some quality cigars, tobacco or smoking accessories? Mecca has a walk-in humidor. You'll find dried herbs, spices and specialty sauces to help home chefs make simple dishes extraordinary. You can always take home some of the gourmet coffee, tea and chocolate. The myriad products at Mecca Coffee Company are as fun to give as to receive. Don't miss this tantalizing coffee shop and gourmet food store.

1143 E 33rd Place, Tulsa OK
(918) 749-3509

Sam & Ella's Chicken Palace, Pizza & Subs

The handsomely restored civil war era building that houses Sam & Ella's Chicken Palace was the site of Tahlequah's beloved Redmen Shoppe a generation ago. With the pizza and sub shop in place, the building bustles with excitement once again. Many who flock to Sam & Ella's may be too young to remember the Redmen Shoppes soda fountain, but they do know that the restaurant serves a divine hand-rolled, stone-baked pizza. Many fans claim it is the best they have ever eaten. Sam & Ella's has pizza for people who like tons of everything. The Big Sloppy Pie features double cheese, double pepperoni and layers of black olives. The Pie Without a Face provides a true veggie feast with red and green bell peppers, red onions, black olives, fresh mushrooms and sweet pineapple. This pie was named in honor of Mike, the headless rooster who became famous after surviving a run in with an ax in the late 1930s. There are many other specialty pies to choose from or you can create your own masterpiece. The cheerful staff also prepares fresh salads (a run through the garden) and tasty subs. The eatery is owned and operated by Jack and Andrea Mullen, also known as Sam and Ella (say it fast and get the joke). For lunch or dinner, Sam & Ella's Chicken Palace is open seven days a week and call-ins are always welcome. They are located in the beautiful, historic downtown Tahlequah.

419 N Muskogee Avenue, Tahlequah OK
(918) 456-1411
www.samandellas.com

Country Cottage Restaurant

The home cooked meals you fondly remember from your past are available in the present at Country Cottage Restaurant, where delicious, homemade meals have been the standard for 20 years. Dale and Linda Moore own Country Cottage, and they are dedicated to creating an environment where their customers will feel at home. The Moores attribute much of their success to their long-time staff, including son and manager Kenny Moore, daughter Kelly, and the Moores' best friends and co-managers, Sheri and R.J. Shatswell. Country Cottage is recognized for its scrumptious entrées, many of which are made from recipes handed down from Dale's and Linda's grandmothers. Menu favorites include mouthwatering fried chicken and chicken-fried steak along with freshly caught catfish, crispy salads and notable desserts, including vanilla cinnamon bread pudding. In addition to the sit-down menu, Country Cottage offers a buffet that draws customers from as far away as Muskogee, Tulsa and Arkansas. Country Cottage can also cater your next special event with a bounty of classic dishes for your guests. The food is highlighted by the restaurant's elegant Victorian décor and friendly, Christian atmosphere. Bring the whole family and enjoy a meal just like grandma used to make with a visit to Country Cottage Restaurant.

6570 N Highway 82, Locust Grove OK
(918) 479-6439

Downtown Tulsa

Sweet Tooth Candy & Gift Company
Fun Foods

Gift giving was never simpler or more rewarding than it gets at Sweet Tooth Candy & Gift Company in Tulsa. Here you have a choice of fine candy or unique gift items, carefully selected for their appeal and originality. Fine chocolates, truffles and a selection of domestic and imported candies always make thoughtful presents, especially when you can hand-select the assortment and have it packaged in a Sweet Tooth candy box. Sweet Tooth also carries a large selection of sugar-free chocolates and other sugar-free candies. Husband-and-wife team Jeff Darby and Janet Dundee have owned Sweet Tooth for 15 years. Sweet Tooth boasts one of the widest selections of candy in Tulsa, with as many as 600 different kinds of candy, including licorice, Jelly Belly Beans, chocolate covered nuts, fruit slices and cordials. Jeff and Janet value original gift ideas and avoid the cookie-cutter gift lines. Look for quality and value in Sweet Tooth's growing gift section with its continually changing selection of jewelry, collectibles and seasonal merchandise. Customer service is a Sweet Tooth standard. Sweet Tooth welcomes special orders and can deliver locally or ship nationwide. When you want your gift to express sweet sentiments as well as sweet flavor, visit Sweet Tooth Candy & Gift Company.

3747 S Harvard Avenue, Tulsa OK
(918) 712-8785 or (800) 514-3191

Copper Canyon Day Spa
Health & Beauty

Copper Canyon Day Spa is a full-service spa offering health and beauty treatments that include massage, mud wraps, Biogenie body slimming treatments and much more. All staff members are licensed, well trained and enjoy years of experience. Copper Canyon is proud of its warm, relaxing atmosphere and personalized service. Biogenie non-surgical face lifting and body shaping is a Copper Canyon specialty. Biogenie lets you target specific areas of the face and body where weight-loss and reduced volume are desirable. The unique electrical energy of this method promotes epidermal regeneration, stimulates lymphatic and venous circulation and enhances energy levels. Copper Canyon's massage therapies include Swedish, sports, therapeutic and deep tissue styles. Facelift massage addresses the face, and reflexology treats the feet. More than half a dozen facials are available. Copper Canyon offers an unusually wide variety of body wraps and polishes that make use of the finest ingredients. Mud and clay treatments employ black mud from the Baltic, red clay from France and Arizona, and European rose body mud. Exfoliating salt treatments use salt from the Dead Sea. As you would expect, Copper Canyon provides manicures, pedicures and waxing services. Eyelash extensions are another popular service. Visit Copper Canyon Day Spa, where the staff strives to make your spa experience one you won't soon forget.

1626 S Boston Avenue, Tulsa OK
(918) 292-8842
www.coppercanyondayspa.com

Island Nation
Retail

Why wait for that vacation to the islands when Island Nation in Jenks is bursting with island-inspired tropical merchandise. Owner Pam Langston has stocked her shop with the very best island art, home décor and apparel. Gift possibilities abound with fragrances from the islands, plus books, jewelry, and bath and body products. Your first glimpse of the shop's Tahitian thatch-and-bamboo ceiling, bamboo walls and woven seagrass floor coverings will conjure up that easy, laid-back island feeling. Tropical clothing lines for men and women, such as comfy rope sandals by Gurkees or easygoing casual wear by Tommy Bahama, will bring the sand and surf a little closer. Island Nation carries bath and body products for an island glow. Discover island secrets to beautiful skin and hair with products from Pure Fiji and Malie Kauai. A significant portion of Island Nation's products come directly from island traders, so whether you're looking for pineapple barware, original artwork or gourmet food, you'll find it here. Representing products from a wide variety of islands, including Hawaii, the islands of the Caribbean and the South Pacific, this store truly is One Nation Under The Sun. Ready for your tropical vacation? Put on those flip-flops and let the islands come to you at Island Nation.

500 RiverWalk Terrace, Suite 110, Jenks OK
(918) 296-9801
www.myislandnation.com

Hastings Entertainment–Bartlesville
Retail

Bartlesville is the City of Legends, a perfect setting for Hastings Entertainment, which is a legend in retail. In the city where Frank Lloyd Wright built his one and only skyscraper and exotic animals roam on an oil baron's ranch, you can find a little bit of everything, and everything is what you'll find at Hastings. From movies to games, books to CDs, Hastings has you covered. The store not only sells entertainment, but rents, trades and buys it as well. Unwind with a good book or watch a movie wearing a cool T-shirt from the Trends section of the shop. Pick up one of the classic board games, such as Twister or Clue. Lines of collectible action figures feature Star War characters and a variety of Ghost Rider figures, as well as celebrities, both real and fictional, such as Lara Croft or Kurt Cobain. The store also has a stock of media accessories, including flash drives and compact disks, digital video disks and iPod covers. Hastings Entertainment is more than just a place to pick up a movie, CD or magazine. Hastings built their business on the Fish! Philosophy, a fun-in-the-workplace concept that promotes a vibrant and entertaining store atmosphere. Stop in and see what they've got—it's the only way to truly discover Hastings Entertainment.

3005 E Frank Phillips Boulevard, Bartlesville OK
(918) 335-0831
www.hastingsentertainment.com

Nouveau Atelier de Chocolat
Fun Foods

This absolutely charming little niche in historic downtown Broken Arrow is a comfort zone all in itself. True to its European beginnings, Nouveau Atelier de Chocolat is elegantly decorated and whimsical at the same time. The owners, Christine Joseph and husband Greg Null, purchased the 1904 building that houses this little treasure and renovated it, restoring the original ceiling tiles, walls and floors. After small beginnings, Christine's business quickly grew through word-of-mouth publicity. Nouveau Atelier de Chocolat is not a secret anymore, and it is now widely known that Christine's Belgian chocolates are simply the best. The charming atmosphere of the shop is only the beginning. You can browse among delightful gifts as you contemplate how many pounds of enchanting chocolate you will carry home. Choose from special gift packaging or chocolate art commissioned for your special occasion. Christine, a Belgian native and a degreed chocolatier, makes all her own chocolates right in the store. You haven't had chocolate until you've had Belgian chocolate! The friendly and welcoming Nouveau Atelier de Chocolat is a place you must stop on your next visit to Broken Arrow.

205 South Main Street, Broken Arrow OK
(918) 258-2877
www.nouveauchocolates.com

Roberts Fine Interiors
Home Décor

Tulsa interior decorators Tom and Juanita Roberts of Roberts Fine Interiors prove homeowners can save money and create designer rooms by working with professionals. Combining 60 years of experience, they often delight in solving the missing piece of a design puzzle. They are experts at working with a customer's existing pieces to create the look and feel a customer desires.

Tom and Juanita offer in-home consultation services free of charge. They understand the personal nature of each project when they respectfully walk into a client's home and offer advice based on professional experience and individual needs. Sometimes a design solution may be as simple as reupholstering old furniture or adding a few well placed accessories. In addition to consultations, Tom and Juanita provide a onestop shop for interior design. Roberts Fine Interiors offers dealer pricing on several fine furniture lines, including Hickory White, Hancock & Moore and Hekman/Woodmark. The Roberts round out their tasteful selections with an array of custom window treatments, bedding and accessories. Tom and Juanita invite you to take them up on their free design assessment and find out how to affordably enhance your home environment at Roberts Fine Interiors.

10021 S Yale Avenue, Suite 106, Tulsa OK
(918) 296-5444

Gourmet's
Retail

Find tasty treats and gadgets galore at Gourmet's on the shores of beautiful Grand Lake O' the Cherokees in Grove. Alan and Janine Caldwell opened the store in 2005. They specialize in providing everything that the professional or recreational chef might need. The Caldwells' engaging staff of wooden helpers, which include Alfred the Doorman, Mr. Dobson the Butler, Mr. Barkley the Head Usher and Chef Teaspoon, make whimsical additions to this sensational place that brims with all of the latest devices needed to create delicious meals in grand style. Gourmet's carries a wide selection of gourmet foods and private blend coffees as well as spices, teas and candy. You will find dipping oils, marinades and sauces to accompany the store's pastas and bruschettas. Gourmet's exceptional gift baskets, loaded with the store's best goodies and kitchen accoutrements, have become one of the most sought after gifts in the Grand Lake area. Either pre-made or made-to-order in your theme and price range, the baskets are sure to delight. For the grilling enthusiast, Gourmet's has a fabulous line of barbeque tools, planks, sauces, rubs and accessories... just the right products to make your grilling an adventure. Spice up your life and then get cooking with a visit to Gourmet's.

2 W 3rd Street, Grove OK
(918) 786-4700

West Southwest Territory
Retail

If you are looking for authentic arts and crafts of the Southwest, plan a trip to West Southwest Territory in Jenks. West Southwest Territory carries an impressive selection of authentic Navajo, Zuni, Cherokee, Kiowa and Southwest-style jewelry. You'll also find Sioux and Pueblo pottery, Navajo rugs, prints, art and more. Every piece is hand-selected by owners Vicki and Wayne Holliday to ensure authenticity. They feature prints by Bill and Tracy Rabbit, Lee Joshua, Jerome Tiger, and more. They carry original paintings by Dana Tiger, White Buffalo, and Diane Star. They also stock such made-in-Oklahoma products as Frankhoma Pottery. Located at Riverwalk Crossing, West Southwest Territory is the only Native American owned and operated store in the area. Visit the Hollidays next time you are in Jenks. Their store is a true expression of the best of the Southwest.

500 RiverWalk Terrace #120, Jenks OK
(918) 296-0957
www.wswterritory.com

Miss Jackson's
Retail

Miss Jackson's is undoubtedly the hub of Tulsa's finest shopping. Located in Utica Square, this store has been the city's merchandise mecca since the early 1900s when Miss Nelle Shields Jackson guided the most elegant shoppers through three floors of botique bliss. Today it is still a paradise boasting the penthouse salon, a second floor of premiere designer fashions and the cozy and elegant main floor. The store possesses collections of many of the worlds most sought after lines of apparel, fine jewelry, cosmetics, handbags, gifts and home selections. The cornerstone of its success is the continued tradition Miss Jacksons staff offers, tailoring their efforts and energies to find and fit your needs. The emphasis is on individual attention, whether you are interested in a complete designer wardrobe or are just in town for a visit and are shopping for a bit of fun. Miss Jackson's is available on the internet, of course, but the shopping experience is well worth the investment of an afternoon.

1974 Utica Square, Tulsa OK
(918) 747-8671 or (866) 688-9702
www.missjacksons.com

Me-O-My Baby Gifts Inc.
Retail

Me-O-My Baby Gifts can widen your gift giving options, thanks to a thoughtful array of baby-specific products. Owner Lois Fish proudly offers quality gifts and personalized service at her Tulsa shop and through her online business. Luxurious christening blankets come in several fun fabrics. Infants rest easy in faux fur blankets that simulate leopard, lamb, mink or fox. Silk christening blankets with Asian flare and exquisitely embroidered flower designs bring beauty and comfort to an important occasion. Colorful diaper bags are always appreciated. Among the accessories carrying the delightful Me-O-My rainbow logo are bibs, hats, baby robes and rattles. Bottles, bowls, sippy cups, eating utensils and baby comb and brush sets also sport the lively logo. The shop offers gift wrapping and cards. Gift certificates include a free gift. Located in a small complex of shops and boutiques near Oral Roberts University, Me-O-My is a great place to browse. The shop also welcomes custom orders. For gifts that will be long remembered for their craftsmanship and thoughtfulness, visit Me-O-My Baby Gifts.

8281 S Harvard, Tulsa OK
(918) 298-4838 or (866)-90MEOMY (906-3669)
www.me-o-my.com

The Flour Sack
Antiques & Collectibles

If you ever find yourself doubting the versatility of a cloth flour sack, a visit to Neva Wasson's shop in Grove will convince you otherwise. The old stone building that houses The Flour Sack is over 100 years old and has been in the Wasson family since 1939. The building housed the family's produce beginning in 1944 when they bought and sold chickens, eggs, seeds, milk, cream and cow hides. During the Great Depression, flour sacks were given a second life as they were used as towels, aprons, shirts, dresses and undergarments. In honor of those sacks and their importance to her family and her community, Neva and her sister, Margarete, established The Flour Sack in 1984. They wrap all purchases neatly in handmade, calico flour sacks. The shop features antiques, primitives and collectibles, plus gifts and crafts made by local artisans. You'll find Depression glass, elegant glass, pottery and porcelain, plus hard-to-categorize odds and ends. Visit Neva at The Flour Sack. You will probably find the perfect present, and maybe a thing or two for yourself. She will send you packing with a flour sack to hold your precious purchases.

307 S Grand Street, Grove OK
(918) 786-4075

Shopping & Services • 175

Tea & Magnolias
Retail

If you are looking for Southern charm and a touch of gracious living, saunter into Tea & Magnolias at the Riverwalk Crossing in Jenks. Susan Ponville has created an oasis of gentility that is stocked with artistic and very well made home décor and gift items that will add a touch of class to any home. Susan, who grew up in Tupelo, Mississippi, will offer you a complimentary glass of iced tea and a confection to nibble on as you browse through her eclectic collection. You'll find the famed fairies of Mark Roberts, and the artistic creations of Jeanette McCall, a renowned baker who produces gorgeous ceramic items such as tea pots and cake plates. Susan also carries Root Candles, cookbooks, kitchenware, coffees, teas and a plethora of both useful and fanciful items. On top of everything else, she carries a selection of items for fans of Oklahoma and Oklahoma State University. Susan is aided in her merchandising efforts by Chamomile, the store mascot who thinks she owns the place, but is really a cat. The next time you are in Jenks, plan a visit to Tea & Magnolias. It's the kind of shop that makes you feel right at home.

500 Riverwalk Terrace, #165, Jenks OK
(918) 296-9832
www.teaandmagnolias.com

Heritage Antiques
Antiques & Collectibles

Collecting antiques is not only a wonderful way to add interest and beauty to your home, it is also a way to connect to your past and feel closer to those who came before you. At Heritage Antiques in Pryor, you can find a wide range of antiques and vintage pieces, including masterfully crafted oak furniture and a delightful array of toys and collectibles. Heritage Antiques is best known for its collection of authentic Civil War bonds, but you will also find a full selection of vintage glassware, primitives and antique lamps. Appropriately, Heritage Antiques makes its home in a historical house that was built around 1900. June Venamon and her partner, Marianne Shrum, first opened Heritage in 1989. They believe that antiques are a link to our pioneer heritage, and they are dedicated to finding and displaying only the finest quality pieces in their shop. Get in touch with your past while adding special, and often one-of-a-kind, pieces of history to your home with a visit to Heritage Antiques.

122 S Adair Street, Pryor OK
(918) 825-5714

Creative Concepts
Home Décor

At Creative Concepts Distinctive Furnishings in Monkey Island, you can envision the changes quality furnishings will make in your home environment, thanks to stylish showroom groupings that help customers hone in on styles that reflect their taste and lifestyle. Creative Concepts offers complete interior decorating services and specializes in creating an atmosphere with just the right set of adornments for your needs, from quality upholstered pieces to flooring, wall décor, window treatments and light fixtures. Unusual furniture pieces can enhance the overall look of a room, and Creative Concepts gives customers a large choice of small side tables, Bombay chests, bookcases, ornate baker's racks, plus room dividers in wood and iron. You'll find a continually changing array of accent pieces to aid in setting a mood and accessories that accent color, texture and style, like vases, florals and statuary. A new or remodeled bathroom might benefit from the distinctive look of a sink chest, a crafted wood vanity topped with fossil stone and a formed metal basin. The overall elegance of a room is deeply influenced by the wall décor, and Creative Concepts not only offers a stunning selection of original oil paintings, designer prints and tapestries, but has the skilled staff who know how to advantageously place that art in relation to your furnishings. You'll also find lighting fixtures that set a mood and make a statement, including chandeliers, table lamps, wall sconces and candles. When your surroundings matter to you, visit Creative Concepts.

29980 South 566 Road, Monkey Island OK
(918) 257-5702

KoKoa Chocolatier

Located in the heart of Brookside, KoKoa is home to Tulsa's most famous chocolatier, Steven Howard. Howard uses the finest chocolate couverture from around the world to create chocolates of exceptional character and diverse flavor. He believes in using only the best, so fresh cream, vanilla beans, pure fruit purees and fine liqueurs are the ingredients for not only extraordinary truffles, but Italian gelato and French pastries. Each evening the shop offers full-table service featuring made-to-order desserts, French-press coffee and an array of choice wine selections. Lunch is served in the afternoons, and twice a month KoKoa hosts an eight-course degustation-style dinner, which includes fine wines and of course, an extraordinary dessert to end the evening. KoKoa Chocolatier invites you to come enjoy one of Tulsa's finest hot-spots for lunch, dessert or coffee.

3410 S Peoria Avenue, Suite 200, Tulsa OK (KoKoa Chocolatier)
(918) 742-4069

510 S Boston Avenue, Tulsa OK (KoKoa Kabana)
(866) 37-KOKOA (375-6562)

www.kokoachocolatier.com

The Quilt Shop
Retail

The old and honorable skill of sewing is alive and well in Grove, thanks to the Quilt Shop and its owner Doris Selvidge. The Quilt Shop, which recently moved from Highway 59 to 290, sells fabrics and quilting supplies, including special threads, needles and quilting frames. It's also the place to buy a Bernina sewing machine or get service and parts for your model. In many ways, the Quilt Shop is an extension of Doris' 14 years of experience in quilting and her active participation in the Grand Lake o' the Cherokee Quilt Guild, a nonprofit organization formed in 1976 and dedicated to promoting the art of quilt-making among Grove residents. The Quilt Shop is an active participant in the guild's annual quilt show, held each 4th of July weekend. In the past, children learned to sew and quilt at their mother's knees. For those who missed this bit of instruction, there's Doris and the Quilt Shop, with sewing and quilting classes and all the encouragement and enthusiasm you need to bring these vibrant beautiful expressions of home and hearth into your life. When you need an idea, a product or a service that involves quilting or sewing, visit Doris at the Quilt Shop.

63153 East 290 Road, Grove OK
(918) 786-2046

Grand Interiors
Home Décor

When Grand Interiors of Grove takes on your new home construction project, the home of your dreams is that much closer to reality. The well-respected Grove interior design company specializes in interior design from the ground up. Owner Jeanne Whiteley and Interior Designer Connie Parsons bring decades of experience to the table and a proven track record of creating new interiors that fit the structure and its occupants. A grand home needs a grand plan; fortunately for homeowners in the Grand Lake area, Grand Interiors has the expertise to turn the myriad details of interior construction and furnishings into a solid and comfortable personalized statement, allowing you to relax and enjoy the process. Grand Interiors works closely with artists and craftspeople to manage all phases of interior planning and execution, including tile, carpet, lighting, wallpaper and paint. They are also experts at window treatments and furniture styling. The company is responsible for the show house at the new luxury community of Apache Coves on Grand Lake. The house is a sample of the architecture and lifestyle residents can expect here with airy rooms, high ceilings and wide expanses of glass that integrate breathtaking views with comfortable interior amenities. Among the many special features of this house is a master bath with etched glass windows over a large Jacuzzi tub, a hand-rendered artistic touch that retains privacy while allowing light to pour in. For an interior with timeless grace and individualized detailing, visit the experts at Grand Interiors.

720 E 3rd Street, Grove OK
(918) 786-6189

Zoller Designs & Antiques, Inc.
Antiques & Collectibles

Located on historic Cherry Street in Tulsa, Zoller Designs & Antiques, Inc. specializes in unique furniture and accessories for the home. Patrons discover a collection of reproduction pieces hand selected from High Point Market and marvel at the store's one-of-a-kind antiques imported from France and Italy. Zoller Designs & Antiques, Inc. carries a large inventory of Lampe Berger lamps and oils as well. Zoller Designs & Antiques, Inc. also takes pride in being a full service Interior Design company. Owner Debbie Zoller and her associates offer clients 20 years combined experience in the interior design industry and have built an infinite library of resources to complete any project. Zoller Designs & Antiques, Inc. provides customers with a friendly shopping experience and unlimited design possibilities for their home or business. For several years their services have been both nationally and locally recognized. They have been named in *Oklahoma Magazine's* Best of the Best competition and have also participated in Tulsa's Designer Showcase. Visit Zoller Designs & Antiques, Inc. at:

1603 E 15th Street, Tulsa OK
(918) 583-1966
www.zollerdesigns.com

Symmetry Salon and Day Spa
Health & Beauty

Relaxation and rejuvenation are the business of Symmetry Salon and Day Spa. Owner Tena Hyde provides a serene and comforting environment for replenishing your mind and body. At the beginning of each service, Symmetry conducts a thorough consultation to customize treatments to the specific needs of each guest. Trained experts restore balance and harmony to the body and mind. Body treatments can increase metabolism, relieve muscle tightness, reduce water retention and detoxify the whole body. Facials, peels and microdermabrasion address issues of skin damage, elasticity, clarity and texture. Symmetry's hair stylists range from senior design stylists to master stylists, and all of them continually update and improve their skills. Symmetry uses the L'oreal sere color line, which contains a patented conditioner that imparts a brilliant shine to hair. Nail care includes paraffin treatments, airbrushing and freehand custom painting. Spa and gift packages can be designed for any occasion and make thoughtful gifts: treat a mother-to-be with an hour of massage, manicure and pedicure, bridal packages include a group discount for the bridal party, and a sports package to work out muscle tension, to name a few. Symmetry Salon and Day Spa is truly a full service salon and spa that will pamper you from head to toe. Visit Symmetry's website for more details.

4860 S Lewis Avenue, Suite 130, Tulsa OK
(918) 491-9873
www.symmetrydayspa.com

Hastings Entertainment–Muskogee
Retail

Whether you are looking for a movie, book, game or music, you can find it all at Hastings Entertainment. Hastings features new and used entertainment that you can buy, rent, trade or sell. If you buy an item and later want to trade it in or sell it back, you can do that, too. The fun items cover every category. Unlike a certain large retailer, Hastings does not sell edited CDs or DVDs, so you always get full original versions. You'll find action figures and board games in the Trends section, along with t-shirts and humorous items. Book Manager April Manes explains that Hastings at Muskogee has a program to collect funds for the Muskogee Literacy Council, and the store does its best to help local teachers and librarians. "We're big on anything that promotes reading," Manes explained. In Muskogee, Hastings offers complementary coffee and tea to visitors. The staff is playful and friendly. There is a large repeat clientele, and staff members know many customers on a first-name basis. Hastings often accommodates school field trips and groups that arrive by bus. The next time you want to read a book, watch a movie or play a game, you know where to go. Head for Hastings Entertainment.

2230 E Shawnee Road, Muskogee OK
(918) 683-7252
www.hastings-ent.com

Stonebridge Garden Center
Home & Garden

Stonebridge Garden Center is the only full-service, locally owned garden center in Claremore. The garden center not only sells plants, but provides landscaping and design as well as total landscape maintenance. The center carries a full line of annuals and perennials, notably potted rosebushes and the Endless Summer hydrangea. Vegetables include 40 varieties of tomatoes. Stonebridge Garden Center offers to create a backyard sanctuary for you through its landscape and design services. The garden center can provide irrigation systems, including sprinklers and water-efficient drip systems. It can install stone walls and landscape lighting. Year-round total landscape maintenance includes mowing, edging, trimming and pruning. Stonebridge's care for flowerbeds includes re-mulching. The center can also handle fertilization, weed control and leaf removal for the entire property. Stonebridge Garden Center has been offering professional services featuring courteous crews, since 1965. Long-term General Manager Matt Jones has recently joined Doree and Ken Broostin as owners of the enterprise, thus freeing up the Broostins for travel and retirement. Still, Doree and Ken will continue to be involved with customer services. Stop by the Stonebridge Garden Center and see what is new.

700 E Will Rogers Boulevard, Claremore OK (918) 341-1228

Nuance Décor
Home Décor

In two short years, Nuance Décor has changed the lives of its owners and the customers they serve. It has given Owner Terry Robinson a new focus in life, showcased the interior design talents of her partner Amber Benson, and brought satisfying transformations to homes in the Grand Lake area and beyond. Terry hired Amber to design her home several years ago; she was so touched by the experience, she asked Amber to team up for a business that would not only sell fine home furnishings but spotlight Amber's design skills. Beyond the monumental statues at Nuance Décor's front door awaits a warm wash of color, glowing lamplight, the gleam of wood and the complex textures and patterns of upholstered pieces. Customers can purchase from the showroom floor or ask for Amber's specialty services. Amber's forté is designing and redesigning interiors from top to bottom, based on the customer's criteria and using many of the customer's own furnishings. She uses a team of nine subcontractors with various specialties, including paint, drapery and custom cabinets. Her favorite part of the project is welcoming clients back to their homes to witness the makeovers. As word spreads about Nuance Décor, Amber is being hired for design projects around the country. Whether you are starting with new construction or renovating an existing structure, visit Nuance Décor—Interiors by Amber Benson for interiors that will satisfy your eye and your lifestyle for years to come.

**2123 South Main Street, Suite C, Grove OK
(918) 786-9300**

Oak Hills Winery & Vineyards

Located just off Historic Route 66 and just 40 minutes northeast of Tulsa, Oak Hills Winery & Vineyards welcomes the whole family to a friendly, park-like environment. While you are here, take a stroll through their gift shop where you are sure to find something interesting. Wines available for tasting range from dry to sweet. Fruit juices let children also enjoy a taste of Oklahoma's harvest. If you're planning a meal of lamb, beef or pasta with a red sauce, you might want to try the winery's medium-bodied, dry Cabernet Sauvignon. On the other hand, a spicy entrée, like barbecue, Thai or Cajun food, pairs nicely with Oak Hill's Traminette, a hybrid grape that blends Seyval Blanc and Gewurztraminer for a spicy, semi-dry experience. Every host can use a red table wine, and Oak Hill's semi-sweet Concord grape-based wine promises to set off cheese, chocolate and finger foods to perfection. Still other Oak Hill offerings include a Catawba that pairs nicely with salads and turkey and a Seyval Blanc that makes the most out of fish, lobster and chicken. Owners Tim and Johnna Decker bottle their wine at the winery, and the wines are available for sale at retailers throughout Oklahoma. Oak Hills is located near the first oil well ever drilled in the state. Special events are scheduled regularly and are announced on the winery's website. Food and music are provided on some weekends. Come pay a relaxing visit to Oak Hills Tuesday through Sunday.

7070 S 4240 Road, Chelsea OK
(918) 789-WINE (9463)
www.oakhillswinery.com

Nuyaka Creek Winery

With free tastings Thursday through Monday and two annual wine festivals, Nuyaka Creek Winery is the place to discover the best of Oklahoma. In addition to a rich variety of classic and specialty Oklahoma wines, Nuyaka Creek Winery offers over a dozen vintages produced and bottled on-site. Owners Dianne and Pete Jones passionately promote this award-winning wine through their annual Harvest Festival in September and Spring WineFest in May, celebrating with live music, crafts and food. The couple enjoys hosting celebrations on the grounds, which are lush with native wild pecan and fruit trees, wildlife and several ponds. Guests are welcome to bring pets and children to witness the wine-making process, explore the nature trails, or even fish or camp by appointment. Nuyaka Creek Winery produces wildly popular handcrafted fruit wines from its own elderberries, chokeberries, peaches and pears. Dianne and Pete also buy local fruit and encourage farmers and citizens to participate in the growth of the Oklahoma wine industry. They promote neighboring wineries and Oklahoma wine in general on their award-winning wine blog, Oklahoma Wine News. Come to the heart of the Oklahoma wine movement with a visit to Nuyaka Creek Winery.

35230 S 177 W Avenue, Bristow OK
(918) 756-8485
www.nuyakacreek.com

Photo by Melissa Claborn/Claborn Photography

Amish Cheese House

If creamy, robust cheeses, lean deli meats and homemade fudge are a few of your favorite things, then take a trip to the Amish Cheese House, where owners Wes and Leah Miller pride themselves on providing a wide variety of quality foods. The Millers established the shop in 2000 and, as members of the Mennonite Church in Pryor, strive to purchase as much product as possible from local Amish and Mennonite communities, including communities in Ohio's Holmes County, which is often referred to as Amish Country. Amish Cheese House carries more than 40 varieties of cheese, such as Bermuda onion, horseradish cheddar and lacy Swiss, along with signature Boar's Head brand meats. The shop offers a choice selection of sugar free products as well as spices, homemade pastas and baking items. Amish Cheese House is also a great place to pick up accessories for the kitchen and gift giving has never been easier, thanks to the store's specialty gift baskets loaded to the brim with gourmet cheeses and tasty treats. Wes and Leah, along with Manager Gina Plank, are happy to assist you with your next special occasion by creating custom made cheese and meat trays that are piled high with your favorite flavors. Enjoy a sampling of the finer things in life, like good food, great service and a friendly atmosphere, with a visit to Amish Cheese House.

Highway 69 N, Chouteau OK
(918) 476-4811
www.amishcheesehouse.com

La Donna's Fancy Foods

La Donna's Fancy Foods provides the ingredients you need to prepare a meal for a special occasion or spice up everyday dishes. Owner La Donna Cullinan wants gourmet meals to be available to everyone and fills her cozy little store on historic Cherry Street with all kinds of fine foods, gifts and kitchenware. For those celebratory dinners when only the best pasta will do, La Donna's offers handmade Italian pastas that are both beautiful and delicious. A drizzle of a special imported olive oil or truffle oil can heighten the flavor of your meals. La Donna's can help you add variety to your basic repertoire with spices, seasonings and accompaniments in new and exciting flavors. Prairie Fire jam is a tasty addition to your morning toast, over the standard cream cheese, and also jazzes up a bowl of vanilla ice cream. The 73 percent dark chocolate from Neuhaus of Belgium is a far cry from the grocery store chocolate bars. The shop packs in a huge number of gourmet cheeses from around the globe and carries a large selection of products made by such local Oklahoma businesses as Maria Rae's, Daddy Hinkle's and Pepper Creek Farms. Add some excitement to your menu with a visit to La Donna's Fancy Foods where you'll find Worldly Flavors at a Local Address.

1523 E 15th Street, Tulsa OK
(918) 582-1523
www.ladonnasonline.com

Cabin Creek Vineyard & Winery

Vintners Pamela and Robert Harris turned their retirement into the manifestation of their fondest dreams by creating Cabin Creek Vineyard & Winery. They attribute their success to numerous inspirational trips to the Napa Valley and the loving support of family and friends. "Family and friends are our dearest harvest and planting partners. Everyone shares in the work, the fun and the rewards," says Pamela. The winery is located near the Cabin Creek battle site on the family's 160-acre Cherokee allotment, in the watershed of Grand Lake o' the Cherokees. They are the only Centennial Farm, Vineyard and Winery in Oklahoma. Their Centennial Celebration has been designated an official celebration by the state of Oklahoma. They will celebrate throughout the month of September 2007, with events related to Oklahoma achieving statehood. Native American grapes flourish here along with many French American hybrids and select Vinifera varietals. There is never a dull moment as this close knit group plants, prunes, picks and plays under the Oklahoma sun. With early morning harvest parties, food and wine pairings, corporate events and even weddings, the winery serves a wide community. At Cabin Creek, the skill of the winemaker and the strength of the earth combine to produce the distinctive flavors of these handmade wines. You can taste these wines and take a winery tour to learn more about the art and science involved in the production of exceptional grapes and luscious wines. You'll also find a delightful gift shop and may get to listen to Nedra Harris, winery partner and storyteller. Cabin Creek's covered pavilion, fully equipped catering kitchen and expanded winery are just waiting for your party reservation. Escape the city, bring a picnic, pop a cork and relax at Cabin Creek Vineyard & Winery.

32153 S 4360 Road, Big Cabin OK
(918) 783-5218
www.cabincreekwine.com

Summerside Vineyards, Winery and Cottages

Summerside Vineyards, Winery and Cottages allow you to combine two of life's great pleasures: travel and wine. The Summerside tasting room is right on Historic Route 66, and the winery is proud to be the home of the Route 66 Red. When you enter, the sounds of music welcome you. Enjoy a delicious range of award-winning Oklahoma wines, from dry reds and whites through sweeter styles. The friendly staff members in the tasting room make choices easy for the casual wine drinker. The Winery Bistro is open limited hours—it's worth calling ahead if you'd like lunch. You can also spend the night at Summerside. Sweet and charming cottages on Grand Lake o' the Cherokees provide a tranquil refuge from the stresses of the outside world. The cottages, which date to 1939, are snuggled safely in a protected cove on the lake. All units sleep four and come with fully equipped kitchenettes, baths with showers and cable television. The people at Summerside Vineyards, Winery and Cottages will treat you like family. Stop by and spend a day at the winery or settle down in one of the cottages. You'll be glad you did.

441251 E Historic Route 66, Vinita OK
(888) 508-WINE (9463)
www.summersidevineyards.com

Black Sheep Winery & Vineyards

It was after David and Becky Brinkley attended a grape stomp at a friend's winery in Texas that they knew exactly what they wanted to do with the 36 acres of family-owned land that they had purchased in 2005. So, Becky Pickle Brinkley and David returned to Poteau to do something unexpected—they planted a vineyard and started a winery. David is the winemaker at Black Sheep Winery. He purchased juice from other quality vineyards and began making wine immediately. Black Sheep's blush, white and red wines are as fun and enjoyable as the whimsical names on each bottle. Some are named to honor family members. There is a wine for every mood and occasion. Pirate Red is a semi-dry, elegant Pinot Noir with subtle cherry and spice flavors that anyone would enjoy. Oh My Darling is as a supple, buttery, fruity semi-dry Australian Chardonnay. Their sweet Pink Flingo! is a White Merlot with tastes of strawberries. The tasting room offers gift baskets and the banquet facility is available for special events. With the variety you'll find at Black Sheep Winery and Vineyards, it will be delicious work to taste your way through and find your favorites. Be sure to call ahead for the hours of operation.

30617 Pickle Lane, Poteau OK
(918) 647-0419
www.blacksheepvineyards.com

Wines & Specialty Foods • 187

Rose Rock—Oklahoma State Rock
Photo by Sven Teschke

188 • Southern

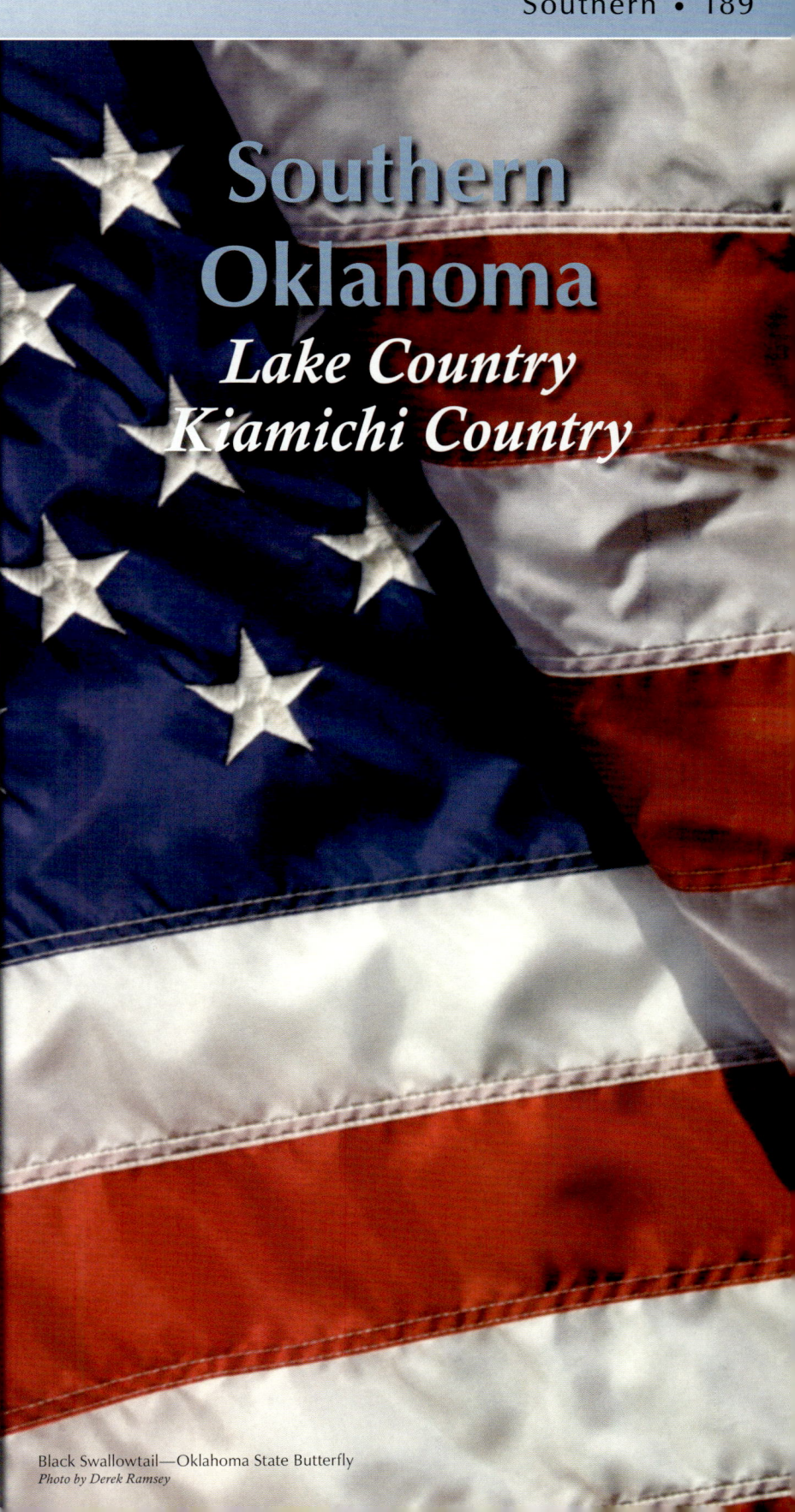

Southern Oklahoma
Lake Country
Kiamichi Country

Black Swallowtail—Oklahoma State Butterfly
Photo by Derek Ramsey

River Bend Lodge

The River Bend Lodge consists of three luxurious log houses on the Washita River in the heart of the Arbuckle Mountains, a few minutes from Turner Falls. The secure and secluded 70-acre grounds offer rest, perspective and plenty of room for the naturalist to roam with serene meadows and woods linked by miles of nature trails. Here you can spot deer and perhaps even wild boar. The lodges, built of sturdy logs, are spanking new. Decks and porches offer relaxing views that speak to the soul. Inside, you'll find lustrous wood everywhere. Robert and Miranda Hottel are your hosts. With an eye for architecture, layout and décor, Miranda ensures that each log home is attractive and well-designed. The westernmost lodge, the first one built, offers two bedrooms and a loft that's great for kids. Next is the romantic honeymoon retreat. The newest lodge is a roomy four bedroom home that exemplifies a refined and rustic décor. All have a therapeutic hot tub, fire pit and Dish Network receiver. Each contains a modern kitchen with everything you need to cook and entertain, including a dishwasher and a complete set of dining and cookware. You just bring the food. Robert is a local cattle rancher, and his persistence was key to the project's success, according to Miranda. Whether you are a family with kids, a group of friends or a family reunion, you'll feel at home at the River Bend Lodge. Come once as a guest, and you'll want to return.

Hottel Road, Davis OK
(580) 247-0147
www.river-bend-lodge.com

Pine Meadow Cabins

Sleep in an authentic teepee when you visit the original Indian Territory of Oklahoma or stay in one of the 12 lovingly maintained luxury log cabins nestled on 47 acres of wooded land across from Hochatown State Park. The cabins offer indoor hot tubs, fireplaces and cable television. Each has a fully equipped kitchen with a refrigerator, stove and microwave. Pots and pans, dishes and a coffeepot are all provided. Each has a private picnic table, charcoal grill and campfire ring. When weather permits, the resort hangs your sheets on the line the old-fashioned way for a crisp, clean feel and smell. A favorite feature of the property is the private pond where your family can enjoy catch-and-release fishing. This is a good place to practice your fly casting prior to heading for the year-round trout stream at Broken Bow Lake or Beavers Bend on the Lower Mountain Fork River nearby. The owners of the cabins live on-site. Clifton and Ruby Jordan built Pine Meadow Cabins in 1999. They are now semi-retired, and their daughter, Dian and her husband, Doug Werhane, are here to make your next visit exceptional. The family furnishes you with everything you might need, and we mean *everything*, including flashlights, candles, pancake mix and coffee. Visit Pine Meadow Cabins, where you really can hear the wind whisper through the pine boughs while you relax on your porch swing.

U.S. Highway 259 N, Broken Bow OK
(580) 494-7391 or (888) SEE-RUBY (733-7829)
www.pinemeadowcabins.com

Beavers Bend Creative Escapes

Beavers Bend Creative Escapes helps you enjoy everything the Broken Bow area has to offer. The company's custom made retreat packages are perfect for the ultimate corporate retreat or for that special family or romantic getaway. Creative Escapes can assist you in booking cabin lodging, food and beverage catering, golf, fishing, trail rides or canoeing and much more. Creative Escapes currently represents 15 cabins, ranging from Eagle Ridge's cozy one-bedroom Hickernet to Mountain Vista, a three-bedroom luxury cabin. The Creative Escapes concierge service can provide anything from housekeeping and cooking to guided fly fishing and even sales/management training. The company's physical office is inside the Girls Gone Wine winery in Hochatown. Of course, you can also call or make 24-hour online reservations. Creative Escapes is the project of Chandra Rickey and Terry Walker, with the help of Janine Carter. During her more than 20 years of hospitality experience, Rickey has owned and operated both resorts and restaurants. Walker, a Certified Hospitality Manager, served 23 years with the Oklahoma Tourism Department and managed Beavers Bend Resort Park and Lodge for the past 13 years. If you'd like this team to pamper you and introduce you to Southeast Oklahoma's best kept secrets, call Beavers Bend Creative Escapes.

U.S. Highway 259 N, Broken Bow OK
(580) 306-2265

Snug Harbor Cabins

Get away from the city and enjoy the water sports and natural beauty of Lake Eufaula from the modern comforts of Snug Harbor Cabins. James Smith opened the lakefront property in 2004 and offers visitors a choice of four beautifully appointed cabins. Though each cabin has the rustic charm of a log home, inside you will find all the modern amenities and conveniences to make your stay enjoyable, including central air-conditioning and heating. Whip up a home-cooked meal in the cabin's full kitchen and relax in the evening in the spacious living room. Each recently remodeled unit offers stylish furnishings and can accommodate up to six guests in two bedrooms. While enjoying the views through the large windows, keep your eye out for the deer and other wildlife from the nearby Eufaula National Wildlife Refuge. Beach access allows swimmers to take a dip in the cool waters, and the on-site boat ramp makes it easy to enjoy boating, fishing and water skiing on Lake Eufaula. Leave your stress at home, and take up refuge at the Snug Harbor Cabins.

Lakeview Drive, Stigler OK
(918) 452-2212
www.snugharborcabins.com

Reuben's Rest Bed and Breakfast

Treat yourself and your loved one to a romantic getaway at Reuben's Rest Bed and Breakfast, located near Beaver's Bend State Park in the scenic Kiamichi Mountains. The Oklahoma Bed and Breakfast Association recently awarded Reuben's Rest the coveted Silver Spoon Award for Excellence. You'll appreciate the luxurious amenities that accompany the three guest accommodations, such as the whirlpool tub in your private bathroom, king-size bed and movie library. In the morning, enjoy a gourmet breakfast. A guest pantry, stocked with complimentary coffee, tea, soft drinks and snacks, is upstairs right next to the guestrooms. The Saunders and Corson rooms are cozy and comfortable. The opulent Rachel's Suite sports a fireplace and a large, private balcony. You may spend the day by the pool, curl up with a good book by the parlor fireplace or play one of the many available games. You'll also discover many great outdoor activities in the Broken Bow area. Your innkeepers are Don and Marilyn Lester. Marilyn's great-great grandfather, Reuben Corson, always kept his home open to friends, mostly preachers, who needed a little R&R. One such guest named the home Reuben's Rest. Thus, carrying on the family tradition of hospitality, Don and Marilyn chose that name for their bed and breakfast. Visit Reuben's Rest Bed and Breakfast, where you'll experience, Old-Fashioned Hospitality and New-Fashioned Conveniences.

E U.S. Highway 70, Broken Bow OK
(580) 584-3155 or (886) 817-0108
www.reubensrest.com

Lago Vista Bed & Breakfast

The Lago Vista Bed & Breakfast sits on a mountainside overlooking beautiful Broken Bow Lake and surrounded by the Ouachita National Forest. A striking, Tuscan-style house in contrast to the usual log cabins of the area, Lago Vista offers plush rooms with amenities galore and spectacular views. Each of the four guest rooms includes a private lake-view balcony, fireplace and Jacuzzi, with oils, salts and bubbles provided. The king-size beds are fitted with 1000-thread-count Egyptian cotton sheets. Guests at Lago Vista can expect the royal treatment. As you arrive, attendants will take your bags and treat you to a complimentary cocktail or tea on the decks. Cocktails are complimentary every evening and breakfast is served every morning in the dining room, or brought to your room if you prefer. If you feel up for some eagle-watching, fishing or rowing, the David Boren Nature Trail will lead you down to Beavers Bend State Park and Broken Bow Lake. For indoor entertainment, Lago Vista offers a home movie theater and pool table. Lago Vista is the realization of a lifelong dream for owners Scott and Chandra Rickey. Find your new dream home-away-from-home at the Lago Vista Bed & Breakfast.

10 miles N of Broken Bow on Highway 259A, Broken Bow OK
(580) 494-7378
www.lagovistabedandbreakfast.com

Wolfe Ranch

Pete and Cheri Wolfe have enjoyed a lifetime of involvement with horses and Wolfe Ranch is the culmination of that experience. Founded in 1980, the ranch is the home of Wolfe Ranch Quarter Horses, which trains, breeds and sells premium quarter horses worldwide. These horses descend from the top bloodlines in the nation, bred for good bones and feet and known for their beauty and longevity. Many have gone on to become champions. For example, Apache Blue Boy has won three AQHA World Championships and seven additional top tens. Two horses sired by Wolfe Ranch Stallions have been exported to the UK and have since been named Top International Champions by the Quarter Horse Association in 2004 and 2005. The Wolfe Ranch also offers Arbuckle Trail Rides, where the Wolfe family takes visitors into the scenic Arbuckle Mountains on half or full-day trail rides. You'll pass historical sites from the days when Oklahoma was known as Indian Territory. Many of these sites can only be seen from horseback or on foot. Trail rides are tailored to fit the group, from beginning riders to advance horsemen. Lesson rides are also offered to teach riders how to communicate with their horses. You can learn how to *work* cattle and American Bison on the ranch as well. Anyone looking for a ranch related experience will enjoy the Wolfe Ranch and Arbuckle Trail Rides.

5311 N Highway 177, Sulphur OK
(580) 622-6326
www.wolferanch.com
www.arbuckletrailrides.com

Turner Falls Park

Turner Falls Park, the oldest park in Oklahoma, has been a favorite recreation area since 1868. Visitors enjoy a spectacular view from the base of Turner Falls as Honey Creek cascades down 77 feet to create the largest waterfall in Oklahoma. Located in the heart of the Arbuckle Mountains, the nine-square-mile park is a geological window into our past. Turner Falls Park offers two natural swimming areas, including one at the base of the falls. You can explore hiking trails, caves and such geological wonders as the Rock Castle. Sandy beaches, picnic areas and a volleyball area add to the fun. In season, a trolley helps you move from place to place. Turner Falls Park offers more than 50 RV sites with water and electricity. Campers choose from more than 500 tent sites available on a first-come first-served basis. You can also reserve cabins in advance. You'll never be too far from one of the park's strategically placed shower houses. The Trading Post is open daily and stocks necessities and novelty items. Owned and operated by the City of Davis, Turner Falls Park is patrolled by police 24 hours a day. Just next door to the park is the 10-square-mile Cross Bar Ranch, which offers primitive camping, horse trails, mountain biking and an ATV area. For natural beauty and a choice of outdoor activities, come to Turner Falls Park, one of Oklahoma's most popular destinations.

I-35 and Highway 77, Exits 47 or 51, Davis OK
(580) 369-2988
www.turnerfallspark.com

Margueritte B. Piers Living Free Sanctuary for Animals & Nature Conservatory

The Margueritte B. Piers Living Free Animal Sanctuary and Nature Conservancy is a non-profit organization that provides a safe and natural habitat for domestic animals and wildlife indigenous to Southern Oklahoma. The conservatory has seven ponds that are the residence of some 200 Canadian geese, blue heron, ducks including mud ducks and other bird life that coexist with the four-legged wildlife. The conservatory has a deer population that it feeds and protects. In addition to protecting local wildlife, the sanctuary serves abused and neglected animals in cooperation with local veterinarians. A major focus of the sanctuary is on cultivating public awareness, which includes educational outreach. The educational outreach programs present the philosophy of nature conservancy, which is to promote the protection and care of animals. The conservatory and sanctuary is located on the Wagon Stop Ranch, a historic site and a working ranch known for its horses. Two cabins on the grounds of the ranch came from Milburn Indian Territory and date back to the 1840s. A stone's throw from the cabins is the original sulfur well used in the days of covered wagons. The sulfur well is Wagon Stop Ranch's landmark. Margueritte B. Piers founded the sanctuary and conservatory in 1999, and today her niece Barbara L. Woodruff serves as executive director. Visits require an appointment, so please call ahead before your visit to the Margueritte B. Piers Living Free Animal Sanctuary and Nature Conservancy.

Ardmore OK
(405) 329-3416

Ada Old Bank Gallery

Ada is the seat of Pontotoc County and the home of the historic Old Bank Gallery. This co-op gallery features the work of talented award-winning artists. Patsy Lane is an outstanding sculptor of Western and wildlife bronze. She encourages viewers to touch her works as she tells them the story. Paul Walsh works in acrylic and watercolor to create captivating Oklahoma landscapes. Glenda Roach enjoys toying with the rules to create her imaginative paintings, sculpture and mixed media works. Bill Roach's art jewelry and drawings are inspired by nature and studies of positive and negative space. Chris Verner's paintings are inspired by her travels and studies abroad and throughout the United States. Cleta Bittle creates portraits by commission as well as still life and landscape paintings. Storm Strickland-Thompson preserves fragile slices of time in light and color through her genre painting and her famous cats. Mary Redman Emerson paints her watercolors in a vivid romantic style. Nedra Sears paints historic subjects and still life with a gentle soft approach. Ada Old Bank Gallery sponsors a National Art Exhibition every spring that brings artists all the way from California to New York. Find your way to the Ada Old Bank Gallery where you will find outstanding art, friendly people and a welcoming atmosphere.

201 West Main, Ada OK
www.adaoldbankgallery.com

Arbuckle Wilderness

Arbuckle Wilderness, Oklahoma's premier exotic-animal theme park, is set on more than 400 acres in the rugged Arbuckle Mountains. It's a recent winner of the Oklahoma Tourism Department's coveted Red Bud award for Outstanding Tourist Attraction. Hundreds of wild and rare animals live among oak thickets and limestone outcroppings—tigers, giraffes, zebras and more. Take the five mile scenic drive in your own car or on a guided safari bus tour with your option of an all-you-can-eat-cookout (advanced reservations required). The animals come right up to feed from special food buckets you hold out. Look for rhinos, camels and a rare white bison. After your drive, stop at the walk-through zoo, which contains monkeys, kangaroos, exotic birds, a petting zoo and more. The Fun Park has turtles and fish you can feed along the way. Race a go-cart, peddle a paddleboat around the lake, get wet on the bumper-boats or ride a camel. For the young ones there are moon-bounce play-ports and the Arbuckle Ark. Discover an array of stuffed animals, souvenirs, educational toys and more in the all new Safari Gift Store. Special events and season passes are available throughout the year. Exotic animals, the Fun Park and the natural beauty of the Arbuckle Mountains are waiting for you. Visit Arbuckle Wilderness soon. Open year-round (rides are seasonal).

I-35 exit 51, Arbuckle Wilderness Access Road, Davis OK
(580) 369-3383 or (800) PET-PARK (738-7275)
www.arbucklewilderness.com

Verner Gallery & Fine Art School

High aesthetics meet the wild spirit of the West at Verner Gallery & Fine Art School. The gallery and school are on Christine Verner's 5,000 acre buffalo ranch in the hills and valleys west of McAlester. Since 1984, the gallery has attracted visitors from all over the country to view rare animals and thematic art handpicked by Christine from around the world. Before 2000, when Oklahoma changed its laws on exotic animals, the ranch was a refuge for western and African animals rescued by the Verners. The cougars, ostriches and bottle-raised white-tailed deer helped to build the gallery's reputation and attracted visitors who then discovered the art inside. Christine featured western and Native American art and stocked her gift shop with African baskets, Native American jewelry and wildlife art. Today, visitors still enjoy the buffalo, cattle and horses on the ranch, and the art has branched out in more contemporary directions while maintaining its Western roots. Christine, who has studied art all over the world, including at the University of Paris, oversees the collection. She is among several local artists who teach at the Fine Art School on the upper floor of the gallery. The school offers weekly classes in a variety of media plus seasonal workshops with world-renowned artists. Discover a treasure trove of fine art and Western spirit at the Verner Gallery & Fine Art School.

2401 N Verner Road, McAlester OK
(918) 423-7267

Greater Southwest Historical Museum

The Greater Southwest Historical Museum works to preserve the history of South-Central Oklahoma through exhibits that detail the area's history from the mid-1800s to the present. The museum tells the fascinating story of human settlement from early Native American history to the time of the farmers, ranchers and townspeople who built strong communities in Oklahoma. Step back a century and explore the history of the region through artifacts, photographs and changing displays. For a look at life at the beginning of the 20th century, peek inside the Eaves-Brady Cabin, a genuine frontier cabin built in 1895. Oil field equipment, one of Ardmore's first fire engines, and an early model electric car are just a few of the treasures you'll discover. Walk the halls of the Military Memorial Museum, which honors our military heroes from the American Revolution through Operation Iraqi Freedom. View the many rare uniforms, medals and weapons exhibited there. Retrace your family history inside the Genealogical Library or find the perfect memento of your visit in the gift shop. Admission is free. The museum also provides exciting educational programming and special events. Come see the Greater Southwest Historical Museum. The past is waiting for you.

35 Sunset Drive, Ardmore OK
(580) 226-3857
www.gshm.org

Grandpa's Catfish Restaurant

At Grandpa's Catfish Restaurant, hearty eating is a family affair. M.D. Bates founded the restaurant on his father's home recipes and makes his own fish batter, cornmeal, hush puppies and peach cobbler. Today, M.D.'s daughter and son-in-law, Allison and Allan Hamilton, continue the legacy. Grandpa's homey atmosphere and family-friendly menu continue to appeal to people from all walks of life. The *Ada Evening News* Reader's Choice poll has honored Grandpa's for best catfish eight years in a row. In addition to fried catfish, butterfly shrimp and oysters, Grandpa's serves hamburgers, chicken-fried steak and all the classic sides. Customers can choose from three or four kinds of potatoes as well as Southern vegetable sides such as okra, corn and coleslaw. Don't forget the homemade peach cobbler. Set in a converted shop decorated with wood siding and clay tile floors, Grandpa's offers a cozy special-occasions room for parties of up to 30. The room evokes a rustic, antique atmosphere with a wood-burning stove. Whether you come to linger or to grab a quick buffet lunch, enjoy the home-style cooking and award-winning catfish at Grandpa's Catfish Restaurant.

16350 Country Road (S on E 32nd Street), Ada OK
(580) 421-9152

Blue Moon Cafe

The Blue Moon Café offers classic food in a classic café. Catfish, chicken fried steak and green fried tomatoes are the stars at this cheerful 1950s-style restaurant. The Blue Moon is one of Ada's most popular spots—readers of the *Ada Evening News* have voted it the town's best value, with the best chicken fry, most awesome burger and best all-around food. The *Discover Oklahoma* television show has featured the café. Snack on the Blue Moon fries, smothered with mozzarella, Monterey jack, cheddar and crumbled bacon. The café takes pride in the catfish, its biggest seller, farm raised and served with a pile of sides. You'll find a dozen kinds of chicken, including charbroiled, barbecue grilled and Santa Fe. You can get these flavorful bird recipes in sandwiches, too. There are 15 burgers and they're customizable. Everyone comes to the Blue Moon Café, from church groups to college students. It's easy to talk, because the noise level is unobtrusive. While you dine, enjoy nostalgic memorabilia celebrating Elvis, Coca-Cola and other 1950s icons. An Elvis impersonator sings several nights a week. Tommy and Judy Miller opened the Blue Moon Café 13 years ago, and their children work in the business as well. Cruise on down to the Moon today.

1104 N Hills Center, Ada OK
(580) 332-4477
www.bluemooncafeada.com

Bob's Bar-B-Que

Located just a few hundred yards from the Ada Municipal Airport, Bob's Bar-B-Que has acquired a national reputation since opening in 1952. Back in the 1960s and 70s when Bob Leonard himself was at the helm, more than 200 planes flew into Ada each week specifically to eat at Bob's or to bring his barbecue back to New York. Together with local custom, this phenomenal popularity created hour-long waits. The restaurant is just as popular today, but you won't have such a long wait. The famous barbecue ribs, chunk pork and sliced beef are still made just the way Bob and his wife Mary did. "People walk in here 20, 30, even 40 years later and say, 'It tastes just like I remember,'" co-manager Patricia Barnett says. Bob's pork ribs are rubbed with a blend of spices, smoked over hickory wood for four hours and basted with a secret sauce. One person staffs the smokehouse from dawn to dusk, ensuring security for the secret recipe. Almost as popular as the ribs is the chunk pork, cooked in a pressure canner with Bob's secret sauce and then hand-picked of fat. Guests can also choose sliced beef, catfish fillet or boneless chicken for an entree and enjoy delicious homemade side dishes

Hastings Entertainment–Ada
Retail

When Hastings Entertainment opened its doors in Ada, locals suddenly found themselves with far more choices than ever before. The books, videos, music and movies are part of the reason, but Hastings sells other items as well. In addition to selling entertainment, the store trades, rents and buys books, CDs, DVDs and games. If you need media storage the shop has flash drives, compact disks, digital video disks and memory cards. Hastings has interactive entertainment such as video games and classic traditional board games such as Sorry, Monopoly and Twister. If you're looking for something to wear for that all night video game-a-thon, check out the World Warcraft t-shirts. Other diversions include coveted collectible action figures. Hastings enjoys an enviable small town community rapport along with the benefits of a corporate identity. The shop promotes a friendly atmosphere and a give-back-to-the-community attitude. It often features seasonal fund-raising drives, such as the clovers for Saint Patrick's Day that support the Muscular Dystrophy Association. A helpful, friendly staff, massive variety and community conscience are all great reasons to make Hastings Entertainment your one-stop shop for home entertainment.

1140 Lonnie Abbott Blvd, Ada OK
(580) 436-0272
www.hastingsentertainment.com

Hastings Entertainment–Ardmore
Retail

A leading multimedia entertainment retailer, Hastings Entertainment was founded in 1968 and opened in Ardmore in 1995. The store is a cornucopia of entertainment of all types, offering books, music, movies, and video games in one 23,000 square foot depot. "Each department is like a separate store within a store," manager Robert Wood said. "The bookstore is closed off to the busyness of the other departments, offering a more relaxed environment and an older, knowledgeable staff. The lifestyles department is more upbeat, with music playing and a younger, trendy staff." The lifestyles department, which includes music and video games, features listening and gaming stations where customers can spend hours sampling the merchandise, just as they do books in the bookstore. The video department, which rents movies as well as sells them, advertises the latest DVDs on big screen televisions. One of Hastings's major benefits is that it buys and sells used media alongside the new. Customers can trade in old music, movies and books for new, or buy used products at a discount under Hastings's quality guarantee. The store also features events for fans of each department, including readings in the bookstore, live music in the cafe and popular video game tournaments. The children's story hour allows parents to leave their charges for a pleasant interval while they browse the rest of the store. Hastings prides itself on offering something for everybody. Find the media that's for you at Hastings Entertainment.

601 N Commerce Street, Ardmore OK
(580) 233-0007
www.hastings-ent.com

Lovera's Italian Grocery

Lovera's Italian Grocery, a provider of authentic Italian sausage and cheese, has been a local institution in Krebs since 1947. This family-owned and operated enterprise makes its Italian sausage on the premises from a recipe the family's grandfather brought with him from Italy. The Alpine recipe, not too spicy, was a success from the start. The most popular of Lovera's cheeses is its own hand-formed Caciocavallo. Made on-site, the gourd-shaped cheese has a mild, creamy, delicate flavor. You can also stock up on sweet Italian garlic in oil and the family's own Old World Style spaghetti sauce. Lovera's has expanded its offerings to include aprons and novelty gifts, as well as pick-your-own gift baskets and boxes. The homemade Parmesan dressing and fresh pestos are packed with zesty flavor. The story began when the family grandparents, Battista and Martha Lovera, immigrated to the area in 1907. In 1946, grandson Mike returned from the Second World War to open Mike's Grocery and Meat Market. Today, Lovera's fan base extends much farther than Krebs and McAlester. Through its website, it can ship its products all over the world. If you love Italian food, get acquainted with the best at Lovera's Italian Grocery.

95 NW 6th Street, Krebs OK
(918) 423-2842
www.iloveitalian.com

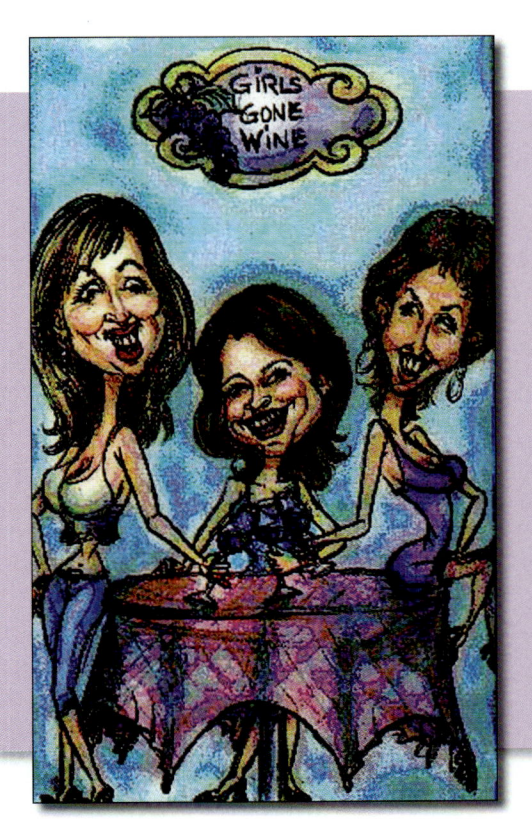

Girls Gone Wine

Chandra, Rhonda and Michelle were three friends looking for a business to go into together. One road trip, a few wineries and a several glasses later, the three dreamt up Girls Gone Wine. A bottle of the winery's Road Trip Red commemorates these origins. The label depicts the three women in a red convertible with Thelma-and-Louise-style scarves flying and wine glasses brandished high. "We don't want to pose as a pretentious, wine-snob place," Chandra explains. "We are a fun place for girlfriends to gather and learn a little about wine." Guests can sample and choose from among the eighteen varieties of Girls Gone Wine, featuring sassy names and custom-drawn labels by Oklahoma's official caricature artist, Teresa Farrington. Girls Gone Wine is more than just a tasting room and gift shop. For a more adventuresome visit, guests can make their own wine. Winemaking parties gather in the back mixing room, where they are outfitted with Girls Gone Wine aprons and photographed. After mixing grape juice, yeast and additions, guests can design their own labels and return weeks later to bottle their own vintage. A batch makes 30 bottles, which make great gifts or conversation pieces for parties, and guarantee lifelong memories. For a fun girl's night out, visit Girls Gone Wine.

10 miles N on Highway 259, Broken Bow OK
(580) 494-6243
www.thegirlsgonewine.com

Whispering Meadows Vineyards & Winery

In 2005, Bob and Karen Stobaugh established the Whispering Meadows Vineyards on 12 acres of the Schwarz Estates, a rolling landscape dotted with ponds and ruffled by breezes. Bob and his eldest son, Douglas, who is studying viticulture and enology, selected both the vinifera and French American hybrid grapes. Karen's parents helped prepare the land. Karen's grandmother Hulda, who stressed the medicinal value of a daily glass of red wine, used to travel home to Germany for half of every year to work at the Schneider family winery. Back in Texas, Hulda's children and grandchildren grew up making backyard wine. Whispering Meadows is entirely run by Bob, Karen and their sons, Douglas and Dylan. The winery is located off-site in the heart of historic downtown McAlester. This boutique-style winery is set in an appealing 1800s former jewelry store with curved glass windows and murals on the walls painted by a local artist. The wine labels are also original watercolor paintings done by an award winning local artist. Visitors are welcome at either the vineyards or the winery. You can enjoy a brief respite in a charming environment with a glass of excellent Cabernet Sauvignon. You won't want to miss a chance to taste wine from the heartland at the Whispering Meadows Vineyards & Winery, a true jewel of Southeastern Oklahoma.

34 E Choctaw Avenue, McAlester OK
(918) 423-WINE (9463)
www.whisperingmeadowswine.com

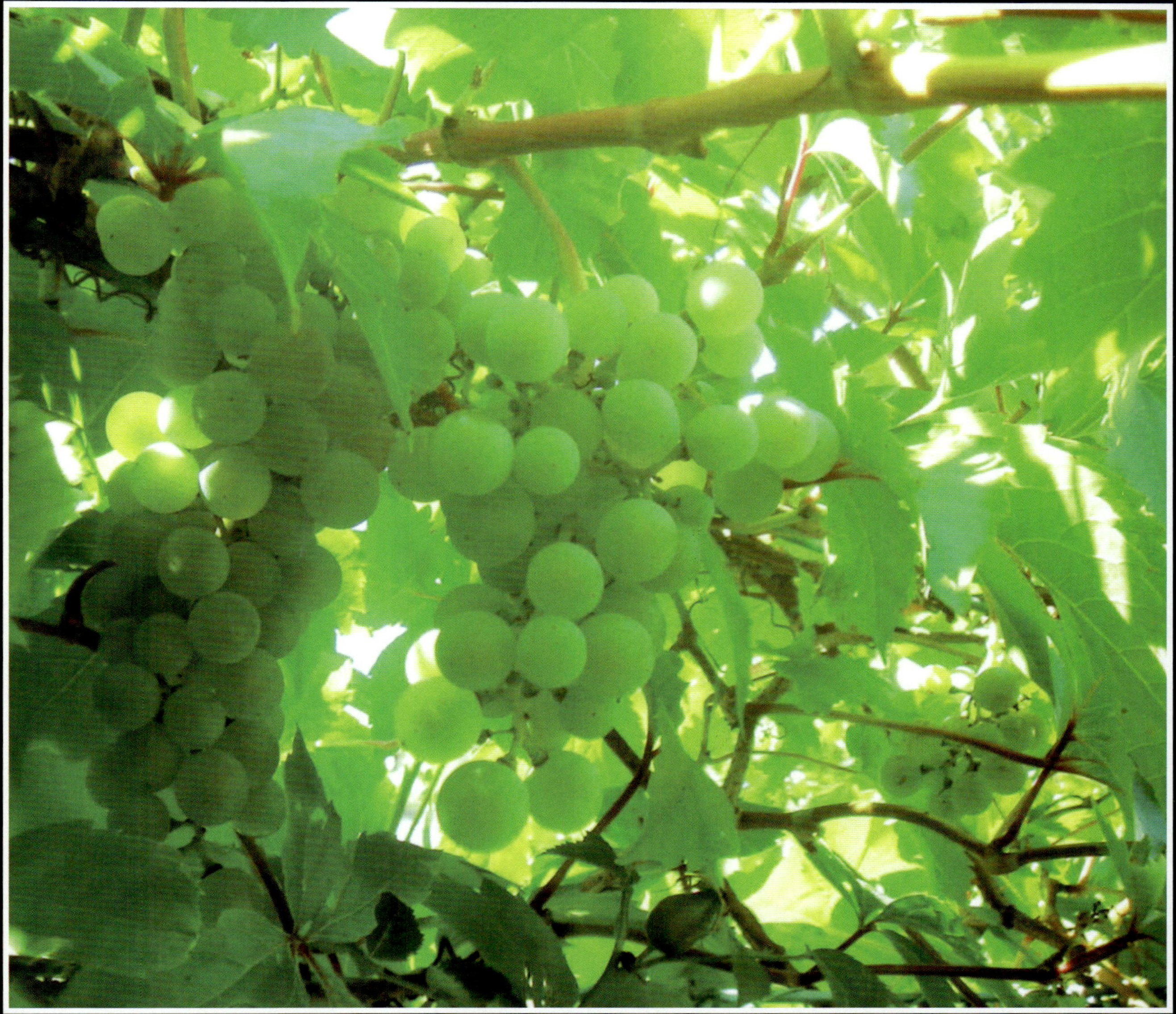

Index by Treasure

A

Ada Old Bank Gallery 196
All American Floats
    & Liquid Lightning Water Slide 128
America's Best Value Inn 6
Amish Cheese House 184
Antique Garden 59
ArabicaDabra's Coffee House 160
Arbuckle Wilderness 197
Arcadian Inn Bed & Breakfast 5
Artichoke Restaurant & Bar 155
Ataloa Lodge Museum 134
Avondale Galleries 25

B

Backyard Deli & Galleria LLC 148
Balliet's 55
Bartlesville Area History Museum 138
Beavers Bend Creative Escapes 191
Big Daddy's Restaurant & Catering 154
Black Sheep Winery & Vineyards 186
Blue Apples Gallery 21
Blue Moon Cafe 200
Bob's Bar-B-Que 201
Brown's Bakery 53

C

Cabin Creek Vineyard & Winery 185
Canadian River Vineyard & Winery 66
Casa Bella Bed & Breakfast 8
Castle Falls 54
Catch the Fever Music Festivals 113
Cattlemen's Steakhouse 50
Chastain's Casual Café & Catering Co. 156
Chesapeake Boathouse 16
Citizen Potawatomi Nation
    Cultural Heritage Center 15, 44
City of Guthrie 11
Clanton's Café 150
Cookson Smokehouse Restaurant 152
Copper Canyon Day Spa 169
Country Cottage Primitives 56
Country Cottage Restaurant 166
Country Inn Bed and Breakfast 102
Creative Concepts 176
Cross Bar Gallery 27
Crucible Gallery and Sculpture Garden 19

D

Dean-Lively Gallery & Frame 28
Deep Deuce Grill 52
Diamondhead Resort 110
Diamond Triple C Ranch at Grand Lake 120
Doubletree Hotel at Warren Place 107
Downtown Art and Frame 18
Dreamer Concepts Studio and Foundation 19
Duchess Creek Marina 116
Dutch Pantry 154

E

E. J. Provence 59
Eagle Bluff Resort 105
Elk City/Clinton KOA 8
Elk Creek Resort 104

F

Fin and Feather Resort 99, 151
Firehouse Art Center 20, 24
FireLake Grand Casino 15
Five Civilized Tribes Museum 142
Flour Sack 174
Flying W Guest Ranch 70

G

Gateway to the Panhandle Museum 75
Gina & Guiseppe's Italian Ristorante 147
Girls Gone Wine 203
Gourmet's 172
Grady County Historical Society 36
Grand Interiors 178
Grandpa's Catfish Restaurant 200
Granny Annie's Amish Furniture 83
Greater Southwest Historical Museum 199
Greenwood Cultural Center 143

H

Hall of Tattoos 21
Harn Homestead 44
Hastings Entertainment–Ada 202
Hastings Entertainment–Altus 82
Hastings Entertainment–Ardmore 202
Hastings Entertainment–Bartlesville 170
Hastings Entertainment–Duncan 84
Hastings Entertainment–Enid 82
Hastings Entertainment–Lawton 84
Hastings Entertainment–Muskogee 180
Hastings Entertainment–Norman 56
Hastings Entertainment–Ponca City 81
Hastings Entertainment–Stillwater 58
Hastings Entertainment–Yukon 54
Heritage Antiques 176
Hilton Garden Inn Tulsa South 101
Holiday Inn at Norman 7
Holiday Inn Express 108
Holiday Inn Express Hotel & Suites 98
Hotel Savoy 108

Index

I
Iguana Cafée 162
Indian Creek Village 71
Indian Trading Post and Art Gallery 40
Island Nation 169
It's All About Moi! At Miss Trudy's 81

J
Jacobson House Native Art Center 20
Jana Jae's Gallery Southwest 130
Jazmo'z Bourbon Street Café 150
Jenks Restaurant & Amazing Clocks 163

K
Katfish Kitchen 152
Kokoa Chocolatier 177
Krawdaddy's BBQ & Suchat Snake Creek Marina 161

L
LaDonna's Fancy Foods 184
LaFortune Park Golf Pro Shop 114
Lago Vista Bed & Breakfast 193
Leslie Powell Foundation and Gallery 74
Lorec Ranch 61
Lovera's Italian Grocery 203

M
Mainsite Contemporary Art 19
Mangum White House Bed & Breakfast 72
Mantel Wine Bar & Bistro 50
Margueritte B. Piers Living Free Sanctuary
  for Animals & Nature Conservatory 195
Mabee-Gerrer Museum of Art 41
Me-O-My Baby Gifts 174
Mecca Coffee Company 164
Melton Art Reference Library 24

Mid American Grille 148
Miss Jackson's 173
Molly's Landing 156
Moonfeathers Winery 66
Moore-Lindsay House Historical Museum 21
MSB Art Gallery 23
Museum of Special Interest Autos 32
Museum of the Great Plains 76
Muskogee Parks & Recreation 123, 137
Myriad Botanical Gardens 12

N
National Cowboy & Western Heritage Museum 37
National Route 66 Museum 79
National Wrestling Hall of Fame and Museum 32
Nonna's Euro-American Ristorante & Bar 49
Norman Arts Council 21
Norman Gallery Association 18–21
Nouveau Atelier de Chocolat 170
Nuance Décor 182
Nuyaka Creek Winery 183

O
Oak Hills Winery & Vineyards 183
Oklahoma Aquarium 117
Oklahoma Centennial Freedom Festival 14
Oklahoma City Museum of Art 33
Oklahoma City National Memorial & Museum 43
Oklahoma City Zoological Park
  and Botanical Garden 10
Oklahoma History Center 31
Oklahoma Music Hall of Fame 138
Oklahoma Opry 17
Oklahoma Sports Museum 36
Oklahoma State Firefighters Museum 46
Oklahoma State University Botanical Garden 12
Ol'Dutchman Bakery 164
Omniplex Science Museum 39
Oxley Nature Center 115

P
Painted Door 62
Panaderia La Harradura 63
Paradise Cove Marine Resort 100
Parsons Vineyard and Winery 64
Performing Arts Studio 18
Peyton's Place 122
Pine Lodge Resort 103
Pine Meadow Cabins 190
Pink House 158
Pioneer Heritage Townsite Center 77
Pioneer Woman Museum 75
Pits Barbecue 153
Plains Indians & Pioneers Museum 80
Plain View Winery 85
Plymouth Valley Cellars 85
Price Tower Arts Center 141

Q
Quilt Shop 178

R
Red Earth, Inc. 33
Red Stone Inn Bed & Breakfast 4
Remington Park Racetrack & Casino 14
Renaissance Oklahoma City
  Convention Center Hotel 4
Reuben's Rest Bed and Breakfast 192
Ring of Fire Studio 20
River Bend Lodge 190
Roadhouse Restaurant 157
Roberts Fine Interiors 171
Room at the Top of the World 106
Rosewood Inn Bed and Breakfast 9
Route 66 Harley Davidson and the 5 & Diner 121
Route 66 Thunderbirds 73

S

S & J Marketplace 57
Safari's Sanctuary 125
Saffron 162
Sam & Ella's Chicken Palace, Pizza & Subs 165
Santa Fe Depot Museum 40
Sapulpa 90–96
Shebang—Wine, Dine, Dance, Sing, Shop 149
Sherwin Miller Museum of Jewish Art 136
Shevaun Williams & Associates 18
Silver Flame 160
Skelly Lodge 111
Snug Harbor Cabins 192
Southern Oaks Resort & Spa 97
Stafford Air & Space Museum 76
Standifer House 72
Stonebridge Garden Center 181
Summerside Vineyards, Winery and Cottages 185
Super Cao Nguyen 65
Sweet Basil Thai Cuisine 52
Sweet Tooth Candy & Gift Company 168
Symmetry Salon and Day Spa 180

T

Talisman Gallery 131
Tara Cottage 114
Taylor's News Stand 58
Tea & Magnolias 175
Tenkiller Lodge 98
TeraMiranda Marina and Resort 100
Terrapin Peak Bed, Breakfast & Beyond 104
Terri's Sixshooter Bed & Breakfast 109
Three Rivers Museum and Thomas-Foreman Historical House 145
Tivoli Inn & The Glass Hall 102
Trattoria il Centro 51
True Grits Restaurant 158
Tulsa Air and Space Museum & Planetarium 134
Tulsa Ballet 129
Tulsa Opera 119
Tulsa Zoo 127
Turner Falls Park 194

U

USS Batfish at the Muskogee War Memorial Museum and Park 144

V

Verner Gallery & Fine Art School 198

W

War Paint Horse Ranch 124
Washington Irving Trail Museum 45
Water Taxi of Oklahoma City 13
Webb 57
West Southwest Territory 172
Whispering Meadows Vineyards & Winery 204
Willard Stone Museum & Gallery 133
Willows Inn 70
Will Rogers Memorial Museums 139
Winery at Greenfield Vineyard 64
Wolfe Ranch 194
Woods & Waters Winery and Vineyards 86
Woolaroc 135
World Organization of China Painters Museum 35

Z

Zackary's Gourmet Grill 159
Zoller Designs & Antiques, Inc. 179

Index by City

A

Ada
Galleries & Fine Art
Ada Old Bank Gallery 196

Restaurants, Bakeries & Cafés
Blue Moon Cafe 200
Bob's Bar-B-Que 201
Grandpa's Catfish Restaurant 200

Shopping & Services
Hastings Entertainment–Ada 202

Afton
Accommodations & Resorts
Paradise Cove Marine Resort 100

Attractions & Recreation
Diamond Triple C Ranch at Grand Lake 120

Altus
Shopping & Services
Hastings Entertainment–Altus 82

Anadarko
Wines & Specialty Foods
Woods & Waters Winery and Vineyards 86

Ardmore
Attractions & Recreation
Margueritte B. Piers Living Free Sanctuary for Animals & Nature Conservatory 195

Museums, History & Culture
Greater Southwest Historical Museum 199

Shopping & Services
Hastings Entertainment–Ardmore 202

B

Bartlesville
Galleries & Fine Arts
Talisman Gallery 131

Museums, History & Culture
Bartlesville Area History Museum 138
Price Tower Arts Center 141
Woolaroc 135

Shopping & Services
Hastings Entertainment–Bartlesville 170

Bethany
Accommodations & Resorts
Rosewood Inn Bed and Breakfast 9

Attractions & Recreation
Oklahoma Centennial Freedom Festival 14

Big Cabin
Wines & Specialty Foods
Cabin Creek Vineyard & Winery 185

Bristow
Wines & Specialty Foods
Nuyaka Creek Winery 183

Broken Arrow
Accommodations & Resorts
Tivoli Inn & The Glass Hall 102

Attractions & Recreation
Safari's Sanctuary 125
Tara Cottage 114

Restaurants, Bakeries & Cafés
ArabicaDabra's Coffee House 160

Shopping & Services
Nouveau Atelier de Chocolat 170

Broken Bow
Accommodations & Resorts
Beavers Bend Creative Escapes 191
Lago Vista Bed & Breakfast 193
Pine Meadow Cabins 190
Reuben's Rest Bed and Breakfast 192

Wines & Specialty Foods
Girls Gone Wine 203

C

Calumet
Museums, History & Culture
Indian Trading Post and Art Gallery 40

Canute
Accommodations & Resorts
Elk City/Clinton KOA 8

Catoosa
Accommodations & Resorts
Skelly Lodge 111

Restaurants, Bakeries & Cafés
Molly's Landing 156

Chandler
Wines & Specialty Foods
Winery at Greenfield Vineyard 64

Chelsea
Wines & Specialty Foods
Oak Hills Winery & Vineyards 183

Chickasha
Museums, History & Culture
Grady County Historical Society 36

Chouteau
Restaurants, Bakeries & Cafés
Dutch Pantry 154

Wines & Specialty Foods
Amish Cheese House 184

Claremore
Accommodations & Resorts
Country Inn Bed and Breakfast 102

Museums, History & Culture
Will Rogers Memorial Museums 139

Restaurants, Bakeries & Cafés
Ol'Dutchman Bakery 164
Pink House 158
Pits Barbecue 153
True Grits Restaurant 158

Shopping & Services
Stonebridge Garden Center 181

Cookson
Accommodations & Resorts
Terrapin Peak Bed, Breakfast & Beyond 104
Terri's Sixshooter Bed & Breakfast 109

Restaurants, Bakeries & Cafés
Cookson Smokehouse Restaurant 152
Krawdaddy's BBQ & Such at Snake Creek Marina 161

D

Davis
Accommodations & Resorts
River Bend Lodge 190

Attractions & Recreation
Arbuckle Wilderness 197
Turner Falls Park 194

Duncan
Shopping & Services
Hastings Entertainment 84

E

Edmond
Accommodations & Resorts
Arcadian Inn Bed & Breakfast 5

Galleries & Fine Art
Dean-Lively Gallery & Frame 28

Shopping & Services
E. J. Provence 59

Elk City
Accommodations & Resorts
Standifer House 72

Museums, History & Culture
National Route 66 Museum 79

Shopping & Services
Granny Annie's Amish Furniture 83

Enid
Shopping & Services
Hastings Entertainment–Enid 82

Eufaula
Attractions & Recreation
War Paint Horse Ranch 124

Restaurants, Bakeries & Cafés
Zackary's Gourmet Grill 159

F

Fairview
Wines & Specialty Foods
Plymouth Valley Cellars 85

Frederick
Museums, History & Culture
Pioneer Heritage Townsite Center 77

G

Gate
Museums, History & Culture
Gateway to the Panhandle Museum 75

Gore
Accommodations & Resorts
Fin and Feather Resort 99

Restaurants, Bakeries & Cafés
Fin and Feather Resort 151

Grove
Galleries & Fine Arts
Jana Jae's Gallery Southwest 130

Shopping & Services
Flour Sack 174
Gourmet's 172
Grand Interiors 178
Nuance Décor 182
Quilt Shop 178

Guthrie
Attractions & Recreation
City of Guthrie 11

Museums, History & Culture
Oklahoma Sports Museum 36

Wines & Specialty Foods
Moonfeathers Winery 66

Guymon
Accommodations & Resorts
Willows Inn 70

J

Jenks
Accommodations & Resorts
Holiday Inn Express Hotel & Suites 98

Attractions & Recreation
Oklahoma Aquarium 117

Restaurants, Bakeries & Cafés
Gina & Guiseppe's Italian Ristorante 147
Jenks Restaurant & Amazing Clocks 163

Shopping & Services
Island Nation 169
Tea & Magnolias 175
West Southwest Territory 172

K

Ketchum
Accommodations & Resorts
Pine Lodge Resort 103

Krebs
Wines & Specialty Foods
Lovera's Italian Grocery 203

L

Lahoma
Wines & Specialty Foods
Plain View Winery 85

Lake Tenkiller
Restaurants, Bakeries & Cafés
Big Daddy's Restaurant & Catering 154

Langley
Accommodations & Resorts
Southern Oaks Resort & Spa 97

Lawton
Galleries & Fine Art
Leslie Powell Foundation and Gallery 74

Museums, History & Culture
Museum of the Great Plains 76

Shopping & Services
Hastings Entertainment–Lawton 84

Lexington
Wines & Specialty Foods
Canadian River Vineyard & Winery 66

Locust Grove
Accommodations & Resorts
Holiday Inn Express 108

Museums, History & Culture
Willard Stone Museum & Gallery 133

Restaurants, Bakeries & Cafés
Backyard Deli & Galleria LLC 148
Country Cottage Restaurant 166

M

Mangum
Accommodations & Resorts
Mangum White House Bed & Breakfast 72

McAlester
Galleries & Fine Art
Verner Gallery & Fine Art School 198

Wines & Specialty Foods
Whispering Meadows Vineyards & Winery 204

Monkey Island
Accommodations & Resort
TeraMiranda Marina and Resort 100

Restaurants, Bakeries & Cafés
Roadhouse Restaurant 157
Shebang—Wine, Dine, Dance, Sing, Shop 149

Shopping & Services
Creative Concepts 176

Muskogee
Attractions & Recreation
Muskogee Parks & Recreation 123

Museums, History & Culture
Ataloa Lodge Museum 134
Five Civilized Tribes Museum 142
Muskogee Parks & Recreation 137
Oklahoma Music Hall of Fame 138
Three Rivers Museum and Thomas-Foreman Historical House 145
USS Batfish at the Muskogee War Memorial Museum and Park 144

Shopping & Services
Hastings Entertainment–Muskogee 180

N

Norman
Accommodations & Resorts
Casa Bella Bed & Breakfast 8
Holiday Inn at Norman 7

Galleries & Fine Art
Blue Apples Gallery 21
Crucible Gallery and Sculpture Garden 19
Downtown Art and Frame 18
Dreamer Concepts Studio and Foundation 19
Firehouse Art Center 20, 24
Hall of Tattoos 21
Jacobson House Native Art Center 20
Mainsite Contemporary Art 19
Moore-Lindsay House Historical Museum 21
Norman Arts Council 21
Norman Gallery Association 18–21
Performing Arts Studio 18
Ring of Fire Studio 20
Shevaun Williams & Associates 18

Restaurants, Bakeries & Cafés
Sweet Basil Thai Cuisine 52

Shopping & Services
Antique Garden 59
Hastings Entertainment–Norman 56
S & J Marketplace 57
Webb 57

O

Oklahoma City
Accommodations & Resorts
Red Stone Inn Bed & Breakfast 4
Renaissance Oklahoma City Convention Center Hotel 4

Attractions & Recreation
Chesapeake Boathouse 16
Myriad Botanical Gardens 12
Oklahoma City Zoological Park and Botanical Garden 10
Oklahoma Opry 17
Remington Park Racetrack & Casino 14
Water Taxi of Oklahoma City 13

Galleries & Fine Art
Avondale Galleries 25
Cross Bar Gallery 27
Melton Art Reference Library 24
MSB Art Gallery 23

Museums, History & Culture
Harn Homestead 44
National Cowboy & Western Heritage Museum 37
Oklahoma City Museum of Art 33
Oklahoma City National Memorial & Museum 43
Oklahoma State Firefighters Museum 46
Oklahoma History Center 31
Omniplex Science Museum 39
Red Earth, Inc. 33
World Organization of China Painters Museum 35

Restaurants, Bakeries & Cafés
Brown's Bakery 53
Cattlemen's Steakhouse 50
Deep Deuce Grill 52
Mantel Wine Bar & Bistro 50
Nonna's Euro-American Ristorante & Bar 49
Trattoria il Centro 51

Shopping & Services
Balliet's 55
Castle Falls 54
Lorec Ranch 61
Painted Door 62
Taylor's News Stand 58

Wines & Specialty Foods
Panaderia La Harradura 63
Super Cao Nguyen 65

P

Park Hill
Accommodations & Resorts
Elk Creek Resort 104
Tenkiller Lodge 98

Ponca City
Museums, History & Culture
Pioneer Woman Museum 75

Shopping & Services
Hastings Entertainment–Ponca City 81

Porum
Attractions & Recreation
Duchess Creek Marina 116

Poteau
Wines & Specialty Foods
Black Sheep Winery & Vineyards 186

Pryor
Attractions & Recreation
Catch the Fever Music Festivals 113

Restaurants, Bakeries & Cafés
Mid American Grille 148

Shopping & Services
Heritage Antiques 176

R

Ringwood
Accommodations & Resorts
Indian Creek Village 71

Ripley
Museums, History & Culture
Washington Irving Trail Museum 45

S

Sand Springs
Restaurants, Bakeries & Cafés
Chastain's Casual Café & Catering Co. 156

Sapulpa
Restaurants, Bakeries & Cafés
Chastain's Casual Café & Catering Co. 156

The Heart of Route 66
City of Sapulpa 91
Downtown Sapulpa 92
Events in Sapulpa 94
Sapulpa Parks 95
Treasures of Sapulpa 93

Sayre
Accommodations & Resorts
Flying W Guest Ranch 70

Shawnee
Accommodations & Resorts
America's Best Value Inn 6

Attractions & Recreation
Citizen Potawatomi Nation Cultural Heritage Center 15
Fire Lake Grand Casino 15

Museums, History & Culture
Citizen Potawatomi Nation Cultural Heritage Center 44
Maybee-Gerrer Museum of Art 41
Museum of Special Interest Autos 32
Santa Fe Depot Museum 40

Shopping & Services
Country Cottage Primitives 56

Wines & Specialty Foods
Parsons Vineyard and Winery 64

Stigler
Accommodations & Resorts
Snug Harbor Cabins 192

Stillwater
Attractions & Recreation
Oklahoma State University Botanical Garden 12

Museums, History & Culture
National Wrestling Hall of Fame and Museum 32

Shopping & Services
Hastings Entertainment–Stillwater 58

Stilwell
Accommodations & Resorts
Room at the Top of the World 106

Sulphur
Attractions & Recreation
Wolfe Ranch 194

T

Tahlequah
Accommodations & Resorts
Diamondhead Resort 110
Eagle Bluff Resort 105

Attractions & Recreation
All American Floats & Liquid Lightning Water Slide 128
Peyton's Place 122

Restaurants, Bakeries & Cafés
Iguana Cafée 162
Katfish Kitchen 152
Sam & Ella's Chicken Palace, Pizza & Subs 165

Tulsa
Accommodations & Resorts
Doubletree Hotel at Warren Place 107
Hilton Garden Inn Tulsa South 101
Hotel Savoy 108

Attractions & Recreation
LaFortune Park Golf Pro Shop 114
Oxley Nature Center 115
Route 66 Harley Davidson and the 5 & Diner 121
Tulsa Ballet 129
Tulsa Opera 119
Tulsa Zoo 127

Museums, History & Culture
Greenwood Cultural Center 143
Sherwin Miller Museum of Jewish Art 136
Tulsa Air and Space Museum & Planetarium 134

Restaurants, Bakeries & Cafés
Jazmo'z Bourbon Street Café 150
Mecca Coffee Company 164
Saffron 162
Silver Flame 160

Shopping & Services
   Copper Canyon Day Spa 169
   Kokoa Chocolatier 177
   Me-O-My Baby Gifts 174
   Miss Jackson's 173
   Roberts Fine Interiors 171
   Sweet Tooth Candy & Gift Company 168
   Symmetry Salon and Day Spa 180
   Zoller Designs & Antiques, Inc. 179

Wines & Specialty Foods
   LaDonna's Fancy Foods 184

V

Vinita

Restaurants, Bakeries & Cafés
   Artichoke Restaurant & Bar 155
   Clanton's Café 150

Wines & Specialty Foods
   Summerside Vineyards, Winery and Cottages 185

W

Weatherford

Attractions & Recreation
   Route 66 Thunderbirds 73

Museums, History & Culture
   Stafford Air & Space Museum 76

Shopping & Services
   It's All About Moi! At Miss Trudy's 81

Woodward

Museums, History & Culture
   Plains Indians & Pioneers Museum 80

Y

Yukon

Shopping & Services
   Hastings Entertainment–Yukon 54